History of Computing

The History of Computing series publishes high-quality books which address the history of computing, with an emphasis on the 'externalist' view of this history, more accessible to a wider audience. The series examines content and history from four main quadrants: the history of relevant technologies, the history of the core science, the history of relevant business and economic developments, and the history of computing as it pertains to social history and societal developments.

Titles can span a variety of product types, including but not exclusively, themed volumes, biographies, 'profile' books (with brief biographies of a number of key people), expansions of workshop proceedings, general readers, scholarly expositions, titles used as ancillary textbooks, revivals and new editions of previous worthy titles.

These books will appeal, varyingly, to academics and students in computer science, history, mathematics, business and technology studies. Some titles will also directly appeal to professionals and practitioners of different backgrounds.

For further volumes:
http://www.springer.com/series/8442

Per Lundin

Computers in Swedish Society

Documenting Early Use and Trends

 Springer

Per Lundin
Centre for Science and Technology Studies
Department of Economic History
Uppsala University
Uppsala, Sweden

ISSN 2190-6831   ISSN 2190-684X (electronic)
ISBN 978-1-4471-5857-8   ISBN 978-1-4471-2933-2 (eBook)
DOI 10.1007/978-1-4471-2933-2
Springer London Heidelberg New York Dordrecht

British Library Cataloguing in Publication Data
A catalogue record for this book is available from the British Library

Preface

Eleven years ago, I was done with the IT industry—or so I thought. Just before the bubble burst at the turn of the millennium and put an end to the Swedish "IT boom," I had—very timely indeed—quit my job as development engineer for a new career as historian of technology. After some comfortable years in the ivory tower, my supervisor by then, Arne Kaijser, one day came into my office at the Royal Institute of Technology (Kungl. Tekniska högskolan, KTH) and mentioned that some senior practitioners affiliated to the Swedish Computer Society (Dataföreningen i Sverige) had been in touch with him. Wouldn't I be interested to join them for a meeting? After all, I had been a programmer. Rather hesitantly I said yes and found myself all of a sudden in a room with a handful of gray-haired gentlemen who since a couple of years had been busy with the idea to present a book on "the heroes of the Swedish IT history," presumably themselves, as an encouraging example to the Swedish youth. Wouldn't we be interested to write this book? We frowned at the idea (of course) but were also caught by their enthusiasm, friendliness, and considerable energy. So instead of dismissing their planned hagiography, we persuaded them that a first step must be to document the computing history and also that the National Museum of Science and Technology (Tekniska museet) must be involved. They bought our argument, and the rock began to roll.

Initial funding from the Bank of Sweden Tercentenary Foundation (Riksbankens Jubileumsfond) and the Marcus and Amalia Wallenberg Memorial Fund (Stiftelsen Marcus och Amalia Wallenbergs Minnesfond) allowed us to run a number of pilot activities and to design a large documentation project named "From Computing Machines to IT: Collecting, Documenting, and Preserving Sources on Swedish IT History" (Från matematikmaskin till IT: Insamling, dokumentation, bevarande och tillgängliggörande av källmaterial om svensk IT-historia) for which we received substantial funding from the above-mentioned financiers as well as the Swedish Arts Council's Access Fund (Kulturrådets accessprojekt). Later, we also received additional funding for specific project activities from the Knowledge Foundation (KK-stiftelsen), the Swedish Governmental Agency for Innovation Systems (Vinnova), the Sven Tyrén Foundation (Sven Tyréns Stiftelse), the National Land Survey of Sweden (Lantmäteriet), the Swedish Tax Agency (Skatteverket), the

Swedish National Road Administration (Vägverket), Volvo IT, and the four banks Handelsbanken, Nordea, SEB, and Swedbank, as well as the three insurance companies Folksam, Länsförsäkringar, and Skandia.

The only drawback with the generous funding was that it had to be spent within a period of 2 years. Thus, I was set with the formidable task to establish and train a large research group with the aim to document Swedish IT history from a user perspective within this given time frame. Several people were instrumental in this process, but without the support of Rolf Berndtson, Peter Du Rietz, Gunnar L. Johansson, Arne Kaijser, Anne Louise Kemdal, and Per Olof Persson, we would not have succeeded.

After completing the project, I was done with documenting IT history—or so I thought. I had just written a final report that contextualized, described, and evaluated the project, and I was on the brink of moving on to tourism history, when Wayne Wheeler at Springer UK contacted me, and encouraged me to revise the final report for the purpose of publishing. Rather hesitantly I said yes …

This book has been special for me to write since it gravitates around a project rather than a well-defined historical problem. My aims have been to describe how we eventually found a rationale for the project "From Computing Machines to IT"; to place it in its proper historiographical, methodological, and theoretical context; and to exemplify how oral evidence can advance our understanding of history of computing. Chapters 1 and 2 of this book are a thoroughly revised version of the final report for the project, while Chap. 3 is newly written. For the completion of this book, I wish to thank the anonymous referees who reviewed the original draft and Isabelle Dussauge, Johan Gribbe, Anna Orrghen, and Gustav Sjöblom for valuable suggestions. Simon Moores and Caroline Wulff have revised the English. Eva Derlow and Anna Gerdén at Tekniska museet have provided me with several images in the book. At Springer UK, I thank Wayne Wheeler and his assistant Simon Rees for both having been enthusiastic, helpful, and most patient publishers. The book has been finalized with financial support from Jan Wallanders och Tom Hedelius Stiftelse.

Contents

Chapter 1
Background and Theoretical Assumptions

Bang, the last file goes in the garbage can. That's how I picture the late summer of 2007 when we at the Corporate Strategy Department move to Stureplan. Full digitization is what counts. I have no intention of riding there and back on the Hässelby–Stureplan metro just because I have forgotten a paper. Most of it is already thrown away, even if some documents were scanned. The 4-cm-thick evaluation study of the TIDAS project is also thrown away. That's typical, just as I was asked to write some lines about it.[1]

1.1 Introduction

Looking at the role of computers in society over the past 60 years, the change has been nothing short of dramatic.[2] While the use of computing technology in the 1950s was narrowly focused on scientific computations and specific administrative routines, it takes an almost infinite number of forms in today's society. Computers are developing into a generic technology. In its various shapes, the technology has become an indispensable part of the world we live in.

The point of departure for this book is that the user and the use of computing technology have to be taken into account in understanding the role of computers in society. During recent years, the historiography of computing also shows a shift in perspective from inventors and innovations toward the more complex relationship between the design and use of computers. Research questions are changing as well. However, finding sources that can help us answer the new questions posed is not always a straightforward task. Historians interested in the use of computing share

---

[1] Erik Sandström, "En resa i TIDas," autobiography no. 54, http://www.tekniskamuseet.se/it-minnen (accessed June 1, 2009).

[2] "Computers" and "information technology (IT)," and also "history of computing" and "IT history" are used synonymously in this book.

P. Lundin, *Computers in Swedish Society: Documenting Early Use and Trends*,
History of Computing, DOI 10.1007/978-1-4471-2933-2_1, © Springer-Verlag London 2012

many of the difficulties that scholars of contemporary history in general face, such as archives not yet accessible, not migrated or even deleted digital sources, etc. In addition, they have to deal with sources that often are complicated and technical in content. The widespread use of computing technology implies, furthermore, that users are found throughout society, which, in many cases, makes it difficult and time consuming to trace written sources. A way to cope with these difficulties is to create and collect new sources with the help of methods of contemporary history.

The project "From Computing Machines to IT" has been such an attempt. Its main objective was to create, collect, and preserve sources on Swedish computing history from a user-centered perspective and make them available on the Web. The project was a collaboration between the Swedish Computer Society, the Division of History of Science and Technology at KTH, and the National Museum of Science and Technology. It became large scale in January 2007 and was finished in December 2008. The approach consisted of several methods and tools. Traditional oral history interviews and collections of autobiographies were used alongside new self-structuring and time-saving methods, such as witness seminars and an Internet-based collection of memories (the Writers' Web). The project resulted in more than 160 interviews, almost 50 witness seminars, and a collection of about 240 autobiographies. The created sources consist of more than 8,000 pages of text (see Appendix I: List of Created and Collected Sources). All in all, nearly 700 people contributed with their stories. The contacts with these people generated, in turn, several donations of archival records, artifacts, movies, and photographs. In addition, the participating scholars and researchers provided meta-documentation on the process of creating sources (see Appendix II: List of Meta-documentation). Also developed within the project was an adapted project model for cooperation between museums, trade and industry, and universities (see Appendix III: Formal Description of Organization and Work Process). The people who participated in the project are listed and presented in Appendix IV: Participants in the Project.

In this book, which consists of three chapters, I consider the methods, organization, and theoretical approach of the project as well as its results.[3] Chapter 1 begins with a discussion of the recent shift toward a more elaborated user perspective in the international historiography of computing. The Swedish historical writing on computing is related to this development, and its lack of explicitly formulated user-oriented approaches is pointed out. After that, the different theoretical traditions on user-technology relations are addressed, and the concept of the user is problematized

---

[3] Earlier accounts of the project are: Per Lundin, *Documenting the Use of Computers in Swedish Society between 1950 and 1980: Final Report on the Project "From Computing Machines to IT"* (Stockholm, 2009); idem, "From Computing Machines to IT: Collecting, Documenting, and Preserving Source Material on Swedish IT-History," in *History of Nordic Computing 2: Second IFIP WG9.7 Conference, HiNC2, Turku, Finland, August 21–23, 2007: Revised Selected Papers*, ed. John Impagliazzo, Timo Järvi and Petri Paju (Berlin, Heidelberg & New York, 2009), 65–73; idem, "Inledning: Projektet och fokusgruppen," in *Användarna och datorerna: En historik 1960–1985*, ed. Birgitta Frejhagen (Stockholm, 2009), 13–20; idem, "Metoder för att dokumentera historia," in *ibid.*, 21–30.

in order to find, if not a precise, at least a loose definition of how this term was understood within the project. The first chapter of the book goes on to discuss the need to create and collect sources on the use of computers in Swedish society by giving a brief account of similar documentation projects both nationally and internationally. This account also considers the different methodological approaches developed and used by these projects.

Chapter 2 outlines the history of the project. It is shown that during this process, methodology, organization, and theoretical approach mutually shaped each other. After a discussion of the methodological considerations made in the project, it is described how oral history interviews and witness seminars were conducted, how written recollections were acquired, and how the Writers' Web was designed. Details are also given about the created and collected sources as well as the meta-documentation. This chapter is concluded by a number of observations on the organization and the methods of the project.

Chapter 3 analyzes how the collected and created sources of the use of computers in Swedish society between 1950 and 1980 can contribute to the Swedish historiography of computing. This final chapter starts out with a critical discussion on the interpretation of oral evidence. Three cases follow, each one considering how oral evidence can inform us about the interaction of computing with large-scale transformations in economies, cultures, and societies. The first case demonstrates how it can help us to examine career patterns, social networks, as well as the transdisciplinary, transsectorial, and transnational character of the flows of computing-related artifacts, expertise, and knowledge. The second case exemplifies how it can contribute to our understanding of how users adapted, modified, reconfigured, and resisted computing technology in order to fit their purposes and the intentions of their organizations. The third case discusses how it can inform us of the materiality and geography of computing.

1.2   Toward a User Perspective in the Historiography of Computing

In a recent article, the American historian of technology Thomas J. Misa argues that, although everybody knows that "computing has changed the world," the existing historiography faces, strangely enough, difficulties in addressing this question directly, and he suggests that scholars shift to focus "on the interaction of computing— including hardware, software, and institutional dimensions—with large-scale transformations in economies, cultures, and societies." Since citizens and policymakers today know that computing has changed the world, Misa continues, historians should help them understand this history.[4]

---

[4] Thomas J. Misa, "Understanding 'How Computing Changed the World,'" *IEEE Annals in the History of Computing* 29, no. 4 (2007), 52 f. A similar shift in perspective for the history of technology in general has previously been advocated by David Edgerton, "From Innovation to Use: Ten Eclectic Theses on the Historiography of Technology," *History and Technology* 16 (1999), 111–36.

He distinguishes three thematic traditions in the field of the history of computing. The first focused initially on identifying the "first" digital computers and understanding the technical, i.e., hardware and software, details, and it was dominated by the practitioners and pioneers of digital computing. Scholars criticized this approach as an "insider history," and they argued for, and pursued, a contextual technical history. The second thematic tradition showed instead an interest in the historical roots of the "Information Age," and, as Misa points out, in this view computers were machines that "first and foremost processed information and only secondarily provided the functions of calculation, control, or communication." The third thematic tradition represents an institutional approach. Instead of emphasizing microstudies of individual computing machines or macrostudies of the information society, scholars shifted focus to the governmental, engineering, or corporate institutions that shaped computing.[5]

Since none of these traditions explicitly address the question of how computing has changed the world, Misa proposes the "making" of a fourth tradition that takes up the challenge of "comprehending the twin-fold shaping of computing and society." On the one hand, "we need to show how developments in computing shaped major historical transformations, that is, how the evolution of computing was consequential for the transformations in work routines, business processes, government activities, cultural formations, and the myriad activities of daily life," and, on the other, our narratives and analysis should "show how major historical transformations shaped the evolution of computing." He, therefore, urges historians of computing to undertake studies that "situate computing within major historical transformations."[6]

I believe that historians interested in undertaking studies in the direction Misa proposes would benefit from addressing the role of the user. They have to understand how businesses and government developed to become leading users of computers. They have to understand how computers entered everyday life and transformed work as well as leisure activities. Nevertheless, they also need to go the other way round and examine how users have shaped digital technology and thoroughly changed our cultural and social understanding of what computers are.

There are examples of recent scholarship, albeit not many, that follow this trajectory. The three-volume *The Digital Hand* written by the remarkably productive American historian and IBM manager James Cortada is perhaps the most notable example. Cortada asks how computers first were used, by whom, and why, and he examines how computing technology was appropriated in American manufacturing, transportation, retail, financial, telecommunications, media, entertainment, and public sector industries (40 in total) during the past half century. He also discusses how the industries in question changed the nature of computing technology. By naming his study *The Digital Hand*, and thus paraphrasing the American business historian Alfred D. Chandler's seminal book *The Visible Hand*, Cortada wanted to emphasize "the crucial supportive role played by computers in helping companies and industries

---

[5] Misa, "Understanding 'How Computing Changed the World,'" 53 ff.
[6] Ibid., 56 ff.

do the work for which they existed."[7] Among Cortada's key findings are that the use varied more by industry than by company, that companies as well as government agencies "preferred to implement new uses in increments," that they concentrated their use of computing to "improve internal business operations and lower operating costs" (and only secondarily to acquire new customers), that they used computers "only if they could both perform a function and support conventional managerial practices," and that users and uses became more alike (regardless of industry) as technology and applications matured.[8] As we shall see below, the outline of our project parallels Cortada's broad approach toward the use of digital technology.[9]

1.2.1 The Swedish Historiography of Computing

How, then, has the history of computing or IT history been written in Sweden? Is it possible to discern "traditions" in the Swedish historiography in a similar manner as Misa has done for the international historiography? And what about the user? Has he or she been taken into account? It must be stressed that Swedish historians in general have paid little attention to the role of computers in society, which makes it difficult to identify traditions in Misa's sense, but the studies undertaken so far can be clustered, albeit loosely, around three different "themes."[10]

---

[7] James W. Cortada, *The Digital Hand: How Computers Changed the Work of American Manufacturing, Transportation, and Retail Industries* (Oxford, 2004); idem, *The Digital Hand: Volume 2, How Computers Changed the Work of American Financial, Telecommunications, Media, and Entertainment Industries* (Oxford, 2006); idem, *The Digital Hand: Volume 3, How Computers Changed the Work of American Public Sector Industries* (Oxford, 2008). He summarizes his three-volume work in James W. Cortada, "The Digital Hand: How Information Technology Changes the Way Industries Worked in the United States," *Business History Review* 80, no. 4 (2006), 755–66; idem, "Studying the Role of IT in the Evolution of American Business Practices: A Way Forward," *IEEE Annals in the History of Computing* 29, no. 4 (2007), 28–39.

[8] Cortada, "The Digital Hand," 760 f.; idem, "Studying the Role of IT in the Evolution of American Business Practices," 33 f.

[9] Examples of other studies pursuing a user perspective in a similar fashion are William Aspray and Paul E. Ceruzzi, eds., *The Internet and American Business* (Cambridge, MA, 2008); David Caminer, ed., *User-Driven Innovation: The World's First Business Computer* (London, 1996); Thomas Haigh, "Inventing Information Systems: The Systems Men and the Computers, 1950–1968," *Business History Review* 75, no. 1 (2001), 15–61; idem, "The Chromium-Plated Tabulator: Institutionalizing an Electronic Revolution," *IEEE Annals of the History of Computing* 23, no. 4 (2001), 75–104; Arthur L. Norberg, *Computers and Commerce: A Study of Technology and Management at Eckert-Mauchly Computer Company, Engineering Research Associates, and Remington Rand, 1946–1957* (Cambridge, MA, 2005); Petri Paju, "National Projects and International Users: Finland and Early European Computerization," *IEEE Annals of the History of Computing* 30, no. 4 (2008), 77–91; JoAnne Yates, *Structuring the Information Age: Life Insurance and Technology in the Twentieth Century* (Baltimore, 2005).

[10] In addition to my own *Documenting the Use of Computers in Swedish Society between 1950 and 1980*, I have found Hans Fogelberg's working paper *Research on IT Use and Users in Sweden, with Particular Focus on 1990–2010* (Stockholm, 2011) useful when compiling this historiographical survey.

The first theme deals with computers and politics. Already in 1970, the political scientist Jan Annerstedt and his coauthors discussed in the book *Datorer och politik* (Computers and Politics) the introduction of computers in the state bureaucracy, the fall of the Swedish computing technology industry, IBM's corresponding strong influence on the Swedish state, and the lack of an official policy on computers.[11] Scholarship that partly questioned, and partly complemented their study followed, with the historian Hans De Geer's *På väg till datasamhället* (Toward the Computer Society) from 1992 as the most important contribution. De Geer identified the government agencies and government committees (independent and powerful in international comparison) as well as the professions and their organizations as the key players in the extensive computerization of the public administration.[12] The historian Lars Ilshammar analyzed, in turn, the debates on computers and integrity as well as the establishment of Swedish legislation on digital information, and in an interdisciplinary study, Jonas Johansson followed the political debate in Sweden (and Norway) on "the information society" during the 1990s.[13] Others focused on aspects of the computerization of the Swedish "welfare state," state-led innovation, and the role of the labor movement in these processes.[14] A reason, perhaps, for the relatively large interest in the relationship between computers and politics is the rise of the welfare state and the quickly expanding public sector in Sweden during the postwar period.

---

[11] Jan Annerstedt et al., *Datorer och politik: Studier i en ny tekniks politiska effekter på det svenska samhället* (Lund, 1970). See also Jan Annerstedt, *Staten och datorerna: En studie av den officiella datorutvecklings- och datorforskningspolitiken* (Stockholm, 1969) and the computer scientist Sten Henriksson's section in Peter Naur, *Datamaskinerna och samhället*, med ett tillägg om svenska förhållanden av Sten Henriksson, trans. Sten Henriksson (Lund, 1969).

[12] Hans De Geer, *På väg till datasamhället: Datatekniken i politiken 1946–1963* (Stockholm, 1992); Hans Glimell, *Återerövra datapolitiken! En rapport om staten och informationsteknologin under fyra decennier* (Linköping, 1989); Sten Henriksson, "Datapolitikens död och återkomst," in *Infrastruktur för informationssamhället: Teknik och politik*, ed. Barbro Atlestam (Stockholm, 1995); idem, "De galna åren – en efterskrift," in *Informationssamhället – åter till framtiden*, ed. Barbro Atlestam (Stockholm, 2004); Kent Lindkvist, *Datateknik och politik: Datapolitiken i Sverige 1945–1982* (Lund, 1984); Thorsten Nybom, "Det nya statskontorets framväxt 1960–1965," in *Statskontoret 1680–1980: En jubileums- och årsskrift*, ed. Arne Granholm and Margot Rydén (Stockholm, 1980), 133–79.

[13] Lars Ilshammar, *Offentlighetens nya rum: Teknik och politik i Sverige 1969–1999* (Örebro, 2002); Jonas Johansson, *Du sköna nya tid? Debatten om informationssamhället i riksdag och storting under 1990-talet* (Linköping, 2006). See also Stefan Karlsson, *Nödvändighetens väg: Världsbildande gränsarbete i skildringar av informationssamhället* (Karlstad, 2005); Åsa Söderlind, *Personlig integritet som informationspolitik: Debatt och diskussion i samband med tillkomsten av Datalag (1973:289)* (Borås, 2009).

[14] See, for instance, Thomas Kaiserfeld, "Computerizing the Swedish Welfare State: The Middle Way of Technological Success and Failure," *Technology & Culture* 37 (1996), 249–79; Per Lundin, "Designing Democracy: The UTOPIA-Project and the Role of Labor Movement in Technological Change during the 1970s and the 1980s," in *History of Nordic Computing 3: Third IFIP WG9.7 Conference, HiNC 3, Stockholm, Sweden, October 18–20, 2010: Revised Selected Papers*, ed. John Impagliazzo, Per Lundin and Benkt Wangler (Heidelberg, 2011), 187–95; Bertil Rolandsson, *Facket, informationsteknologin och politiken: Strategier och perspektiv inom LO 1976–1996* (Göteborg, 2003).

The second theme focuses in a rather straightforward manner on different aspects of the construction of Swedish mainframe computers by the Swedish Board for Computing Machinery (Matematikmaskinnämnden, MMN), the companies Åtvidabergs Industrier (later Facit Electronics) and Saab (later Datasaab/Stansaab/ Ericsson Information Systems), as well as other players involved in the establishment of a domestic computer industry. A number of these studies have been undertaken by practitioners and pioneers in digital technology and focus, above all, on technical details. Most notably, the control theorist Karl Johan Åström broadens the perspective and provides an apt analysis of the early development of automatic control in Sweden.[15] Other studies have been accomplished by historians and deal with cultural discourses, institutional settings, and social networks centered around these early Swedish computers. The business historian Tom Petersson explains, for instance, the crisis and stagnation of the above-mentioned Swedish company Facit—once one of the world's largest producers of office machines—in the late 1960s and the early 1970s by personal relations and an inability to solve internal organizational problems rather than a miscalculation of the accelerating technological development as have been claimed in earlier research.[16] Studies addressing the physical

---

[15] Karl Johan Åström, "Early Control Development in Sweden," *European Journal of Control* 13 (2007), 1–24; Tord Jöran Hallberg, *IT-gryning: Svensk datahistoria från 1840- till 1960-talet* (Lund, 2007); Jörgen Lund, *Från kula till data* (Stockholm, 1989); Kjell Mellberg, Gunnar Wedell and Bo Lindestam, *Fyrtio år av den svenska datahistorien: Från Standard radiofabrik till ...?* (Stockholm, 1997); Per Arne Persson, "Transformation of the Analog: The Case of the Saab BT 33 Artillery Fire Control Simulator and the Introduction of the Digital Computer as Control Technology," *IEEE Annals in the History of Computing* 21, no. 2 (1999), 52–64. Valuable historical information is also found in the computer club Datasaabs vänner's book series on the history of Datasaab: Conny Johansson, ed., *Tema gudar* (Linköping, 2002); Bertil Knutsson, ed., *Tema bank: Datasaab och bankerna* (Linköping, 1996); Viggo Wentzel, ed., *Tema D21* (Linköping, 1994); idem, ed., *Tema flyg: Flygets datorpionjärer* (Linköping, 1995); Sven Yngvell, ed., *Tema D22–D23: Tunga linjens uppgång och fall* (Linköping, 1997). Of interest are also several of the essays in Janis Bubenko, Jr., John Impagliazzo and Arne Sølvberg, eds., *History of Nordic Computing: IFIP WG9.7 First Working Conference on the History of Nordic Computing (HiNC1), June 16–18, 2003, Trondheim, Norway* (New York, 2005). On the Swedish difference engines of the nineteenth century, see Michael Lindgren, *Glory and Failure: The Difference Engines of Johann Müller, Charles Babbage and Georg and Edvard Scheutz*, trans. Craig G. McKay, 2nd ed. (Cambridge, MA, 1990).

[16] Anders Carlsson, "Tekniken – politikens frälsare?: Om matematikmaskiner, automation och ingenjörer vid mitten av 50-talet," *Arbetarhistoria* 23 (1999), 23–30; idem, "Elektroniska hjärnor: Debatten om datorer, automation och ingenjörer 1955–58," in *Artefakter: Industrin, vetenskapen och de tekniska nätverken*, ed. Sven Widmalm (Hedemora & Möklinta, 2004), 245–85; Magnus Johansson, "Early Analog Computers in Sweden—With Examples From Chalmers University of Technology and the Swedish Aerospace Industry," *IEEE Annals in the History of Computing* 18, no. 4 (1996), 27–33; idem, *Smart, Fast and Beautiful: On Rhetoric of Technology and Computing Discourse in Sweden 1955–1995* (Linköping, 1997); idem, "Big Blue Gets Beaten: The Technological and Political Controversy of the First Large Swedish Computerization Project in a Rhetoric of Technology Perspective," *IEEE Annals in the History of Computing* 21, no. 2 (1999), 14–30; Tom Petersson, *I teknikrevolutionens centrum: Företagsledning och utveckling i Facit, 1957–1972* (Uppsala, 2003); idem, "Facit and the BESK Boys: Sweden's Computer Industry (1956–1962)," *IEEE Annals of the History of Computing* 27, no. 4 (2005), 23–30; idem, "Private and Public Interests in the Development of the Early Swedish Computer Industry: Facit, Saab and the Struggle for National Dominance", in *Science for Welfare and Warfare: Technology and State Initiative in Cold War Sweden*, ed. Per Lundin, Niklas Stenlås and Johan Gribbe (Sagamore Beach, 2010), 109–29.

establishment and the institutional settings of computer networks in Sweden, most notably the Internet, can be added to this body of literature.[17]

Historical scholarship that adopts an interdisciplinary perspective on the relationship between man, information technology, and society (*människa, informationsteknik och samhälle*) forms a third thematic cluster. Since these studies normally put their main emphasis on developing economic or sociological theories, the historical understanding of the role of computers in society usually comes second. The historical case studies undertaken in these investigations are often of rather limited value for the historian, since they are subordinated to the main objectives (discussing and developing theories).[18] However, in this body of literature, we also find the few user-oriented approaches in the Swedish historiography of computing. The librarian and social scientist Lena Olsson investigates how librarians computerized the Swedish research libraries during the 1970s. The musicologist Per Olov Broman and the art historian Gary Svensson describe and analyze how musicians and artists appropriated computing technology during the postwar period in order to develop new artistic expressions.[19]

To conclude, the question of how "computing has changed the world" has not really been addressed by Swedish scholars. Likewise, explicitly formulated user-oriented approaches, save for the examples mentioned above, are, by and large,

[17] Lena Andersson-Skog, "Från normalspår till bredband: Svensk kommunikationspolitik i framtidens tjänst 1850–2000," in *Omvandlingens sekel: Perspektiv på ekonomi och samhälle i 1900-talets Sverige*, ed. Lena Andersson-Skog and Olle Krantz (Lund, 2002), 117–43; Barbro Atlestam, "Datornät," in *Infrastruktur för informationssamhället: Teknik och politik*, ed. Barbro Atlestam (Stockholm, 1995), 113–27; Inga Hamngren, Jan Odhnoff and Jeroen Wolfers, *De byggde Internet i Sverige*, 2nd ed. (Stockholm, 2009); Kaarina Lehtisalo, *The History of NORDUnet: Twenty-Five Years of Networking Cooperation in the Nordic Countries* (Hørsholm, 2005). Although the historical findings are limited, the essays in the interdisciplinary anthology *The World's Largest Machine: Global Telecommunications and Human Condition* (Linköping, 1995) edited by Magnus Karlsson and Lennart Sturesson as well as Lars Ilshammar's chapter, "Från supervapen till supermarket: Utvecklingen av Internet 1957–1997," in *Den konstruerade världen: Tekniska system i historiskt perspektiv*, ed. Pär Blomkvist and Arne Kaijser (Stockholm & Stehag, 1998), 323–43, and Bernt Skovdahl's book, *Den digitala framtiden: Om förutsagda informationssamhällen och framväxande IT-realiteter* (Stockholm, 2009), might be of interest.

[18] Joakim Appelquist, *Informationsteknik och organisatorisk förändring: Teknik, organisation och produktivitet inom svensk banksektor 1975–2003* (Lund, 2005); Christer Johansson and Jörgen Nissen, *Människa, informationsteknik, samhälle: MITS – en forskargrupp* (Linköping, 1996); Magnus Karlsson, *The Liberalisation of Telecommunications in Sweden: Technology and Regime Change from the 1960s to 1993* (Linköping, 1998); Jörgen Nissen, *Pojkarna vid datorn: Unga entusiaster i datateknikens värld* (Stockholm, 1993).

[19] Per Olov Broman, *Kort historik över framtidens musik: Elektronmusiken och framtidstanken i svenskt 1950- och 60-tal* (Stockholm, 2007); Lena Olsson, *Det datoriserade biblioteket: Maskindrömmar på 70-talet* (Linköping, 1995); Gary Svensson, *Digitala pionjärer: Datorkonstens introduktion i Sverige* (Stockholm, 2000). See also Ulf Sandqvist, *Digitala drömmar: En studie av svenska dator- och tv-spelsbranschen 1980–2005* (Umeå, 2007).

absent.[20] This is perhaps even more surprising for the Swedish historiography than for the international one, given that Sweden has been prominent in involving the user in the design of computing technology and in systems development.[21]

1.3   But Who Is the User?

At this juncture, when I have urged historians to address the question of how computing has changed the world by adopting a user perspective, it is time to scrutinize the user as a concept. Who is the user? How has the category been defined and discussed by scholars? And how do we define it?

As a point of departure for my discussion in this section, I will take Nelly Oudshoorn and Trevor Pinch's introduction to the book *How Users Matter* from 2003, since it gives a good survey of the state of the research on user-oriented approaches in the quickly growing field of Science and Technology Studies (STS).[22] Thereafter, I will give an account of the criticism that their work has attracted from historians, and, in the next section, I will present an approach and a definition that we advocate.

Oudshoorn and Pinch are concerned with "the role of users in the development of technology in general," and they pay attention to how users consume, modify, domesticate, and resist technologies. Even if they put the main emphasis on "what users do with technology," they also claim to be interested in "what technologies do to users."[23]

Oudshoorn and Pinch notice that users and technology are too often seen as separate objects of research (it should be noted here though that when they refer to

---

[20] Other exceptions are a number of short essays in *Dædalus*, the annual of the National Museum of Science and Technology and the papers presented at the Third IFIP Conference on the History of Nordic Computing. Mats Höjeberg, ed., *Dædalus 2002: Tekniska museets årsbok: Dator till vardags* (Stockholm, 2001); John Impagliazzo, Per Lundin and Benkt Wangler, eds., *History of Nordic Computing 3: Third IFIP WG9.7 Conference, HiNC 3, Stockholm, Sweden, October 18–20, 2010: Revised Selected Papers* (Heidelberg: Springer 2011).

[21] Pioneering was the so-called Scandinavian school in systems development. Jørgen Bansler, *Systemutveckling: Teori och historia i skandinaviskt perspektiv*, trans. Geije Johansson (Lund, 1990); Kristo Ivanov, *Systemutveckling och ADB-ämnets utveckling* (Linköping, 1984); Markku I. Nurminen, *People or Computers: Three Ways of Looking at Information Systems* (1986), trans. Päivi Käpylä and Ellen Valle (Lund, 1988).

[22] Nelly Oudshoorn and Trevor Pinch, "Introduction: How Users and Non-Users Matter," in *How Users Matter: The Co-Construction of Users and Technologies*, ed. Nelly Oudshoorn and Trevor Pinch (Cambridge, MA, 2003). See also their recent update: Nelly Oudshoorn and Trevor Pinch, "User-Technology Relationships: Some Recent Developments," in *The Handbook of Science and Technology Studies*, ed. Edward J. Hackett et al., 3rd ed. (Cambridge, MA, 2008), 541–65. It should be noted here that the concept of user is also a matter for discussion in information systems research and other related ICT-disciplines. See, for instance, Roberta Lamb and Rob Kling, "Reconceptualizing Users as Social Actors in Information Systems Research," *MIS Quarterly* 27, no. 2 (2003), 197–236.

[23] Oudshoorn and Pinch, "Introduction," 1f.

earlier research, it is usually STS they have in mind). Instead, they want to view users and technology as "two sides of the same problem—as co-constructed." Their aim with the anthology is to go beyond "technological determinist views of technology and essentialist views of users' identities," and they suggest studies of the coconstruction of users and technologies as a way to reach this goal.[24] They distinguish four different approaches to user-technology relations in the earlier literature: the social construction of technology (SCOT) approach, feminist approaches, semiotic approaches, and cultural and media studies.

The SCOT approach was one of the first in technology studies that drew attention to the user. Its founding fathers Trevor Pinch and Wiebe Bijker saw users as a social group that played a part in the construction of technology. They observed that different social groups could construct radically different meanings of a technology—a phenomenon they denoted as interpretive flexibility. As a technology eventually stabilized, the interpretive flexibility vanished, and a dominant design, a dominant meaning, and a dominant use emerged in its place. Since many of the classic SCOT studies focused on the early stage of technologies, they, as Oudshoorn and Pinch point out, did not show any greater interest in how users could modify stable technologies.[25]

Moving on to feminist scholars, as Oudshoorn and Pinch denote them, these have played an important role in drawing attention to users. Their point of departure was the neglect of women's role in the development of technology. By focusing on users and use rather than on engineers and design, it would be possible to go "beyond histories of men inventing and mastering technology." The work of Ruth Schwartz Cowan played a crucial role, and her concept of "the consumption junction," defined as "the place and time at which the consumer makes choices between competing technologies," played a pivotal role.[26] Gender studies as well as technology studies reflect, as emphasized by Oudshoorn and Pinch, a shift in the conceptualization of users from "passive recipients to active participants." Feminist scholars have also acknowledged that "users come in many different shapes and sizes," and have tried to cope with the diversity of users (and the implicit difference in power relations) by differentiating between "end users," "lay end users," and "implicated actors."[27] Oudshoorn and Pinch underline that feminist studies include an explicit political agenda: "to increase women's autonomy and their influence on technological development."[28]

---

[24] Ibid., 2f.

[25] An exception is Ronald Kline and Trevor Pinch's article "Users as Agents of Technological Change: The Social Construction of the Automobile in the Rural United States," *Technology and Culture* 37, no. 4 (1996), 763–95; Oudshoorn and Pinch, "Introduction," 3f.

[26] Ruth Schwarz Cowan, "The Consumption Junction: A Proposal for Research Strategies in the Sociology of Technology," in *The Social Construction of Technological Systems: New Directions in the Sociology and History of Technology*, ed. Wiebe E. Bijker, Thomas P. Hughes, and Trevor Pinch (Cambridge, MA, 1989), 263; Oudshoorn and Pinch, "Introduction," 4ff.

[27] End users are "those individuals and groups who are affected downstream by products of technological innovation," the concept lay end users highlights "some end users' relative exclusion from expert discourse," and implicated actors are "those silent or not present but affected by the action." Oudshoorn and Pinch, "Introduction," 6.

[28] Ibid., 4ff.

The semiotic approach was, in turn, introduced by STS scholars who extended semiotics, studies on how meanings are constructed, "from signs to things." My account of this approach will not be detailed here, but it should be mentioned that the concepts of "configuring the user" and "script" are central to this approach. The former refers to how designers configure users, but also to how designers are configured by both users and their own organization, while the latter tries to "capture how technological objects enable or constrain human relations as well as relationships between people and things." Oudshoorn and Pinch largely dismiss this approach, since, they argue, it stays too close to the old linear model of technological innovation, which gives priority to the agency of designers and producers over the agency of the users.[29]

Cultural and media studies have, in contrast to technology studies, always had users and consumers as its major topic of analysis. As Oudshoorn and Pinch point out, their central thesis is that "technologies must be culturally appropriated to become functional." In the 1980s, many prominent intellectuals, such as Pierre Bourdieu, Mary Douglas and Baron Isherwood, and Jean Baudrillard, made important contributions to this tradition. It should also be mentioned that the semiotic approach eventually made its way into cultural and media studies. But perhaps the most interesting contribution to the study of user-technology relations from cultural and media studies is the notion of "domestication" introduced by Roger Silverstone. With the concept, he describes how the integration of technological objects involves "a taming of the wild and a cultivation of the tame," and he has specified four phases of domestication: appropriation, objectification, incorporation, and conversion.[30] Domestication is understood as a process in which both technical objects and people may change, and may thus, according to Oudshoorn and Pinch, inspire to conduct research that will "transcend the artificial divide between design and use" and reconceptualize "the traditional distinction between production and consumption."

With *How Users Matter*, Oudshoorn and Pinch want to bridge the above-presented approaches to user-technology relations and explore "the creative capacity of users to shape technological development in all phases of technological innovation."[31] In order to reach a thorough understanding of "the role of the users in technological development," they argue that "the multiplicity and diversity of users, spokespersons for users, and locations where the coconstruction of users and technologies takes place" have to be taken into account.[32]

---

[29] Ibid., 7ff., 15.

[30] "Appropriation occurs when a technical product or service is sold and individuals or households become its owners. In objectification, processes of display reveal the norms and principles of the 'household's sense of itself and its place in the world'. Incorporation occurs when technological objects are used in and incorporated into the routines of daily life. 'Conversion' is used to describe the processes in which the use of technological objects shape relationships between users and people outside the household. In this process, artifacts become tools for making status claims and for expressing a specific lifestyle to neighbors, colleagues, family, and friends." Ibid., 14f.

[31] Ibid., 16.

[32] Ibid., 24.

But exactly what kind of users do they have in mind? They do not give an explicit definition, but their discussion makes it clear that they are only interested in users or nonusers that *matter* in the development of technology (*or* in the design, the production, and the selling of technologies *or* in the stabilization and destabilization of technologies). Users or nonusers that do *not shape* the technological development lie outside the scope of their book and are not included in their (implicit) definition of users.

Indeed, as the US-based historian of science and technology John Krige points out in an insightful review of *How Users Matter*, Oudshoorn and Pinch, although pioneering in bringing in the user, still focus "on their shaping of the process of technological design and innovation." Their book, thus, only addresses a small subset of users: those that are "articulate, organized, and living in rich industrialized countries where spaces are created for the individual consumer and the citizen to express their interests." However, most "end users" do not have this capacity; they are, as he remarks, "the sometimes passive, sometimes willing, sometimes resentful 'victims' of technological change, deeply affected by it, yet effectively powerless to shape its trajectory."[33] A focus on them, Krige continues, "and on that category of intermediate users, notably the coercive apparatus of the state and some major corporations, who demand technologies that disempower people, and peoples, would provide a far less positive picture of the role of human agency in shaping technology."[34]

The British historian of technology David Edgerton elaborates Krige's comments on the first-mentioned group of users by delivering a powerful critique of the innovation-centric historiography. His general argument is that most historiography of technology (including STS) deals with innovation rather than technology and that it has led to an "unfortunate conflation between the two." Distinguishing innovation from use not only facilitates a dialogue between history of technology and history in general, it is also essential in addressing questions concerned with gender, ethnicity, and class. Furthermore, the innovation-centered historical writing often excludes histories of technology in use. Edgerton asserts that processes of maintenance, repair, remodeling, reuse, and recycling have been fundamental to material culture, but that they are ignored in the current historiography because of the emphasis on initial creation. A use-centered history, he contends, will overcome these shortcomings.[35]

Thus, Oudshoorn and Pinch's implicit definition of the user excludes two very important groups: those not contributing to the process of technological design and innovation, i.e., the majority of the people in the world, and those empowered by government or corporations with the authority to adapt technology to fit their needs.

---

[33] John Krige, "Review: How Users Matter: The Co-Construction of Users and Technology by Nelly Oudshoorn and Trevor Pinch," *Contemporary Sociology* 35, no. 1 (2006), 32.

[34] Ibid.

[35] Edgerton, "From Innovation to Use", 111–120; idem, *The Shock of the Old: Technology and Global History Since 1900* (Oxford, 2007), ix–xviii.

That they address far from *all* users that *matter* in the development of technology (technological innovation) is also a point made the American business historian by JoAnne Yates in her 2006 article "How Business Enterprises Use Technology." She criticizes the SCOT approach, including Oudshoorn and Pinch's *How Users Matter* in that tradition, for only taking the individual user into account. In the SCOT (or the STS) approach, firms only enter the picture as the producers and the distributors of technological artifacts or of products of technology to individuals.[36] Yates argues for broadening the concept of "technology users or consumers to include business enterprises as well as individuals." Manufactured items are, in many cases, "created and sold to only other institutional users, whether a business enterprise or a government or nonprofit organization." An example of artifacts involved in these kinds of "business-to-business (B2B) transactions" is, or rather was, mainframe computers.[37] In fact, according to Yates, critical decisions in Cowan's "consumption junction" (see above) are, in many cases, taken by an organization consisting of many individuals with different roles and interactions.[38]

Furthermore, Yates argues for extending the focus on users to also include studies on technology use, or "technology in practice." By studying technology use, she continues, we will be able to understand "the early and ongoing influence of technology on firms and individuals, and these users' influences on the technology and on innovation in general."[39]

The criticism leveled at Oudshoorn and Pinch's discussion of user-technology relations may be summarized in three points. First, they are still caught in the powerful master narrative of invention and innovation when discussing user-technology relations. Their interest in the role of users or nonusers is limited to technological invention and innovation. However, as Edgerton has pointed out, most users in the world are not involved in these processes. Second, they do not address all users that matter in technological development, i.e., intermediate users of technology, such as corporations and governments. Third, and related to the second, they only consider individual users, not institutional users, such as firms, governments, or nonprofit organizations.

1.4 Introducing the "Elite" User

How do we understand the term "user" then? As the above discussion shows, it is obviously difficult to reach "closure" on a definition of the concept. The different positions are, nevertheless, helpful for us in defining what we mean by users and which groups we primarily identify as users.

---

[36] JoAnne Yates, "How Business Enterprises Use Technology: Extending the Demand Side Turn," *Enterprise and Society* 7, no. 3 (2006), 426f.

[37] Ibid., 430.

[38] Ibid., 434.

[39] Ibid., 424f. It should be noted here that the above-mentioned James W. Cortada examines Yates' argument when discussing the *raison d'être* for his monumental study *The Digital Hand*. Cortada, "Studying the Role of IT in the Evolution of American Business Practices," 30f.

We are primarily interested in the groups of users that have the power to shape major historical transformations. These may be bureaucrats, businessmen, managers, but most of all professionals. We call them "elite" users.[40] This is not to say, however, that users in Oudshoorn and Pinch's sense do not have the possibility to change the world. They sometimes do, as the cases in their book indeed show, but they are obviously not in the same privileged position as elite users. They are not supported by political and economic power to the same extent. Moreover, they are not educated, organized, and trained in the same fashion as elite users, and, therefore, they do not share beliefs, values, and norms to the same extent as these. It may be added that these men and women did not denote themselves users. Rather, they identified themselves with, and drew legitimacy from, their professional basis. Thus, we understand the user as primarily an analytical category, not as a historical category.

While Yates eloquently argues for extending the user concept to include organizations, such as firms, government agencies, and nonprofit organizations, we will reserve the concept of elite users for individuals or groups of individuals.[41] We borrow the argument for limiting the concept to the individual from the historical scholarship on the study of elites, which has moved from a position where class and state were central analytical concepts to a position where agency, exclusivity, and mode of relationship are placed in the foreground.[42] As George E. Marcus points out, the notion of elites has a personal, informal trait:

> In modern societies, elites are creatures of institutions in which they have defined functions, offices, or controlling interests, but in relation to institutions, they re-create a domain of personal relationships that extends across functional and official boundaries. Institutions seem to have a life of their own, and society can be explained wholly in terms of the working of formal organizations. But what if the behavior of the same organizations is attributed to the activities of their controlling elites in closed informal communities? The theoretical

---

[40] There are alternative notions to elite users, but we argue that they are too narrowly defined and do not fully capture the group of users that have the power to shape major historical transformations. With the notion "lead users," Eric von Hippel emphasizes that innovation often is user-driven. We want, however, to cover more than the role of users in "product innovation," which is von Hippel's main focus. Eric von Hippel, *Democratizing Innovation* (Cambridge, MA, 2005), 1–17; Oudshoorn and Pinch, "User-Technology Relationships," 542f. Other alternative concepts that we have considered, but, in the end, rejected, are "qualified" users as well as "critical" users. An objection raised against the first is that many users that can be identified as qualified do not necessarily have the position or the possibility "to change the world," i.e., that they are qualified does not mean that they possess elite attributes. An objection to the second concept is that it is already used by researchers on user-centered design and they do it with a different purpose. With "critical users," they refer to "users with severe disabilities (motion, sensory or cognitive impairments) who can illustrate the extreme end of the usability spectrum and on whom the impact of poor design is greatest in terms of function and stigma. [---] Such users are in a valid critical position because they have similar lifestyles, aspirations and tastes as creative designers, but have to adapt to ill thought out products that may not have been designed with consideration of their capability limitations." See, for instance, Hua Dong et al., "Critical User Forums: An Effective User Research Method for Inclusive Design," *Design Journal* 8, no. 2 (2005), 49–59.

[41] We do, however, acknowledge the analytical value in discussing users at an aggregated level.

[42] George E. Marcus, "Elite as a Concept, Theory, and Tradition," in *Elites: Ethnographic Issues*, ed. George E. Marcus (Albuquerque, 1983), 7–13.

vision of modern society then is less a model of the workings of formal organizations than it is an image of the internal cultures of ruling groups and of the effects of their activities upon deceptively monolithic, automatic institutional processes in which or against which they operate.[43]

Ultimately, power is connected to individuals, rather than impersonal processes or institutions. I would like to distinguish between elite users as we define them and the scholarly understanding of "elites." Scholars devoted to the study of the latter usually deal with economic and political elites—those with the utmost power. Elite users do not necessarily possess the utmost economic or political power, but we argue that they, nevertheless, are in a position to shape major historical transformations due to their organizational, technical, and scientific skills and positions.

We do not see elite users as a distinct, given group of individuals. Elite users can change arenas, functions, or positions, i.e., they have careers. Designers or producers of a certain technology may shift arena, function, or position and become highly qualified users of the very same technology. Qualified users occupying a key role in an organization may, on the other hand, modify or transform technology to a unique product that they, after a while, start to manufacture and sell as producers and salesmen. Moreover, while a scientist develops a certain technology, he or she uses other technologies. The composition of elite users thus differs depending on the arena or time period studied as well as the perspective taken. The concept elite user, as we understand it, is, therefore, necessarily dynamic.[44]

It also means that users are given the attribute "elite" *in relation* to other users (hence seen as being "nonelite"). The advent of the PC in the 1980s, for instance, eventually led to a mass use of computers, and people who previously had been elite users found their elite status challenged, when the digital technology suddenly became accessible to the majority.

To summarize, we are certainly interested in users as Oudshoorn and Pinch define them, and we do not neglect "end users" in Krige and Edgerton's sense, but, above all, we direct our attention to elite users of computing technology (and their interaction with designers, producers, purchasers, and salesmen as well as manufacturers and suppliers in the public, the private, and the military sector). The reason for doing that is a simple one: we want to understand how computing has changed the world.

1.5   The Need for Documenting the Recent Past

But do we really need to collect and create sources on the use of computers in Swedish society during the latter part of the twentieth century? Are there not already an abundance of sources on the history of computing in Swedish archives and libraries

---

[43] Marcus, "Elite as a Concept, Theory, and Tradition," 16f.

[44] Elite users' involvement with technology can, furthermore, be described with Oudshoorn and Pinch's notion of users and technology as coconstructed. Yates even suggests that this notion could be extended from individual to firm users. Yates, "How Business Enterprises Use Technology," 437.

just waiting to be "discovered" by historians? At first glance, the situation in general for the historian devoted to the twentieth century is certainly one of sources in abundance. The salient (source-critical) problem for this historian is to find methods to navigate through the plethora of sources rather than scrutinize a scarcity of resources. A set of historical questions often makes a point of departure. Are the sources relevant given the questions posed? Are they representative of the historical phenomena that interest the scholar?[45]

This is, of course, the situation in general. As always, there are exceptions. Some archives may have restricted access to the relevant sources. Documents may be in private hands. Records in archives of firms and nonprofit organizations may have been sorted out due to lack of space or change of ownership. Mergers of firms have occasionally led to the disappearance of whole archives. And catastrophes, fire, and wars have destroyed many archives in the past. Even government authorities now and then throw away archival records because of ignorance (the worst sinners in this respect are, somewhat ironically, universities and cultural institutions), and throughout history it has often occurred that the official who produced or originally collected a given document did not find it worth saving. Moreover, sources deteriorate because of the quality of paper and ink. Poor archival conditions accelerate the degradation.[46] But these kinds of particularities are, of course, not exclusive to the twentieth century. Evidence has always disappeared and will probably continue to disappear. We have to acknowledge that a complete historical record is an illusion.

Of greater concern for us, as the American historian Roy Rosenzweig points out, is that the general situation changes dramatically as we move into a "digital era." Practices are rapidly being transformed. Government records are digitized. Traditional works, like books, journals, and films, are increasingly "being born digitally." Paper correspondence is being replaced with e-mails. And Web-based media, such as today's Facebook, MySpace, Twitter, and YouTube, will probably increase in scale and scope at the cost of "analog" media.[47]

At first glance, it seems that the future historian will have access to even more sources. Almost everything seems to leave digital footprints. Phone calls have, for instance, at least, to some extent, been replaced by e-mails. Perhaps an essentially complete historical record is not an illusion after all? But then we forget that evidence in the digital era is fragile. Even if the digital sources are here today, they may be gone tomorrow. While paper-based media deteriorate slowly and unevenly, digital media may fail completely—a single damaged bit can render an entire document

---

[45] Maria Ågren, "Synlighet, vikt, trovärdighet – och självkritik: Några synpunkter på källkritikens roll i dagens historieforskning," *Historisk tidskrift* 2005:2, 249–62.

[46] See, for instance, Martha Howell and Walter Prevenier, *From Reliable Sources: An Introduction to Historical Methods* (Ithaca, 2001), 37–39.

[47] Roy Rosenzweig, "Scarcity or Abundance? Preserving the Past in a Digital Era," *The American Historical Review* 108 (2003), 735–62. The Center for History and New Media (CHNM) at George Mason University also provides on their Web site several insightful essays and discussions on history in the digital era: http://chnm.gmu.edu/ (accessed June 10, 2009).

unreadable. The life spans of digital media are also considerably shorter than the ones of acid-free paper and microfilms, but, Rosenzweig stresses, changes in hardware and software pose far greater problems than the media itself. Platforms and programs change constantly.[48] A solution is to "migrate" the data stored in old formats to up-to-date formats. Migration costs will be very high, however, given that hardware and software will continue to change.[49] While the preservation of digital sources is linked with numerous technical problems, Rosenzweig argues that the social, economic, legal, and organizational problems are far worse.[50] There are yet no established practices on how to handle digital sources. Web pages come and go. E-mails to or from an organization are usually administered by the organization's IT support, with little or no knowledge at all of archival practices and obligations, instead of the same organization's archivists. And how shall national archives and libraries deal with the international Web? To conclude this short digital detour, we cannot at all be assured that there will be an abundance of sources on our contemporary history. We may even have to cope with scarcity in the future.

But, on the other hand, since we are dealing with the period between 1950 and 1980, one could argue that most of the documents are not digital and not really affected by the changes described above. So the question basically remains: do we really need more sources?

Ultimately, the answer depends on which set of questions we are interested in. If sources that are relevant and representative given our historical questions exist, it will, of course, not be critical to create new sources (although these can still be valuable as a complement to existing ones). But that is not always the case. Our existing archival records often display a strong bias. The activities of the nation-state and organizations (governmental as well as nongovernmental) are, in general, well documented, while the activities of other historical actors may not be documented at all. As the British historian John Tosh points out, written sources are primarily the result of grown-up men's work, and, therefore, it is difficult to find sources on the experiences of women (those who did not belong to the letter-writing bourgeoisie) and children. And, on many other social groups, such as nonunion labor, peddlers, or immigrants, there is an almost complete lack of written sources.[51] This bias in the written sources has often been reflected in the historians' investigations and choice of questions. Although there are notable exceptions, labor history deals with trade union officials more often than the rank and file, history of housing with housing

---

[48] Rosenzweig, "Scarcity or Abundance?" 741–5.

[49] A more straightforward solution is to print out digital documents on paper, but then there remain, of course, complex, dynamic, and interactive objects, such as computer games, digital art, and Web pages generated from databases. This is because virtually every Web page is linked to every other and retaining the full complexity requires ultimately the whole Web to be preserved. Thomas J. Misa, "Organizing the History of Computing: 'Lessons Learned' at the Charles Babbage Institute," in *History of Nordic Computing 2*, 8f.; Rosenzweig, "Scarcity or Abundance?" 742.

[50] Rosenzweig, "Scarcity or Abundance?" 743f.

[51] John Tosh, *The Pursuit of History: Aims, Methods and New Directions in the Study of Modern History*, 4th ed., with Seàn Lang (Harlow, 2006), 314f.

policies and sanitary reforms rather than the everyday life of tenants, the history of technology with planning and construction of large technological systems (in the Western world) rather than their use (in the rest of the world), and the history of science with prominent scientists and laboratories rather than amateur scientists.

With the turn toward (Marxist) social history during the 1970s, historians began to explore new fields in the landscape of the past. The history of everyday life (*Alltagsgeschichte*) and micro history (*microstoria*) as well as the "linguistic turn" during the following decade accelerated this development.[52] New research questions forced them to reflect on the apparent bias in the archival records. In doing so, they started to look for alternative sources in a more systematic manner than before. A multitude of unwritten sources, such as artifacts, landscapes, movies, oral sources, pictures, radio, and television, attracted their attention. Intense and often innovative methodological and theoretical discussions and developments followed this "discovery" of alternative sources, and today, most historians use a combination of sources in their daily work, and as a consequence, they have broadened the scope of the potential historical problems that can be addressed.[53]

To sum up, if the existing sources are not relevant to and/or representative of the historical problems and questions that interest us, it is necessary to "find" or create alternative sources. In what follows, it will be discussed how scholars have documented the recent past by creating sources. My survey will, at the same time, give arguments for why we need more sources on the use of computers in Swedish society.

1.6   Creating Oral and Written Sources

At this point, I would like to introduce two distinctions. Sources can roughly be divided into two categories: those which are created in retrospect and those which are not.[54] The former category can, in turn, be divided into sources created in the meeting between scholars and their like, on the one hand, and historical subjects on the other, and sources created by the historical subjects themselves. Diaries, memoirs, etc., belong to the latter type. We are interested in the former type

---

[52] Georg G. Iggers, *Historiography in the Twentieth Century: From Scientific Objectivity to the Postmodern Challenge*, with a new epilogue by the author (Middletown, CT, 2005), chaps. 7 and 9.

[53] See, for instance, Anders Brändström and Sune Åkerman, eds., *Icke skriftliga källor: Huvudtema I* (Umeå, 1991); Mats Burström, *Samtidsarkeologi: Introduktion till ett forskningsfält* (Lund, 2007); Ronald E. Doel and Thomas Söderqvist, eds., *The Historiography of Contemporary Science, Technology, and Medicine: Writing Recent Science* (New York, 2006); David W. Kingery, *Learning from Things: Method and Theory of Material Culture Studies* (Washington, 1996); Steven Lubar and David W. Kingery, eds., *History from Things: Essays on Material Culture* (Washington, 1993); Simon Schama, *Landscape and Memory* (London, 1996); Bosse Sundin and Sverker Sörlin, "Landskapets värden: Kring miljö- och kulturmiljövård som historiskt problemfält," in *Miljön och det förflutna: Landskap, minnen, värden*, ed. Richard Pettersson and Sverker Sörlin (Umeå, 1998), 3–19.

[54] This distinction corresponds roughly to the difference between documentary and reported evidence. Seldon and Pappworth, *By Word of Mouth*, 4f. Cf. Howell and Prevenier, *From Reliable Sources*, chap. 1.

of sources, which basically are of two kinds: oral sources and written recollections.[55] These are, to use Pinch and Oudshoorn's terminology, coconstructed by the historian and the historical subject.

How, and for what purpose, have sources been created, or coconstructed, by scholars? My main focus in this section will be on oral sources. To begin with, I give an account of how a "cousin" of oral history, written recollections, has been acquired.[56]

1.6.1 Early Ethnographical Collections

In Sweden, folklorists and philologists became interested in documenting different aspects of *folkkultur* (popular culture) already in the 1870s and created the ethnographical collections that eventually led to the establishment of Nordiska museet, today the oldest and largest museum of Swedish cultural history, as well as the world's first open-air museum Skansen in Stockholm.[57] They developed so-called *frågelistor* (questionnaires) as a method for creating sources on popular culture, and documentation work along these lines was institutionalized during the first decades of the twentieth century. The documentation focused on peasant culture and dealt with various subjects, such as "arbete, trötthet och vila" (work, fatigue, and rest), "lynne och karaktär" (temper and character), "brott och straff" (crime and punishment), "källor och brunnar" (springs and wells), and "belysning" (lighting). During the 1940s, folklorists at Nordiska museet began to document *arbetarminnen* (workers' memories) in order to cope with the bias toward agrarian culture in the earlier collections. They acquired memories from more than 30 different occupational groups with the help of questionnaires and published the resulting documentation in several volumes with titles, such as *Sågverksminnen* (Sawmill Memories), *Järnvägsminnen* (Railroad Memories), *Bokbindarminnen* (Bookbinder Memories), and *Stenhuggarminnen* (Stone-Cutting Memories).[58] Acquiring written recollections

---

[55] Other kinds of sources of this type could be the (re)constructions of artifacts and the like.

[56] Seldon and Pappworth, *By Word of Mouth*, 13f.

[57] Cecilia Hammarlund-Larsson, "Samlingarna och samlandet," in *Nordiska museet under 125 år*, ed. Hans Medelius, Bengt Nyström and Elisabet Stavenow-Hidemark (Stockholm: Nordiska museets förlag, 1998), 180–239; Mátyás Szabó, "Fältarbeten och forskning," in *ibid.*, 240–71.

[58] Nationalmuseet in Denmark, Norsk Folkemuseum in Norway, Svenska Litteratursällskapet i Finland (The Society of Swedish Literature in Finland) and Finska Litteratursällskapet (The Finnish Literature Society) also acquired workers' memories in a similar fashion. Charlotte Hagström and Lena Marander-Eklund, "Att arbeta med frågelistor," in *Frågelistan som källa och metod*, ed. Charlotte Hagström and Lena Marander-Eklund (Lund, 2005), 11f.; Knut Kjeldstadli, *Det förflutna är inte vad det en gång var*, trans. Sven-Erik Torhell (Lund, 1998), 185; Sune Åkerman, "Mjukdata," in *Usynlig historie: Foredrag fra den 17. Nordiske fagkonferensen for historisk metodelære i Tranum Klit 19.–23. mai 1981*, ed. Bjørn Qviller and Birgitte Wåhlin (Oslo, 1983), 47–54. An interesting parallel is the British mass-observation project, which ran between 1937 and the early 1950s. Dorothy Sheridan, "Ordinary Lives and Extraordinary Writers: The British Mass-Observation Project," in *Frågelist och berättarglädje: Om frågelistor som forskningsmetod och folklig genre*, ed. Bo G. Nilsson, Dan Waldetoft, and Christina Westergren (Stockholm, 2003), 45–55.

with the help of questionnaires has up to the present continued to be a prominent feature in Swedish ethnology and folklore.[59] A selection of the collected life stories of engineers published by Nordiska museet in the volume *Framtiden var vår* (The Future Was Ours) serves as a recent example. The written recollections that this volume contains give a comprehensive and nuanced picture of the engineering profession and its role in Swedish society.[60]

1.6.2   History from Below

The dominating method, however, for coping with the bias in the written sources has been to create and use oral sources. Historians since ancient Herodotus and Thucydides have relied on the spoken word, but the nineteenth-century development of an academic history discipline led to the primacy of archival research and documentary sources, and a marginalization of oral evidence. Although oral sources continued to be consulted by historians, they were not treated as genuine documents, i.e., they were not footnoted.[61] If historians were hesitant about using oral sources, folklorists and social scientists took a more positive stance. A pioneering project devoted to creating oral accounts of the past was launched in the USA in the late 1930s. The Federal Writers' Project, as it was called, produced, in particular, oral histories on labor and slave memories in the form of life histories, but without the methodological rigor that the documentation of oral histories later became associated with.[62] The development of new recording techniques, i.e., the wire recorder and later the tape recorder, aroused the interest in preserving the spoken word. Allan Nevins, who also coined the term "oral history," carried out the first modern oral history project at the University of Columbia in the late 1940s. His project differed markedly from the above-mentioned collections since it focused on elites— the leaders in business, the professions, politics, and social life—from the outset,[63] and, as will be discussed below, the elite approach has remained an important part of oral history. Soon, however, scholars once again turned their attention toward marginalized or neglected social groups whose voices, by and large, remained silent

---

[59] See, for instance, Charlotte Hagström and Lena Marander-Eklund, eds., *Frågelistan som källa och metod* (Lund, 2005); Nilsson, Waldetoft, and Westergren, *Frågelist och berättarglädje*.

[60] Dan Waldetoft, ed., *Framtiden var vår: Civilingenjörer skriver om sitt liv och arbete* (Stockholm, 1993).

[61] Soraya de Chadarevian, "Using Interviews to Write the History of Science," in *The Historiography of Contemporary Science and Technology*, ed. Thomas Söderqvist (Amsterdam, 1997), 54f.; Alistair Thomson, "Four Paradigm Transformations in Oral History," *The Oral History Review* 34, no. 1 (2006), 51.

[62] The project had, for instance, to rely on human notetakers because there were no audio recorders. Linda Shopes, "Making Sense of Oral History," *History Matters: The U.S. Survey Course on the Web*, http://historymatters.gmu.edu/mse/oral/, February 2002 (accessed March 9, 2009).

[63] Ibid.

in the existing sources. The use of oral history grew rapidly among anthropologists and historians of preliterate societies. The interest in recording the experiences of "ordinary" people was especially salient in Great Britain and became an important part in the "history from below" movement among politically committed social historians from the 1960s onward.[64] Paul Thompson, one of the movement's leading figures and author of the pioneering book *The Voice of the Past*, understood oral history as synonymous with history from below, and he emphasized its emancipatory qualities.[65] Today, however, most scholars prefer to see oral history as a method and not as a field or subdiscipline (such as social history).[66] Their practice has inspired them to reflect on methodological and theoretical issues, such as the question of subjectivity in the historical sciences, the relation between history and memory, individual versus collective memory, as well as memory and narrativity.[67]

1.6.3   Oral Sources on Elites

As a method, then, oral history has, above all, been justified and used for giving voices to the "invisible" historical subjects,[68] but since Nevins' project elites have also been its subjects. While Nevins' approach had an almost hagiographic stance— "great" men were interviewed about great events—I would like to underscore that elite oral history over the last decades has had a rather different purpose. Elite oral history as well as the study of elites is justified by the fact that elites and their activities have had considerable influence on social change, and to examine different aspects of elites will increase our knowledge of how they function and exercise power.[69] Scholars today argue that, although it is true that elites already have a voice in history,

---

[64] Thomson, "Four Paradigm Transformations in Oral History," 49–70. See also Shopes, "Making Sense of Oral History."

[65] Paul Thompson, *The Voice of the Past: Oral History* (Oxford, 1978).

[66] de Chadarevian, "Using Interviews to Write the History of Science," 52; David Gaunt, "Oral history och levnadsöden," in *Icke skriftliga källor: Huvudtema I*, ed. Anders Brändström and Sune Åkerman (Umeå, 1991), 64f.; Seldon and Pappworth, *By Word of Mouth*, 4; Tosh, *The Pursuit of History*, 334.

[67] A good overview of the critical developments in oral history is given in Thomson, "Four Paradigm Transformations in Oral History," 49–70. See also Geoffrey Cubitt, *History and Memory* (Manchester, 2007), 70; Anna Green, "Individual Remembering and 'Collective Memory': Theoretical Presuppositions and Contemporary Debates," *The Journal of the Oral History Society* 32, no. 2 (2004), 35–44; Alessandro Portelli, "The Death of Luigi Trastulli: Memory and the Event," in *The Death of Luigi Trastulli and Other Stories* (Albany, NY, 1991), 1–26.

[68] "Invisible" could here be replaced by "forgotten" or "hidden" without losing its essential meaning. Birgitta Odén, "Den 'osynliga' historien," in *Usynlig historie: Foredrag fra den 17. Nordiske fagkonferensen for historisk metodelære i Tranum Klit 19.–23. mai 1981*, ed. Bjørn Qviller and Birgitte Wåhlin (Oslo, 1983), 9–24.

[69] Seldon and Pappworth, *By Word of Mouth*, 6. See also Lewis Anthony Dexter, ed., *Elite and Specialized Interviewing* (Evanston, 1970); Eva McMahan, *Elite Oral History Discourse: A Study of Cooperation and Coherence* (Tuscaloosa, 1989).

the existing sources often remain silent about several important aspects of elites. The written sources rarely record lobbying. Compared to oral history as practiced in the "history from below" movement, elite oral history has to cope with different methodological challenges. Elite persons may, for instance, have been interviewed several times before, and they are more likely to have a canonical way in which they tell their story. The interviewer has to find ways to probe and question this canonical account.

I would like to mention a methodological development regarding elite oral history that has been taking place in Great Britain. Since 1986, the Centre for Contemporary British History (CCBH) has been developing witness seminars as a method for documenting the recent past.[70] These are a category of oral history methods where a number of individuals who have participated in, and/or witnessed, a certain series of historical events gather to discuss and debate their often-different interpretations of the past events. We can thus consider them as group interviews. As a method, the witness seminar is not exclusively directed at elites but has, by and large, been adopted as such. CCBH has, for example, dealt with top-level political events and processes, such as "The Berlin Crisis," "Britain and the Marshall Plan," "The British Response to the Strategic Defence Initiative (Star Wars) in the 1980s," and "Conservative Government Difficulties 1961–64."[71] The witness seminars designed by CCBH have become the model for similar documentation projects at a number of centers and institutes around the world. In Sweden, the Institute for Contemporary History at Södertörn University has held witness seminars essentially modeled on CCBHs. These have often, but not always, paid attention to top politicians, leading officials, and prominent intellectuals as in the witness seminar on "löntagar-fonder" (wage-earners' investment funds), on "grön politik" (green politics), or on "makten i Stadshuset" (the power in Stockholm Town Hall). As such, they have illuminated the hidden and more savory aspects of politics and policymaking as well as highlighted informal structures and political networks.[72]

1.6.4 Oral Sources on Recent Science, Technology, and Medicine

Related to elite oral history is a rather long tradition of conducting oral history in the history of science, technology, and medicine. Scholars have, in particular, used oral history in the study of leading engineers and scientists, such as Nobel Laureates, or

---

[70] "What Is a Witness Seminar?" http://www.ccbh.ac.uk/witnessseminars.php (accessed June 15, 2009).

[71] Ibid.

[72] Torbjörn Nilsson, personal communication, August 24, 2007; "Vittnesseminarier: Samtidshisto-riska institutet" (unpublished document). In 2004, Södertörn University also initiated a pilot project on elite oral history aiming at central political decision-makers. Ylva Waldemarsson, "Politiska makthavare som historisk källa," *Arkiv, samhälle och forskning* 2007:2, 6–23; idem, "Den redi-gerade källan," *Arbetarhistoria* 2008:1, 32–5.

outstanding laboratories, research facilities, or research groups, such as Niels Bohr's group in Copenhagen, the Manhattan Project, or the Radiation Laboratory at MIT.[73] They have found oral sources useful as a supplement to written sources. Since official records and scientific papers often are not very representative of the everyday life and work of engineers and scientists, conversations with the historical subjects may help the scholar to understand the component of "tacit knowledge" in engineering and scientific work as well as to grasp the often complex and complicated content that characterizes recent science. Oral history may also enhance their understanding of professional identities and ideologies.[74] Although oral history in the history of science, technology, and medicine does not necessarily have to deal with elites, the main emphasis on engineering and scientific elites still remains today. The influential professional communities and organizations of engineers and scientists are a part of the explanation. These have been instrumental in the creation of oral history archives in fields such as physics, chemistry, and medicine. The American Institute of Physics (AIP) is home to the Center for History of Physics, which dates back to the early 1960s, and that has completed some 1,500 oral history interviews with physicists, astronomers, and others.[75] The US-based Chemical Heritage Foundation (CHF) also runs a comprehensive oral history program, which has produced a substantial oral history collection over the years. Today, it contains more than 400 oral history interviews with "leading scientists and entrepreneurs."[76] Crossing the Atlantic, the British medical research charity the Wellcome Trust established in 1990 the Centre for the History of Medicine. As in the cases of AIP and CHF, it aims to build archives and conduct historical research related to the professional community of medical scientists. A salient feature is to create oral sources, and since 1993, the Centre for the History of Medicine has held witness seminars modeled on those of the above-mentioned CCBH. To date, more than 50 such meetings have been held, and they have dealt with subjects, such as "Monoclonal Antibodies," "Early Heart Transplant Surgery in the UK," and "Neonatal Intensive Care."[77] The many comprehensive oral

---

[73] Alex Soojung-Kim Pang, "Oral History and the History of Science: A Review Essay with Speculations," *International Journal of Oral History* 10, no. 3 (1989), 270–85. See also de Chadarevian, "Using Interviews to Write the History of Science," 51–70; Lillian Hoddeson, "The Conflict of Memories and Documents: Dilemmas and Pragmatics of Oral History," in *The Historiography of Contemporary Science, Technology, and Medicine: Writing Recent Science*, 187–200; E. M. Tansey, "Witnessing the Witnesses: Potentials and Pitfalls of the Witness Seminar in the History of Twentieth-Century Medicine," in *ibid.*, 260–78.

[74] de Chadarevian, "Using Interviews to Write the History of Science," 51f.; Hoddeson, "The Conflict of Memories and Documents," 187; Soojung-Kim Pang, "Oral History and the History of Science," 271ff.; Tilli Tansey, "Telling Like It Was," *New Scientist*, December 16, 1995, 49.

[75] "Center for History of Physics," http://www.aip.org/history/ (accessed June 10, 2009). See also "Sources for History of Quantum Physics," http://www.amphilsoc.org/library/guides/ahqp/ (accessed June 10, 2009).

[76] "Oral History Collection," http://www.chemheritage.org/exhibits/ex-nav2.html (accessed June 10, 2009); Rasheedah S. Young, "Oral History at CHF," *Chemical Heritage* 23, no. 2 (2005), 34–5.

[77] Tansey, "Witnessing the Witnesses," 260f.; "Wellcome Witnesses to Twentieth Century Medicine," http://www.ucl.ac.uk/histmed/publications/wellcome_witnesses_c20th_med (accessed June 10, 2009).

history programs in the history of science, technology, and medicine have contributed to establishing oral history as an accepted and widely used method in these disciplines.

During the last decade, historians of science, technology, and medicine have also shown a renewed interest in acquiring written recollections. Some oral historians have dismissed the method, arguing that written recollections can be guarded, bland, and difficult to evaluate.[78] It is certainly true that oral history interviews are preferable, but since they are time and resource consuming, it may not be possible to conduct interviews with a substantial number of people, for example, users. Acquiring written recollections, on the other hand, is rather cheap, and with Internet solutions it is possible to increase the scope of the documentation. A pioneering project in this respect was carried out at MIT, namely, the "History of Recent Science and Technology on the World-Wide Web," between 2000 and 2003. It appears that it did not take full advantage of the benefits of the method since it was only intended for a limited number of top scientists and engineers.[79] However, the use of this method will probably increase as it already today is much easier to design Web solutions of this kind.

It seems to me that there are at least two reasons for the comprehensive oral history programs in the history of science, technology, and medicine. First, more than 90% of all science has been produced during the last half century, and the majority of the scientists who have existed are still alive, which makes it possible to talk with them—something that historians increasingly begin to see as an opportunity, and less as a problem, since conversations with the historical subjects may help them to navigate in the multitude of sources as well as to interpret these.[80] It would be no wild guess that this statement also is valid for the engineering community— although I do not have any statistics to support it. Second, and more important, the professional communities themselves have played an active, and even crucial, role in preserving "their" heritage for posterity by initiating large oral history programs. Oral history in the history of science, technology, and medicine thus differs from oral history in social history or political history in one important aspect: the active and often intense collaboration between the members of the professional communities and historians. This relation is by no means unproblematic since it introduces dependencies and biases, but as Arne Hessenbruch has somewhat provocatively argued, collaboration with scientists and their like will be necessary for historians of recent science "in order to determine what will remain as a historical source in the future."[81] As we shall see, collaboration with the professional community played a very important role also in our project.

---

[78] Seldon and Pappworth, *By Word of Mouth*, 14.

[79] Arne Hessenbruch, "The Trials and Promise of a Web-History of Materials Research," in *The Science–Industry Nexus: History, Policy, Implications*, ed. Karl Grandin, Nina Wormbs, and Sven Widmalm (Sagamore Beach, 2004), 397–413; idem, "'The Mutt Historian': The Perils and Opportunities of Doing History of Science On-Line," in *The Historiography of Contemporary Science, Technology, and Medicine*, 279–98.

[80] Hessenbruch, "'The Mutt Historian,'" 279f.; Thomas Söderqvist, "Preface," in *The Historiography of Contemporary Science and Technology*, vii.

[81] Hessenbruch, "'The Mutt Historian,'" 294.

To summarize, scholars have created and used oral sources in order to approach three areas, or, rather, set of areas, in the historical landscape: social history or "history from below," political history, and the history of science, technology, and medicine. All of these categories aim at the "hidden" history in the sense that the existing sources do not reveal the complexity and details of these areas.

1.7   Documenting History of Computing

To what extent, how, and by whom has the history of computing been documented up to the present? Which methods and tools have been used? And which aspects of the history of computing have these efforts aimed to cover? Has a user-centered perspective been taken into account? In this section, these questions will be answered by surveying the major international documentation efforts.

Research and documentation in the history of computing have, above all, been undertaken in the USA with the Charles Babbage Institute (CBI) as the pioneering organization. CBI was established in 1978 in Palo Alto, California, and moved 2 years later to Minneapolis. Especially during its first years of existence, the professional community played a pivotal role through the Charles Babbage Foundation (CBF), an advisory and supporting organization consisting of corporate executives, historians, and museum staff. Since 1989, CBI has been part of the University of Minnesota where its director also holds a chair. CBI has a small staff consisting of historians, archivists, and administrative personnel. Its three core activities were, from the outset, the collecting of archives, manuscripts, media materials, corporate records, historical research, and oral histories. Over the years, there has been a substantial cross-fertilization between these three different areas. Oral histories have usually been conducted within research projects, and the contacts with informants that these have generated have, in turn, stimulated donations of archives, etc., which, in the long run, has created an entire infrastructure for future research. When it comes to oral histories, CBI has developed a so-called research-grade model for conducting them. The model includes extensive research beforehand by the interviewer (4 days on average for one interview), tape recording of the usually 2–3-h-long interviews, and a subsequent process of transcription and editing.[82] To date, CBI has completed more than 300 oral histories, and if permitted these are published on the Web. A glance at the conducted interviews shows that they mainly deal with pioneers in computing technology.[83] But during the last couple of years, CBI has responded to the recent shift in the historiography toward the users of computing and nonpioneering figures, companies, and nations by developing

---

[82] Misa, "Organizing the History of Computing," 2ff.; Arthur L. Norberg, "A Perspective on the History of the Charles Babbage Institute and the Charles Babbage Foundation," *IEEE Annals of History of Computing* 23, no. 4 (2001), 12–23; Thomas J. Misa, personal communication, May 25, 2007.

[83] "Oral History Database," http://www.cbi.umn.edu/oh/index.phtml (accessed November 4, 2011).

new research tools and methods, such as blog-, database-, and wiki-based technologies as a way to create and collect sources on the "many" users.[84]

Another important institution is the IEEE History Center in New Brunswick, New Jersey. The center, which was founded in 1979, is supported by two organizations: IEEE and Rutgers State University. I would like to stress two important aspects of this organizational solution. It helps give the IEEE History Center credibility both in academia and in the professional community of electrical engineers, and it also makes the center more economically robust since it receives funding from different trustees.[85] Like CBI, it has a small staff consisting of historians, archivists, and administrative personnel. The center is devoted to furthering the preservation, research, and dissemination of information about the history of electrical science and technology, and in particular, it focuses on the technological and organizational history of IEEE, its members, and their professions, which means that it covers important aspects of the history of computing. Conducting, recording, and transcribing oral histories are part of the IEEE History Center's core activities, and to date almost 500 oral histories have been completed. The majority of them are available and published on the Web. Almost all of the oral history interviews are conducted with members of the professional community of electrical engineers. Oral history as a method is very well established at the center. Professional historians always conduct the oral history interviews, and whenever it is possible in relation to ongoing research projects. Lately, the center has developed a Web-based solution for acquiring the IEEE members' stories.[86]

Besides CBI and the IEEE History Center, a number of American institutions have done, and are doing, important documentation work. The National Museum of American History as well as National Air and Space Museum at the Smithsonian Institution Archives in Washington, DC, host a large collection of artifacts and a number of oral history interviews with American pioneers in computing, such as J. Presper Eckert, Douglas Engelbart, Bill Gates, and Steve Jobs.[87] The MIT Museum in Cambridge, Massachusetts, focuses quite obviously on MIT, and the history of computing is only dealt with if related to MIT, but the museum is worth mentioning in this matter since it has a substantial collection of oral histories on the subject.

---

[84] See, for instance, the project on FastLane conducted at CBI. Misa, "Organizing the History of Computing," 9; Thomas J. Misa and Joline Zepcevski, "Realizing User-Centered Computer History: Designing and Using NSF's FastLane (1990–Present)" (paper presented at the SHOT meeting, October 12–14, 2008, Lisbon, Portugal).

[85] Also CBI was initially supported by two organizations. The above-mentioned Charles Babbage Foundation (CBF) governed the institute together with the University of Minnesota until 1989 when the university assumed complete authority for CBI. Norberg, "A Perspective on the History of the Charles Babbage Institute and the Charles Babbage Foundation," 20ff.

[86] "Oral-History: IEEE Oral History Collection," http://www.ieeeghn.org/wiki/index.php/Oral-History:IEEE_Oral_History_Collection (accessed November 4, 2011); Frederik Nebeker, personal communication, May 22, 2007.

[87] The list is not long, but quite impressive. "Computer History Collection," http://americanhistory.si.edu/collections/comphist/ (accessed June 10, 2009); "Oral History on Space, Science, and Technology," http://www.nasm.si.edu/research/dsh/oralhistory.cfm (accessed June 10, 2009).

The vast majority of these are conducted with engineers and scientists affiliated with MIT. Both the Smithsonian and the MIT Museum publish the interviews on the Web if permitted.[88]

Also the Computer History Museum in Mountain View, California, which was established in 1996 and currently is the world's largest museum on the history of computing, creates oral histories in the form of interviews and panel discussions. These are videotaped, transcribed, and edited, and to date almost 300 of them are made available online. The oral histories have mainly been completed by senior practitioners from the field, and not by scholars, unlike the above-mentioned institutions.[89]

Finally, I would like to mention a recent interesting effort, the international and multicultural WiWiW project (Who is Who in the Internet World), which, since the late 1990s, has recorded almost 200 oral history interviews with Internet pioneers around the world. Along with interviews, archive materials are also collected. Many of these interviews, like the Computer History Museum's, have been conducted and processed by a "distributed" global network of practitioners from the field. The WiWiW project has, as in the cases of CBI and the IEEE History Center, experimented with Internet-based tools for creating and collecting sources.[90]

The last two examples show that there is no patented best practice for how to proceed when creating and collecting oral sources on the history of computing. While CBI, the IEEE History Center, and others have established and used a successful, but time-consuming model for conducting oral history interviews that includes extensive research and preparations by scholars, alternative models cannot be dismissed a priori. It is worth noting, however, that all of the above-mentioned institutions and projects consider it necessary to transcribe and edit the conducted oral history interviews. They seem to agree that audiotapes, and even audio clips made available online, are of limited practical value for researchers. All of them strongly favor Web-publishing the edited transcripts if possible.

Few similar documentation efforts can be found in Europe. A notable exception is the UK National Archive for the History of Computing in Manchester that was created in 1987. Like its American peers, the archive also focuses on archival collections, oral histories, and research on the history of computing, although the

---

[88] More precisely, the Institute Archives and Special Collections and the MIT Museum have them. "Oral History@MIT," http://libraries.mit.edu/archives/oral-history/index.html (accessed October 17, 2007); Deborah Douglas, personal communication, October 25, 2007.

[89] "Oral Histories Collection," http://www.computerhistory.org/collections/oralhistories/ (accessed November 4, 2011); Kirsten Tashev and Dag Spicer, personal communication, May 25, 2007. Similar in approach is Silicon Genesis, a collection of oral history interviews with pioneers of the semiconductor industry hosted by Stanford University. "Silicon Genesis: An Oral History of Semiconductor Technology," http://silicongenesis.stanford.edu/index.html (accessed November 4, 2011).

[90] Andreu Veà, "Internet History and Internet Research Methods: Engineering the Worldwide WiWiW Project" (paper prepared for the SHOT meeting, October 12–14, 2008, Lisbon, Portugal); "WiWiW project," wiwiw.org/(accessed November 4, 2011).

task of documenting oral sources has been very much subordinated to its other activities.[91] In Sweden, the archives, museums, and libraries are the organizations that traditionally have initiated and led documentation projects, but the history of computing has, by and large, not been favored. To my knowledge, only two Swedish museums have shown an interest in the subject. The first one is the National Museum of Science and Technology in Stockholm, which held its first exhibition on computers in 1978, and the second one IT-ceum, a small regional museum exclusively devoted to the history of computing that was established in 2004 in Linköping. However, none of these two museums has carried out any systematic documentation of the history of computing on their own.[92]

How can the apparent lack of European efforts to document the history of computing be explained? Four reasons should primarily be considered. To begin with, oral history as an archival practice has led a rather obscure life in Europe (with the possible exception of Great Britain) compared with the USA.[93] It is only during the last couple of decades that European scholars have begun to create oral sources in a more systematic way. Furthermore, history of science and technology is, above all, an American phenomenon, and this is even more so for the subdiscipline history of computing. Admittedly, changes are underway, but in comparison there still are relatively few European historians devoted to science, technology, or computing. A related point, which has been touched upon earlier, is that the historiography of computing shows an overwhelming bias toward pioneers in computing technology, and, consequently, toward the USA, since the majority of the computing technology was developed there. My guess is that the lack of European interest in documenting the history of computing is largely a reflection of this bias. Why document the development of domestic computing technologies whose impact only has been marginal? Although such efforts could easily be justified intellectually (failed technologies are as interesting for the scholar as successful ones), it is not difficult to imagine that the interest from the national archives, museums, and libraries as well as the general public in the "nonpioneering" countries for such a project would

---

[91] John Pickstone and Geof Bowker, "The Manchester Heritage," *IEEE Annals of the History of Computing* 15, no. 3 (1993), 7–8; Geoffrey Tweedale, "The National Archive for the History of Computing," *Journal of the Society of Archivists* 10, no. 1 (1989), 1–8; "UK National Archive for the History of Computing," http://www.chstm.manchester.ac.uk/research/nahc/ (accessed June 10, 2009); James Sumner, e-mail, June 19, 2009. There are also a number of pilot projects that have been carried out in other European countries. The research project "Information Technology in Finland after World War II: The Actors and Their Experiences" that was completed between 2002 and 2005 collected, for instance, 744 stories with the help of an Internet questionnaire. Satu Aaltonen, "Tunteita, tulkintoja ja tietotekniikkaa: 'Milloin kuulit ensimmäistä kertaa tietokoneista?' -kyselyn tuloksia" (Turku, 2004), 21; Petri Paju, e-mail, June 22, 2009.

[92] *Dædalus 1978/79: Tekniska museets årsbok* (Stockholm, 1978–1979), 171; "IT-ceum: Det svenska datamuseet," http://www.itceum.se/ (accessed June 15, 2009).

[93] The American historian Ronald J. Grele argues that the origin of oral history in the United States lay as an archival practice, while in Europe, it was the work of research-oriented social historians. Ronald J. Grele, "Oral History as Evidence," in *History of Oral History: Foundations and Methodology*, ed. Thomas L. Charlton, Lois E. Myers, and Rebecca Sharpless (Lanham, 2007), 34–40.

be lukewarm at the most. However, with the shifting emphasis from pioneers and nation-centered history to users and transnational processes in the recent historiography, the interest will, however, probably increase.[94] Finally, the powerful professional communities in the USA, which have initiated and supported extensive oral history programs aiming to document their own members' activities and lives, have no corresponding European counterparts.

In summarizing the main findings of this section, extensive documentation efforts in the history of computing have, in particular, been carried out in the USA, and these have, above all, dealt with (American) pioneers in computing technology. Even if the picture is beginning to change, as the example of CBI shows, the user-centered perspective is, by and large, absent. The method *par preference* for nearly three decades has been the oral history interview—which, in turn, has become a major source for history of computing. This should come as no surprise since the method has proved very well suited for in-depth studies of key persons. But the examples given in this section also indicate that oral history is transforming as it enters the "digital" era (the Australian historian Alistair Thomson even talks about a paradigmatic revolution).[95] Many of the above-mentioned institutions and projects use the Web to increase the accessibility of their collections, and they also experiment with information technology in order to find novel and innovative tools and methods for creating and collecting oral sources and the like. This recent trend, which, in part, is spurred by the shift in the historiography toward the user and technology in use, has especially been visible during the latter part of our current decade.

1.8   Approaching the (Elite) User

From my discussion in the previous sections, it has become apparent that there are many reasons for the historian to create oral (and written) sources in retrospect. In particular, we can find arguments for the need to document the activities of elite users in the history of computing. It is obvious that many aspects of elites are not covered by the existing sources. The same is true for the component of tacit knowledge in technical and scientific work. Furthermore, it is difficult for the layman to comprehend and assess the often complex and complicated computing technology with the help of written sources only. And the fragmented character of the use of computing, which indicates that users are found throughout society, makes it difficult and time consuming to trace written sources. From the previous section, we can also conclude that there has not been any comprehensive oral history program on users

---

[94] A notable example of this shift is the large, pan-European research project Soft-EU that investigates computing in Europe from a transnational perspective. See, for instance, Gerard Albert's introductory piece "Appropriating America: Americanization in the History of European Computing" to a number of thematic articles on the subject in *IEEE Annals of History of Computing* 32, no. 2 (2010).

[95] Thomson, "Four Paradigm Transformations in Oral History," 68–70.

and the uses of computing technology. Most of the efforts have dealt with pioneers in computing technology. These are, in a sense, elite people, but their activities differ, in many cases, from the elite users' (while they conflate in other cases). We had, therefore, no obvious oral history program or documentation model that we could copy or adopt. Finally, the discussion has made it clear that research tools and methods must be adapted to the historical questions and themes that are addressed. Oral history is, for instance, conducted and interpreted differently in different historical fields. That we have chosen to document the history of computing from an elite-user perspective implies that we cannot solely rely on the methods used by the above-mentioned oral history programs, since these mostly have developed and refined them—in particular the oral history interview—for the task of documenting pioneering figures in computing technology.

With which methods do we then approach the elite user? The question has no simple, straightforward answer. The elite users in the history of computing occupy, in a sense, a middle ground between the "few" pioneers and the "many" users. They are neither that few nor that many. While pioneering engineers and scientists in computing technology are concentrated to a limited number of organizations and physical locations (large companies, research institutes and laboratories, universities, etc.), elite users are scattered among many industries, public authorities, and other organizations. Still, they are easier to identify than the "ordinary" user, since they to a larger extent share an educational background and, in many cases, belong to the same professional organizations and networks. Usually, but not as a rule, they share similar beliefs, values, and norms. Because of this "in-between" character, because we had no obvious model to blueprint, and because different methods are needed for different purposes and for different historical subjects, we hypothesized that the elite user probably would be best approached by a combination of different methods (but as we shall see, this hypothesis was shaped by organizational concerns as well).

The oral history interview that has been so successful in documenting the activities of pioneers and elites can certainly be adapted to the documentation of elite users. It is also possible to acquire written recollections on the use of computing technology with the help of detailed questionnaires published in the media or sent by mail—a method that frequently has been used in Sweden to create sources on the everyday life experiences of the "ordinary" man. A promising method for targeting the elite user is the witness seminar. When firms, government authorities, and other organizations appropriated, modified, and transformed computing technology to meet their needs, teams of individuals rather than individuals carried out much of the work, and it seems beneficial to invite the individuals in these teams to discuss their experiences and recollections together. Also, we should not refrain from experimenting with information technology when developing and using the above-mentioned tools and methods. In a sense, methods are always in the making, and this is, in particular, true for the history of computing when it comes to addressing users.

Chapter 2
Documenting the Use of Computers

[H]istory is inherently an eclectic discipline and the skills it requires are correspondingly diverse. And therein lie its strengths.[1]

Ludmilla Jordanova

2.1 The Mutual Shaping of Methodology and Organization

Above, the case has been made for the necessity of the project from a scholarly point of view. If we want to understand how computing changed the world, we need to address the users and the uses of computing technology, and therefore we need sources on these actors and processes. But besides these scholarly criteria, the project was also shaped by *nonscholarly* criteria. These may be divided into factors *internal* and *external* to the project. Among the internal factors that affected the outcome were the choice of organization, the participating parties (organizations as well as individuals), and the work process. Among the external were funding, conditions for grants, and, perhaps, most important, that the first generation of IT actors were getting old. In this section, the role of these factors in shaping the methodological approach and organization as well as the type of sources created and collected will be considered by giving an account of the history of the project.

The project has a history that dates back to 2002, when senior practitioners with an interest in IT history formed the first network at the Swedish Computer Society. They had recognized that the first generation of pioneers in computing, including themselves in this category, were increasingly fragile and wished to pass on this generation's experiences to future generations before it was too late. Originally, this network aimed at writing a Swedish IT history, and its members approached a number of interest organizations, museums, and universities with this purpose. Among these were IT-ceum, IT-företagen, the Museum of Work (Arbetets museum),

---

[1] Ludmilla Jordanova, *History in Practice*, 2nd ed. (London, 2006), 171.

the Royal Swedish Academy of Engineering Sciences (Kungl. Ingenjörsvetenskaps-akademien, IVA), and Nordiska museet. A steering group with a couple of senior practitioners and representatives from the above-mentioned organizations was formed in 2003. The senior practitioners also formed small networks, which they decided to call focus groups, interested in certain industries or technologies, which they, in turn, called focus areas. According to the senior practitioners themselves, IBM's sales organization, divided according to industries, inspired the chosen organizational form. Ideally, they wanted the members of the focus group to represent different experiences, knowledge, and organizations. It should be noted here that the concept of a focus group usually is used as a tool for the researcher in market research and social sciences to acquire a group of people's attitude toward a product, service, concept, idea, or packaging.[2] The senior practitioners saw, in contrast, the focus group as an autonomous network that formulated research questions and strategies and also did the actual work. The ultimate aim of the network activities was to pass on the lessons learned by the pioneering generation. They wished to convey the experiences of Swedish industry, trade and business, and the public sector for the benefit of future generations. Four focus groups were established during 2004 for this purpose: financial industries, healthcare, hardware and software (later renamed early computers), and systems development. The same year the steering group entered discussions with the Division of History of Science and Technology at KTH and the National Museum of Science and Technology, which both showed an interest in the project. Scholarly discussions on the theoretical approach and methodology started. The idea that documentation of the Swedish IT history must be a first step toward writing a Swedish IT history now began to take shape, and eventually it was concluded that this should be the main objective of a joint project with the Swedish Computer Society, the Division of History of Science and Technology at KTH, and the National Museum of Science and Technology as participating parties. The *raison d'être* for such a project was formulated in a straightforward manner: people were passing away.

The senior practitioners in the focus groups made the first documentation efforts. They conducted a number of interviews, mainly with each other, but without following the established practice in oral history to, firstly, record them with sound (or, secondly, to make careful notes). Inspired by the curators at Nordiska museet, the members in one focus group also decided to write their own autobiographies, but it resulted in no more than half-a-dozen autobiographies. Although the outcome of these first steps may seem poor at first glance, they, nevertheless, were important, since they forced the participants to reflect on methodological questions. It became clear that interviews had to be conducted in another way and that written recollections, given the low response rate, had to be acquired on a large scale.

Meanwhile, the first steering group was dissolved in 2005 and replaced with a new composition where representatives from museums, trade and industry, and universities took their place. With initial grants from the Bank of Sweden Tercentenary

---

[2] "Focus group," http://en.wikipedia.org/wiki/Focus_group (accessed November 3, 2011).

Foundation, the Marcus and Amalia Wallenberg Memorial Fund, and the Knowledge Foundation, a number of oral history interviews[3] as well as a number of witness seminars[4] were completed under scholarly guidance during 2005 and 2006. The witness seminars, which were held in public, appealed, in particular, to the senior practitioners, since it gave them a well-defined role as co-organizers as well as an opportunity to socialize. These experiences gave important methodological insights, and they also made it clear that large-scale documentation had to involve professional historians, but, above all, they highlighted the need for a robust organization. How should sources be gathered, processed, administrated, preserved, and disseminated? And by whom? By the senior practitioners or by scholars or by museum curators? Who should be responsible for the project? And who should lead and oversee the work?

With a research program written by the participating scholars, the project managed to obtain funding for a 2-year period from Riksbankens Jubileumsfond and the Marcus and Amalia Wallenberg Memorial Fund at the end of 2006. The research program marked a shift in emphasis from documenting the activities of the first generation of pioneers in computing technology to documenting the activities of computer users between 1950 and 1980. There were three reasons for choosing a user-oriented approach. First, one of the parties, the Swedish Computer Society, had been a user organization since its establishment in 1949. Originally named the Hollerith Club (Hollerithklubben), it turned to IBM users exclusively. Soon, however, the club decided to invite users of other computer brands as well. This expansion was manifested by a change of name to the Punch Card Club (Hålkortsklubben). In 1990, after a number of changes of name and a merger, the organization received its present name.[5] It should be underscored that mainly "elite" users in the form of data processing managers were members of this organization. So-called end users were rarely represented in it during the given period. Second, two of the focus

---

[3] Börje Langefors, interview from 2005 by Janis Bubenko, Anita Kollerbaur and Tomas Ohlin; Werner Schneider, interview from 2005 by Hans Peterson and Urban Rosenqvist; Ulla Gerdin, interview from 2005 by Hans Peterson; Paul Hall, interview from 2005 by Hans Peterson; Bengt Olsen, interview from 2006 by Urban Rosenqvist and Isabelle Dussauge, Div. of History of Science and Technology, KTH, Stockholm.

[4] Milena Dávila, ed., *Datorisering av medicinsk laboratorieverksamhet 1: En översikt: Transkript av ett vittnesseminarium vid Svenska Läkaresällskapet i Stockholm den 17 februari 2006* (Stockholm, 2008); idem, ed., *Datorisering av medicinsk laboratorieverksamhet 2: Massanalyser och hälsokontroller: Transkript av ett vittnesseminarium vid Tekniska museet i Stockholm den 20 september 2006* (Stockholm, 2008); Per Lundin, ed., *Att arbeta med 1950-talets matematikmaskiner: Transkript av ett vittnesseminarium vid Tekniska museet i Stockholm den 12 september 2005* (Stockholm, 2006); idem, ed., *Tidig programmering: Transkript av ett vittnesseminarium vid Tekniska museet i Stockholm den 16 mars 2006* (Stockholm, 2007); idem, ed., *Databehandling vid Väg- och vattenbyggnadsstyrelsen/Vägverket 1957–1980: Transkript av ett vittnesseminarium vid Tekniska museet i Stockholm den 22 maj 2006* (Stockholm, 2007); Björn Thodenius, ed., *IT i bank- och finanssektorn 1960–1985: Transkript av ett vittnesseminarium vid Tekniska museet i Stockholm den 13 mars 2006* (Stockholm, 2008).

[5] Gert Persson, "Från Svenska Dataföreningen till Dataföreningen Sverige," in *EDB historik: I nordisk perspektiv*, ed. Erik Bruhn (København, 1988).

groups—finance and healthcare—already dealt with the use of computing technology. Third, as mentioned above, there has been a recent shift toward a user perspective in the historiography of technology in general and computing technology in particular. The research program also suggested the combination of different documentation methods: oral history interviews, witness seminars, and written recollections.[6] The reason for choosing an eclectic methodological approach reflected partly a desire to continue along the chosen (methodological) path, partly a conviction that a methodological best practice could not be singled out beforehand (if at all).

In the meantime, another four focus groups had been established by the senior practitioners and quite independent of the research program: defense, manufacturing industries, transportation industries, and user organizations and user participation.[7] It became essential to solve the organizational problems for three reasons: the project had grown quickly in terms of both scale and scope, the funding was limited to 2 years, and since the historical actors were passing away, the documentation efforts had to start as soon as possible.

The steering group identified especially two potential organizational threats to the realization of the project. First, the collaboration consisted of three parties with, to say the least, different organizational cultures and aims. There are few Swedish examples, if any, of successful collaborations between museums, trade and industry, and universities. Second, the collaboration contained senior practitioners from the field working on a nonprofit basis, on the one hand, and professional scholars and museum curators working on a profit basis on the other. International documentation efforts by organizations, such as the above-mentioned CBI and IEEE History Center, have indeed shown the importance of cooperating with practitioners, but have also made it clear that a project has to be very careful in not relying too much on the efforts made on a nonprofit basis when it comes to meeting time schedules and delivering products.[8]

After intense discussions, the steering group decided that these potential threats should be resolved through a meticulous design of the project's organization and work process. Making the organizational structure and the different parties' responsibilities explicit from the beginning, it was argued, would remove many potential pitfalls in the organization and chain of command and thus minimize possible misunderstandings between the three participating parties. It would also clarify the

---

[6] Originally, we also intended to create artifact biographies, a method that aims to contextualize artifacts by creating stories about them. Since it was not possible to systematically and regularly collect artifacts, it became very difficult for us, given the time schedule, to plan and allocate resources for the task. Therefore, we abandoned the method. On artifact biographies, see Igor Kopytoff, "The Cultural Biography of Things: Commoditization as Process," in *The Social Life of Things: Commodities in a Cultural Perspective*, ed. Arjun Appadurai (Cambridge, 1986), 64–91; Lubar and Kingery, *History from Things*.

[7] The name "user organizations and user participation" may, in retrospect, seem confusing since the whole project has a user perspective, but when the focus group was established, the project had not yet decided its direction.

[8] Nebeker, personal communication, May 22, 2007; Misa, personal communication, May 25, 2007.

different roles of those individual participants working on a nonprofit basis and those working on a profit basis. It would, furthermore, make it easier for individuals to enter (and to leave) the project. At the beginning of 2007, we, therefore, devised a formal description of the organization, the workflow, and the different participants' responsibilities. We presented it in a project manual, which in addition contained descriptions of the methods and the archival routines as well as a collection of template documents for agreement forms, covering letters, oral history skeleton question lists, questionnaires, etc. We distributed the project manual to all project members and discussed its content with them at a specially designed workshop during the spring of 2007. The purpose was to get the project and the practically autonomous focus groups to go in the same direction. The general organization, the agreed-upon deliverables, and the structure of the work process for each focus area are described in Appendix III: Formal Description of Organization and Work Process.

The decision to organize the project in focus groups had achieved a momentum already when we wrote the research program, and it also fitted well with the chosen user perspective. When the steering group addressed the organizational problems, it was also decided that the funding allowed 16 focus groups in total. The choice of the eight remaining groups became the subject of intense negotiations between the participating parties, and eventually it was concluded that these groups should be information technology industries; public administration; telecommunications industries; higher education; archives, libraries, and museums; media; schools; and retail and wholesale industries. In each and every group, there was a "research secretary." The research secretary was usually a trained historian in a postdoctoral position. With research secretaries entering the organization, the role of the senior practitioners changed to an advisory one. The research secretaries belonged to a research group, which became the project's primary forum for methodological discussions. In addition, a scientific council was established with the purpose of both advising the research group in its methodological work and the steering group in scholarly matters. These organizational changes, by and large, led to a shift from a project driven by the senior practitioners to a research-driven project.

To conclude, I argue that the resulting project organization has to be conceived as a trade-off between different, and sometimes conflicting, interests. The methodological choices must also be seen in this light. Both are shaped by social and intellectual circumstances. In fact, methods, organization, and theoretical approach are closely intertwined and mutually interdependent, and cannot be analyzed as separate entities.

2.2 Reflections on Methodology

As my survey of oral history projects on computing in Chap. 1 of this book suggests, documentation and research should, if possible, be conducted together. Unfortunately, the specific conditions of the project—in particular its urgent nature and time-limited funding—did not allow us to relate our documentation efforts to ongoing research projects. We, therefore, introduced an element in the work process that served to substitute research: the knowledge outline.

Compiling a knowledge outline consists of drawing a rough map of the landscape of the past. The purpose of the knowledge outline is to give a guide for the principal task of creating and collecting sources. Which parts of the past should be documented and why? If there, for instance, are abundant written sources on the events and processes in a certain part of the past, it becomes less important to create and collect complementary oral sources. If, on the other hand, the events and processes have left no traces, or few, in the existing archives, it becomes more important to create and collect new sources about precisely these events and processes. However, an unexplored area in the landscape of the past is, at the same time, not a sufficient reason to start documenting. Such a project will easily become insurmountable. There are many unexplored areas. The documentation efforts should, therefore, ideally be linked to those problems that have been addressed in the historiography on the given part of the past. The role of the knowledge outline is to identify these as well. Thus, the compilation of a knowledge outline includes two stages: first, to obtain a picture of the existing historical research dealing with a certain part in the landscape of the past, for instance, a focus area; and, second, to identify existing sources on it by compiling bibliographies and listing relevant archives. If completed as described, the knowledge outline will become an important preparatory work for the documentation efforts to follow.

As discussed in Chap. 1, the oral history interview has been used extensively for decades as a method for creating oral sources. Consequently, there is a vast and increasing literature on the subject.[9] Only a number of aspects on the subject that have guided us when conducting interviews (and witness seminars) will be highlighted. All of the oral history projects mentioned in the previous chapter primarily conduct interviews for archival purposes, and this is also our aim. To begin with, it is, therefore, helpful to distinguish between the "archival" interview and the "research" interview. While the former aims to create sources for a future use by any researcher and, consequently, needs to be as broad and open as possible, the latter typically focuses on the interviewee's participation and interpretation of particular events or processes. The archival interview usually, but not always, takes the form of life-story or career interviews.[10]

---

[9] A couple of useful introductions to the subject are Robert Perks and Alistair Thomson, eds., *The Oral History Reader*, 2nd ed. (New York, 2006) and Donald A. Ritchie, ed., *The Oxford Handbook of Oral History* (New York, 2011). There also exist a number of straightforward handbooks on oral history, for instance, Donald A. Ritchie, *Doing Oral History: A Practical Guide*, 2nd ed. (Oxford, 2003). See also Thomas Haigh, "The Historian for Hire: Conducting a Career Oral History Series in a Technical Area" (lecture at the summer school Oral History and Technological Memory: Challenges in Studying European Pasts, August 10–15, 2009, Turku, Finland).

[10] Soraya de Chadarevian distinguishes between "life-story" interviews and "directed" interviews, while Arthur Norberg classifies interviews into career interviews and focused interviews. These distinctions are of course not clear-cut. In many cases, the interviews both functions as archival and research interviews. de Chadarevian, "Using Interviews to Write the History of Science," 60; Arthur Norberg, "How to Conduct and Preserve Oral History," http://www.ithistory.org/resources/norberg-article.pdf (accessed August 15, 2009), 5.

Oral history interviews and witness seminars (as well as written recollections) belong to a category of sources that are coconstructed by the historian and the historical subject. Lilian Hoddeson compares the process of creating sources to the study of the kind of phenomena, such as the quantum mechanical, in which the process of observation changes what is being observed. But how much influence should the historically trained scholar exert when conducting interviews? Hoddeson makes a distinction between "passive" and "interactive" interviews. While many suggest that historians should play as small a role as possible, and thus making the interview more reliable, she argues for "conducting fully interactive interviews whose content is self-consciously tailored by the historian with the help of questions based on considerable research."[11]

Hoddeson considers the "mask," a concept introduced by the Flemish historian Jan Vansina, which is "the public account, the one people reveal readily, as a cover story." This mask is "built up in terms of roles and statuses, values and principles." Behind the mask lies "the hidden portrait, or 'face,' the authentic account." According to Hoddeson, "[b]oth mask and face are important objects of study for the oral historian; exploring their relationship helps her to understand how interviewees see themselves in relation to their culture. But to construct a deeper history, she must go farther and dislodge the mask, to discover the face."[12]

Hoddeson urges the historian to use jolts as an interviewing technique that helps probe the mask. There are two principal techniques for stimulating jolts. Since the question concerns the interviewer's principal tool, the "two-sentence format" introduced by the American oral historian Charles Morrissey is of particular interest. With this technique, the first of the two sentences presents the agreed-upon knowledge, while the second uses the interviewee's response to the first sentence to probe deeper and question it.[13] Bringing artifacts, documents, pictures, and the like may also help to trigger and expand the memories of the interviewee. The Swedish ethnologist Lars Kaijser compares them to *konversationspjäser* (pieces of conversation). He sees the pieces of conversation as specific historical items that may ease the conversation by allowing the interviewee to (seemingly) talk about something else than herself/himself. They can also help the interviewer to direct the interview toward events and processes of particular interest.[14] A drawback of bringing items when conducting "archival" interviews is, of course, that the resulting transcript may be difficult to comprehend for other researchers or scholars. This problem can rather easily be avoided by providing meta-documentation in the form of careful annotations and, perhaps, including reproductions of the items in question in the transcript.

---

[11] Hoddeson, "The Conflict of Memories and Documents," 188 f.

[12] Ibid., 190.

[13] Charles Morrissey, "The Two-Sentence Format as an Interviewing Technique in Oral History Field Work," *Oral History Review* 15 (1987), 43–54.

[14] Lars Kaijser, e-mail, November 2, 2009. David K. Allison, e-mail, October 23, 2007.

Ideally, the interviewer should show both suspicion and trust. Suspicion, the distance which implies objectivity, cannot, however, be too marked. Ultimately, the interviewer is dependent on the interviewee's benevolence. Since the interviewee volunteers for the interview, there is simply a need to collaborate. As Hoddeson puts it, the historian has to surrender part of her or his objectivity in order to gain the interviewee's trust. Referring to her own experiences, it was not until she had established a trusting relationship with the interviewees that they were prepared to offer more intimate details of their professional life or even agreed to extensive interviewing. In Vansina's words, interviews are "social processes of mutual accommodation during which transfers of information occur." If the interviewer fails to establish a social relationship, it will affect the information transfer negatively.[15]

The witness seminar is not all as common as the oral history interview, and the literature on the method is scarce. However, many of the aspects on interviews discussed above can be generalized to include witness seminars as well. E. M. Tansey, who has arranged the meetings at the Wellcome Trust, emphasizes, for instance, the necessity of "some semi-formal structure" for the seminars in order to keep the participants focused on the topic and give the meeting coherence. Thus, using Hoddeson's terminology, she argues for a considerable degree of "interactivity" between the chair, or moderator, of the session and the participating witnesses. This can be contrasted with group interviews, where the main emphasis usually is on the interaction between the participants themselves, and therefore are more "passive."[16]

According to Tansey, witness seminars, when compared to particular interviews, stimulate an entirely different interaction between the participants, who, in a sense, jolt each other's memories. However, Tansey strongly dismisses the notion that the seminars explore "collective" memory. Rather, she argues, "they expose many *overlapping* memories, collective and individual, which frequently span a wide spectrum of recollections and opinions."[17] A witness seminar can thus serve to highlight different interpretations of an event and thereby contribute to a deeper understanding of the complexity of historical processes.

However, Tansey also points out that the method has some obvious disadvantages. Critical to the outcome of the seminar is the lineup of participants. If potential witnesses are unable or unwilling to participate, there is not much one can do. Furthermore, an inherent risk with the method is that conflicts may be suppressed and that dissentients will not be able to make their voices heard, with too "streamlined" recollections as a result (although Tansey argues that this is not what the Wellcome Trust has experienced). Another danger she identifies is that the reminiscences may be too anecdotal; a feature witness seminars, of course, share with other forms of oral history.[18]

---

[15] Hoddeson, "The Conflict of Memories and Documents," 192, 194f.

[16] Admittedly, the group interview and the witness seminar have a lot in common. Hugo Slim and Paul Thompson, with Olivia Bennett and Nigel Cross, "Ways of Listening," in *The Oral History Reader*, ed. Robert Perks and Alistair Thomson, 2nd ed. (New York, 2006), 147f.; Tansey, "Witnessing the Witnesses," 264.

[17] Tansey, "Witnessing the Witnesses," 271.

[18] Ibid., 265ff.

To acquire written recollections with the help of questionnaires, in contrast to conducting oral history interviews and witness seminars, is a laborsaving way to document memories. Another advantage of the method, besides being effective and time saving, is that it makes it possible to collect large amounts of sources. The role of the intermediary is less pronounced than in, for example, interviews, and it has been argued that the sources, therefore, become autobiographical in a unique sense.[19] Nevertheless, it is also important to be aware of the drawbacks of the method. These include that several individuals have difficulty expressing themselves in writing, thus leaving only short answers or no answers at all, and that the written recollections may appear too carefully prepared and revised.[20] Furthermore, it is important to bear in mind that the majority of those invited to contribute choose not to participate. This disadvantage of the method can be explained by the relative lack of a social relationship between the collector and the potential contributors. The method does not build a trusting relationship, and as a consequence, the transfer of information will not be high. Thus, the response rate to advertisements is usually kept at a low level, and written recollections have, therefore, to be acquired on a large scale. The Internet is, of course, a very promising tool in this respect. Although Internet-based methods and tools are still in the making, it should be evident that they will stimulate entirely new ways of organizing collections.[21] A flexible and powerful way to manage digital collecting is to develop a Web site. Today, a number of free or inexpensive platforms offer tools and modules for building robust Web sites, and with new techniques such as digital scanning, individual contributors can easily digitize documents and images and upload them to a site. Contrary to "traditional" ways of acquiring written recollections, Internet-based methods and tools, for example, the blog, allow for interactivity between the contributing individuals.[22] Another example is the wiki-based solutions, which create accounts that, in a sense, are collectively molded.

My survey of oral history projects in Chap. 1 has made it clear that different methods and tools have their pros and cons. Oral history interviews and witness seminars as used in the history of science, technology, and medicine (including history of computing) are more elite oriented, while to acquire written recollections using advertisements or Internet-based solutions may reach the rank and file to a larger extent. A routine-like application of any method entails a risk of collecting sources of less value to scholars. I would like to emphasize the necessity of reflecting over which method is most suitable in relation to the events and the processes to be

---

[19] Hagström and Marander-Eklund, "Att arbeta med frågelistor," 16f.

[20] Ibid.

[21] See, for instance, Daniel J. Cohen and Roy Rosenzweig, *Digital History: A Guide to Gathering, Preserving, and Presenting the Past on the Web* (Philadelphia, 2006); Hessenbruch, "The Trials and Promise of a Web-History of Materials Research," 397–413; idem, "'The Mutt Historian'," 279–98; Kelly Schrum et al., "Oral History in the Digital Age," in *The Oxford Handbook of Oral History*, ed. Donald A. Ritchie (New York, 2011), 499–515.

[22] On the blog as a method, see, for instance, Liisa Avelin, "Oral History and E-Research: Collecting Memories of the 1960s and 1970s Youth Culture," in *Oral History: The Challenges of Dialogue*, ed. Marta Kurkowska-Budzan and Krzysztof Zamorski (Amsterdam, 2009), 35–46.

documented. The relationship between the methodological approach and the stories one wants to collect is crucial. Depending on what is required, this relationship may be more or less formalized, structured, or guided. Is it the historical subjects themselves or the historical events and processes, of which the subjects only constitute a small part, that are the focus of the documentation efforts? In particular, the use of the witness seminar seems to be delicate. Looking at the pioneering use of the method by the Centre for Contemporary British History and the Centre for the History of Medicine at the Wellcome Trust, it has mostly been used for challenging narratives and for creating general overviews.

Finally, it is necessary to acknowledge that the choice of method will sometimes be determined by chance rather than strictly methodological considerations. Some people may, for instance, find themselves uncomfortable with the witness-seminar form and, therefore, prefer being interviewed. Others may happen to attend a witness seminar as part of the audience and give their "testimony" there and, as a consequence, cancel the planned interview session.

2.3 Conducting Oral History Interviews and Witness Seminars

The knowledge outline acted, in a way, as a substitute for the research that documentation ideally should be linked with. It gave the research secretary a general overview of the focus area in question. Informal consultations and discussions with the senior practitioners in the focus group also proved to be of great value in this explorative phase. With the help of the knowledge outline and the advice of the senior practitioners, the research secretaries identified the potential interview subjects as well as potential themes and subjects for witness seminars. The research secretaries also discussed their knowledge outlines and choices of oral history sessions with each other in the research group.

Once the interview subject had been identified, the next steps were to prepare, conduct, transcribe, and finally edit the oral history interview, and in this process we drew heavily on the experiences of CBI and the IEEE History Center.[23] The research secretaries prepared for the interview by gathering as much information as possible about the potential subject given the time they had at their disposal. If possible, they contacted him or her by telephone to set the time and date for the interview. Ideally, they conversed informally with the interviewee for about half an hour. The purpose of this introductory conversation was to gather information for preparing the interview, to see if the interviewee was reliable (i.e., did not suffer from amnesia and the like), and above all to gain the interviewee's trust. The research secretaries also asked if the subject could compile a CV as an aid for preparing the questions. The career-oriented oral history skeleton question list compiled by the Center for History of Physics at AIP proved to be a useful template for this task.[24]

---

[23] See, for instance, Norberg, "How to Conduct and Preserve Oral History."
[24] "Oral History Skeleton Question List," http://www.aip.org/history/oral_history/questions.html (accessed July 20, 2009).

The usual setting for the sessions was one interviewer and one interviewee. Some settings consisted of two interviewers (usually a research secretary and a senior practitioner) and one interviewee. In a number of cases, there were two interviewees, and in exceptional cases three or more. If possible, the location was the interviewee's home, but, in many cases, it turned out to be the interviewer's office and, in some cases, the interviewee's office. Before the session started, the interviewer described the project as well as the purpose and the outline of the interview. He or she also asked the interviewee to sign an agreement form to ensure that the Web publishing of voice clips or the edited interview transcript would not infringe copyright.[25] After the session finished, the interviewer inquired if the interviewee had any archival records, artifacts, photographs, and the like that he or she wished to donate.

The sessions were typically between 1 and 3 h long and recorded with sound in MP3 format with the help of digital voice recorders. A professional bureau transcribed the interviews in verbatim, added necessary information (such as the names of the interviewer and the interviewee), and highlighted possible obscurities in the transcript (usually caused by mumbling voices, the poor quality of the recording, or unfamiliar concepts and spellings).[26] The research secretaries then edited the transcript regarding readability and comprehension. At the same time, they aimed at preserving the transcript's oral character and consequently kept colloquial expressions as far as possible. During the editing process, the interviewees had the opportunity to clarify, correct, or comment on their contributions. Minor changes, such as corrections of names, dates, and technical concepts, were inserted in the transcript without comments. In individual cases, the research secretaries added sentences or subordinate clauses, as suggested by the interviewee, to make lines of thought or conversations more complete. Furthermore, they included extensive comments from the interviewee using addenda. They completed the transcript by adding 5–10 keywords and an abstract in English. The final edited transcripts consist normally of 15–45 pages. If permitted, we made them available on the Web as fully searchable PDF files.

Of great value to us, when planning and conducting witness seminars, were the experiences of the Centre for History of Medicine at the Wellcome Trust.[27] After choosing the theme and the appropriate witnesses, we looked for a suitable moderator. Since the witness seminars involved several participants and different organizations, they required careful planning. Invitations had to be sent out in advance. The auditorium and the technical personnel had to be reserved. In the invitation, we described the purpose and the outline of the witness seminar. We discouraged the prospective witnesses from bringing pictures, PowerPoint presentations, and the like to the seminar, since it could disrupt the session. We also advised them not to prepare manuscripts in advance. Finally, we asked them to send in their CVs in advance.

---

[25] The agreement form also gave the interviewees the possibility to classify the content of the interview, but they only invoked this clause in rare cases.

[26] Initially, we let students transcribe the interviews, but since they often had no experience at all of transcription work, it proved to be a very tedious and time-consuming process. These initial experiences led us to hiring the services of the company Rappa Tag.

[27] Tansey, "Witnessing the Witnesses," 260–78.

The usual setting for the witness seminars consisted of 5–10 witnesses and a moderator. If possible, a professional historian with knowledge of the field moderated the seminar, but since only a few Swedish historians are specialized in the history of computing, we usually followed the practice of the Wellcome Trust and let a senior practitioner carry out this task. In these cases, the research secretaries discussed the organization and the outline of the seminar with the appointed moderator and assisted in preparing questions. As the project proceeded and the research secretaries gained more experience, they occasionally moderated the sessions. In several cases, an expert commentator, either a historian or a senior practitioner, assisted the moderator. It proved to be valuable, since the moderator, besides questioning the witnesses, had to keep all the practical details in mind. We held the majority of the seminars in a large auditorium at the National Museum of Science and Technology in Stockholm. Usually, a small audience of interested historians, museum curators, and senior practitioners (often old colleagues of the witnesses) attended the seminar. On a number of occasions, we held the seminars behind closed doors and then often in a smaller room (Fig. 2.1).

Our witness seminars took between 3 and 4 h and were divided into two sessions, separated by a short coffee break. They normally started with a lunch with the participating parties. The museum staff or the research secretary photographed the participants and asked them to fill in the above-mentioned agreement form. Short introductions by the museum curator and the research secretary and/or some other representative of the project followed. The curator specifically asked if the participants had materials that they wished to donate. The moderator began the session by introducing the theme (or asked the expert commentator to introduce it), and after that followed an informal discussion based on a number of questions prepared by the research secretary and the moderator. We generally allowed the audience to complement and comment on the testimonies and pose questions to the witnesses. While some moderators were keen on following an outline carefully prepared in advance, others allowed the conversation to take freer forms. The structure of the seminar varied considerably depending on the interplay between the moderator, the witnesses, and the audience.

We recorded the witness seminars with both sound and images in digital video format (DVCAM).[28] On the technicians' recommendations, we used two cameras: one for getting a panorama view of the whole session and one for zooming in on specific participants. We then mixed the images into one film. We transcribed the sound files and edited the transcripts roughly in the same way as with the oral history interviews with two important exceptions. Firstly, the research secretary added explanatory footnotes to the edited transcripts. The footnotes contain biographical information about the people as well as explanatory descriptions of individuals, organizations, technical artifacts, and other historical peculiarities mentioned during the seminar. The research secretary worked on the footnotes in close cooperation with the participants, and they, therefore, in many cases, function

---

[28] Due to special circumstances, we recorded three of the seminars with sound only.

Fig. 2.1 The project "From Computing Machines to IT" held its first witness seminar in September 2005 on the theme "Working with the Computing Machines of the 1950s." On picture (**a**) from *left to right*: Erik Stemme and Gunnar Stenudd. On picture (**b**) Lars Arosenius, who moderated the seminar. On picture (**c**) from *left to right*: Carl-Ivar Bergman, Bengt Beckman, Hans Riesel, Elsa-Karin Boestad-Nilsson, Erik Stemme, Gunnar Stenudd, Bert Bolin, and Gunnar Wahlström (Photo: Courtesy of Pär Rittsel)

as complementary sources. Documents or images frequently referred to during the seminar, as well as complementary testimonies, comments, or disagreements supplemented in retrospect by panelists or audience, were included using addenda. Secondly, we published the edited transcripts (about 40–55 pages long) both in print and electronic versions, the latter in the form of fully searchable PDFs.

Since the conduct and questions of the interviewer or the moderator affect the outcome of the interview or the seminar, as emphasized in the previous section, it is important to take a critical stance vis-à-vis the problems that occur when historians and historical subjects actively create sources together. In order to facilitate source criticism, we did two things: first, we preserved the different steps in the processing of oral sources (recording of sound and images, transcript, and edited transcript), and second, the research secretaries contextualized the process of creating and collecting sources in a final report of their work (see the Sect. 2.6 for further details).

2.4 Acquiring Written Recollections and Designing the Writers' Web

In addition to the oral histories, we acquired autobiographies in the form of written recollections with the help of advertisements in the media as well as a specially designed Web interface called the Writers' Web.

The project's research group acquired the written recollections in collaboration with Nordiska museet and the National Museum of Science and Technology. A model for us was the written recollections that ethnologists and folklorists at Nordiska museet in Sweden have acquired since the 1940s with the help of detailed questionnaires sent out en masse by mail or advertised in the media.[29] Based on Nordiska museet's template, we developed a career- or life-story-based questionnaire aimed at users of computing technology. We featured the questionnaire in different advertisements between April and July 2007 in the daily press, specialist press, trade union press, and on the television. A key target group was Swedish pensioners, and we approached the National Organisation of Pensioners (Pensionärernas Riksorganisation, PRO) with c. 400,000 members and the Swedish Pensioners' Association (Sveriges Pensionärsförbund, SPF) with c. 250,000 members and advertised in their print and electronic media. We wrote some of the advertisements for the general public; others were for specific occupational groups, such as metalworkers, nurses, and doctors. In the latter case, we slightly modified the questions to fit the specific group. The experience of Nordiska museet is that a firm deadline not too far from advertising the call for autobiographies is essential for receiving replies. We, therefore, set the end of September as deadline (but of course we included the autobiographies of latecomers in our collection) (Fig. 2.2).

The curators at the National Museum of Science and Technology assessed the replies received. They weeded out replies that merely consisted of simple inquiries and the like. The curators contacted the autobiographers and asked them if we could publish their recollections on the Web. We did not edit the autobiographies. If permitted, we made them available on the Web as fully searchable PDF files (if originally in electronic form) or as indexed PDFs (if originally in paper form).

The research group also designed an interface for acquiring written recollections over the Internet in collaboration with the National Museum of Science and Technology and the Swedish Computer Society. At least one similar attempt occurred internationally, although the outcome of this pioneering work was rather poor. One of the participants implicitly admitted that the virtual platform developed was too complicated.[30] We considered this experience when developing our Writers' Web—a simple interface based on the above-mentioned questionnaire—in May 2007.[31]

---

[29] See, for instance, Hagström and Marander-Eklund, *Frågelistan som källa och metod*; Nilsson, Waldetoft, and Westergren, *Frågelist och berättarglädje*.

[30] Hessenbruch, "The Trials and Promise of a Web-History of Materials Research," 397–413; idem, "'The Mutt Historian,'" 279–98.

[31] We followed the American historians Daniel Cohen and Roy Rosenzweig's advice in *Digital History* to streamline the functions.

LIST OF QUESTIONS

1. BIOGRAPHICAL DATA
Name, year of birth, place of birth, your parents' professional status, years at school

2. FUTURE PROSPECTS
Interests in your young days (also other than technical or scientific ones), anticipated career choices, the importance of primary and secondary school, your social activities as a student, higher education.

3. HOW YOUR CAREER STARTED
The reasons for choosing your educational and professional direction, the influence from those closest to you, people and experiences of vital importance (parents, brothers and sisters, fellow students, teachers, books, journals, films and other things). Please feel free to write about significant events!

4. THE INTRODUCTION TO COMPUTERS/COMPUTING TECHNOLOGY
The first time you used a computer (main frame computer, personal computer) and the first assignments, your first employment involving work with computer/computing technology and/or "numerical" assignments, cooperation with special persons, routines, special difficulties, machines and coding techniques, important relations within or outside your organization or your assignment.

5. MACHINES AND TECHNIQUES
What machines and/or programming techniques have you been working with professionally? If possible describe some special, important changes in this respect which have influenced you. How did these changes influence your working experience and the "quality" of its result? Did you choose any specific machine and programming technique and if so, please tell why?

6. KNOWLEDGE, INFORMATION, SKILLS
Did different periods of time involve different demands for acquiring the knowledge, information and skills needed to perform the work in question? If so, why? What countries and institutions – universities, companies, authorities – did you visit and with what purpose? Has the nature of the international contacts needed been changing? Have you been striving for changes of competence within your field?

7. THE VIEW ON COMPUTERS AND COMPUTING TECHNOLOGY
How du you experience that the view on you as a computer user and/or producer has been changing during your professional life. Do you find that the status of computer technology has been changing, according to your point of view?

8. LIFE IN GENERAL (optional)
Have you developed recreational interests related to your professional life? Has anyone in your family a profession similar to yours? Have you been forced to move because of changes in your professional life or did you yourself choose to move? Have you belonged to any union? Please feel free to write about the matters that you find important.

Skriv in dig i den svenska it-historien!

Vår kunskap om it-historien handlar i första hand om den tekniska utvecklingen. Nu vill Tekniska museet, Dataföreningen i Sverige och KTH fördjupa bilden och dokumentera de tidiga användarnas historia.
   Du som arbetade med it under perioden 1950–1980, skriv om dina minnen och erfarenheter och om hur du uppfattat de förändringar du varit med om. Berätta också om dig själv. Om din bakgrund, om din väg in i yrket, och om ditt liv vid sidan av yrkesarbetet.
   Skicka ditt bidrag senast den sista september 2007 till intendent Peter du Rietz, Tekniska museet, Box 27842 115 93 Stockholm.
peter.durietz@tekniskamuseet.se
Har du frågor kan du höra av dig till projektadministratör Åsa Hiort af Ornäs, tel 0706-120252, asa.hiortafornas@dfs.se
   De insamlade berättelserna kommer att tillsammans med projektets övriga dokumentationsmaterial förvaras i Tekniska museets arkiv och finnas tillgängligt för forskare, studenter och andra. Information om projektet hittar du på www.dfs.se/ithistoria eller www.tekniskamuseet.se

Fig. 2.2 The project's questionnaire (*on the left*) and its call for autobiographies in the journal *Ny teknik*, no. 18, May 2, 2007 (*on the right*)

We constructed it with the help of the open source software Drupal. In order to minimize the risk of hacking or unauthorized computer access, we required the contributor to create an account with a login name and a password before using the site. At the Writers' Web, which has the URL http://ithistoria.se, the visitors are invited to record their recollections. It is also possible for them to upload different kinds of files, for instance, pictures. We, furthermore, provided the Writers' Web with a function that allows the visitors to comment on earlier uploaded contributions, and thus making an interaction between the platform's visitors possible. We did not edit postings for grammar or checked them for "accuracy." Except to demand the individual contributor to create an account, we required no further verification. In contrast to the oral histories, we did not provide the collected autobiographies or Web postings with metadata (Fig. 2.3).

Fig. 2.3 The project launched its Writers' Web in June 2007. The picture shows the homepage of the Writers' Web

2.5   Created and Collected Sources

As mentioned in the previous sections, the sources we created and collected in the project "From Computing Machines to IT" consist of oral history interviews, witness seminars, autobiographies in the form of written recollections, Writers' Web entries, and finally archival records, artifacts, movies, and pictures. Appendix I: List of Created and Collected Sources lists all the created and collected sources.

We completed 166 oral history interviews in total. Of the interviews, 153 were recorded with sound, transcribed, and edited; 7 of them were recorded with sound, transcribed, but not edited; 6 of them were recorded with notes only. The resulting recordings and transcripts are all deposited in the National Museum of Science and Technology's archival collections. The 153 edited transcripts consist of 3,905 pages of text in total. The 137 edited transcripts, for which we have the interviewer/interviewee's permission to publish on the Web, are available at the National Museum of Science and Technology's Web page: http://www.tekniskamuseet.se/it-intervjuer. The remaining transcripts (edited or not edited) are deposited in the museum's archival collections and are available for researchers only.

We, furthermore, arranged 47 witness seminars. We recorded 44 of them with both sound and images in digital format, and the remaining with sound only. We transcribed and edited all of the seminars. The resulting recordings and transcripts are deposited in the National Museum of Science and Technology's archival collections. The edited transcripts consist of 2,417 pages of text in total, and 44 of them are published both in print and electronic versions (2,271 pages of text) in KTH's working paper series TRITA-HST. Both the published and unpublished transcripts are available electronically at the National Museum of Science and Technology's Web page: http://www.tekniskamuseet.se.

In the project, we made two types of calls for autobiographies: a general call and a number of focused calls. The project's research group completed the general call for autobiographies in collaboration with the National Museum of Science and Technology and Nordiska museet, and the call resulted in 249 replies consisting of 1,461 pages of text in total. We considered 190 of the replies to have autobiographical qualities. The 129 autobiographies, for which we have the autobiographers' permission to publish on the Web, are available electronically at the National Museum of Science and Technology's Web page: http://www.tekniskamuseet.se/it-minnen. The remaining autobiographies are deposited in the museum's archival collections and are available for researchers only.

Several of the focus groups also made separate calls for autobiographies. These were mainly aimed at the senior practitioners in the focus group in question and people around them. The resulting 24 autobiographies consist of 534 pages of text in total. We have the autobiographers' permission to publish 6 autobiographies on the Web, and these are available electronically at the National Museum of Science and Technology's Web page: http://www.tekniskamuseet.se/it-minnen. The remaining autobiographies are deposited in the museum's archival collections and are available for researchers only.

In addition to the call for autobiographies, we designed a virtual platform, the Writers' Web, with the URL http://ithistoria.se/. Between May 2007 and February 2009, 35 autobiographies and 19 comments on these were posted on the Writers' Web site. All these entries are available on the Web site http://ithistoria.se/, which currently is hosted by the Swedish Computer Society.

When conducting interviews, arranging witness seminars, and acquiring written recollections, we asked if the subjects were willing to donate archival records, artifacts, movies, on pictures in their possession to the National Museum of Science and Technology. We acquired a substantial number of archival records, artifacts, movies, and pictures through this procedure. These are deposited in the museum's collections.

2.6   Contextualizing the Process of Documentation

If present and future generations of researchers and scholars can place a documentation project in its proper intellectual and social context, the American historian Linda Shopes argues, it will allow them to understand how the context unavoidably shaped the inquiry and it will help them to assess the strengths and weaknesses of the project. If they have knowledge of the particular circumstances for a single oral history, they will be able to read it more astutely.[32] Meta-documentation increases the usefulness as well as the life length of a collection, and consequently it is a crucial part of any professionally run documentation project.

The knowledge outlines produced by the research secretaries as part of their preparatory work, their correspondence with informants as well as invitations to the witness seminars, attendance lists to the seminars, questionnaires, and calls for autobiographies are all documents that help contextualize the created and collected sources. In addition, the research secretaries also summarized in a final report the documentation work done in each and every focus group. In the report, they considered the criteria that were decisive for the choice of documentation efforts. They also gave an account of the planning and realization of interviews and witness seminars, and they discussed the editing and publication process. Finally, they identified which kind of additional documentation that would be desirable to carry out in the focus area, and they suggested a number of potential research problems that could be addressed with the help of the created and collected sources.

As mentioned above, we also preserved the different steps in the process of transcribing and editing the oral histories and witness seminars. The witness seminars were provided with a preface containing information that helped contextualize the event (such as the attendants, possible special circumstances, and if the seminar had been co-organized with someone else). The extensive footnoting of the seminars and possible addenda also contributed to the contextualization.

Finally, we archived all the documentation that helps contextualize the project as a whole such as correspondence, contracts, minutes, and research applications, and we also contextualized, described, and evaluated the project in a final report.[33]

Altogether, the mentioned meta-documentation informs researchers and scholars about the provenance of the collection. The meta-documentation is deposited at the museum's archival collections (see Appendix II: List of Meta-documentation).

2.7 Concluding Observations

My conclusions on the process of documentation the organization and the methods. I point out that the methods, the organization, and the theoretical approach have mutually shaped each other, and I suggest that the project, besides the development of methods and the creation of sources, has resulted in an adapted project model for cooperation between museums, trade and industry, and universities. The possibility of a more permanent form of organization is also considered. I will then go on to discuss our experiences of methods and tools at a micro- and a macrolevel. The collaboration between historians and senior practitioners is especially emphasized, and I argue

---

[32]Linda Shopes, "Oral History and the Study of Communities: Problems, Paradoxes, and Possibilities," in *The Oral History Reader*, 263–4. James E. Fogerty, "Oral History and Archives: Documenting Context," in *History of Oral History*: 197–226.

[33]Lundin, *Documenting the Use of Computers in Swedish Society between 1950 and 1980*.

for the importance of creating events where practitioners are given the chance to come together to discuss and remember their historical past and at the same time socialize.

2.7.1 Organization

My first observation is that the project is the result of a historical process that has mutually shaped the methods, the organization, and the theoretical approach. The interplay between these factors has, to a large extent, formed the resulting collection of sources. It is, therefore, necessary to consider the organization when discussing and evaluating the documentation efforts. Two examples illustrate my argument.

That a user organization, the Swedish Computer Society, was one of the parties involved in the project aroused the curiosity of the researchers, who saw the possibility of exploring and developing a user perspective on the history of computing. Their reaction would probably have been different if, for example, an organization, such as Datasaabs vänner (Friends of Datasaab), an informal club that focused mainly on the development of hardware, had been a party. It was, furthermore, not without importance for the chosen approach to "elite" users that the National Museum of Science and Technology, with its long history of cooperating with engineers and the engineering industry, was a party instead of, for instance, Nordiska museet or the Museum of Work with their preeminent focus on skilled and unskilled labor. The choice of user perspective legitimized and cemented, in turn, the organization of the project in focus groups and focus areas.

Addressing users and technology in use also implied an empirical focus on the use of computing technology in different sectors and areas instead of the "usual" focus on hardware and software in the history of computing. The participating researchers, therefore, needed a historical understanding of these sectors and areas rather than of computing technology. As a result, the project chose to enlist scholars specialized in the history of the focus area in question (defense, financial industries, healthcare, manufacturing industries, etc.) rather than in the history of computing.

My second observation concerns the choice of a project organization as an overarching organizational form. Even if it has become more common to carry out documentation in the form of projects, the choice is far from obvious. The international documentation efforts in the history of computing have overwhelmingly been accomplished by single institutions (although these sometimes have been backed by several trustees).[34] The institution as an organizational form represents, in many aspects, an ideal solution. It guarantees permanence and facilitates long-term planning. A small staff can do the work over a long period of time. It is possible to relate the

---

[34] These institutions have, of course, realized the documentation in the form of projects but then within the existing organization.

documentation to ongoing research at the institution. CBI and the IEEE History Center have, for instance, conducted oral history interviews for almost 30 years and can afford to spend up to 2 years, including lead times, to process an interview. Institutions can build and maintain competence as well as ensure quality.

However, we faced strikingly different conditions. In comparison with CBI and the IEEE History Center, we started about 25 years late and could not possibly create and collect sources in relation to ongoing research. The advanced age of the historical subjects called for urgency. Our funding was limited to a period of 2 years. We were set the task of accomplishing a large-scale documentation of the use of computers in Swedish society within a limited time frame. We, therefore, decided to choose the project form as an organizational form. We had to hire many researchers on short contracts (6 months or less), the majority of whom had not systematically worked with documentation before. Training became, therefore, a crucial part of the project. We arranged an introductory workshop with invited speakers, which we followed up with frequent working meetings, and we circulated the key literature. We used "auscultation" as a method to familiarize the research secretaries with the interview and witness-seminar settings. The auscultator learned how to conduct an interview and arrange a witness seminar by observing a more experienced researcher in action. We also introduced the knowledge outline as a substitute for the research that documentation ideally should be linked with. Preparing, conducting, editing, and preserving oral history interviews and witness seminars as well as acquiring written recollections are activities that involve many steps and several parties. The many activities required formalized management and control. Here we drew upon the long experience of large projects, several of whose members in the steering group had come from trade and industry, and we developed an adapted project model.

This formalized approach was probably a necessary measure given the different organizations and the many participants involved. It made it possible for them to plan and predict their work. It made the project less vulnerable and less dependent on key persons. It became a way to cope with the many uncertainties that arise when one has to do many things for the first time. A drawback of this formalized approach was the loss of flexibility. The scope for improvisation was limited, i.e., for following up unexpected or newly discovered threads, such as interview subjects that suddenly fall ill (for instance, Jan Freese) or focus areas that we did not consider when planning the project (for instance, the energy sector). This has been true both at the project level and that of the individual research secretaries and focus group. In retrospect, a way to introduce flexibility could have been to allocate resources for taking possible urgent measures.

I would like to suggest that the organization of the project could serve as a model for carrying out the documentation of historical events, processes, and matters in the future. The design of organizational bodies, the explicit delegation and distribution of responsibilities, and the structured work process (described in Appendix III: Formal Description of Organization and Work Process) would certainly be of great value to other bi- or tripartite collaborations with similar objectives.

But why primarily recommend a collaboration between two or three parties? Why not let a single institution carry out all the work? There are a couple of reasons. First, Swedish research foundations distinguish between documentation and research. This development is due to a professionalization and demarcation of the work done by academia, on the one hand, and archives, libraries, and museums on the other. Thus, academia has become less inclined to carry out documentation, and archives, libraries, and museums less inclined to carry out research.[35] But research is often needed for documentation and vice versa. Collaboration between academia and archives, libraries, and museums is, therefore, desirable, perhaps even essential, when it comes to documentation. Second, as I will discuss in more detail in the following section, documentation projects will most likely be more successful if, from the beginning, they involve the subjects whose stories are to be documented. There are, of course, certain risks in such collaborations, but based on our experiences, I would argue that the gains far outweigh the losses.

The project as an organizational form has been useful, and probably necessary, for us to accomplish large-scale documentation within a limited period, and similar efforts in the future will most likely have to face similar challenges and, therefore, benefit from organizing themselves in the project form. Nevertheless, the project as an organizational form has an obvious drawback when it comes to the preservation of created and collected sources—it is supposed to end at a certain date (in our case December 31, 2008). Thus, projects—in contrast to institutions, such as archives, libraries, and museums—cannot guarantee permanence. There are a number of reasons for making a project like ours permanent in the form of an institute or a foundation. First, existing institutions, such as the National Museum of Science and Technology, have difficulty receiving, administering, and preserving new collections, since their old ones need all available resources. Second, the experiences created, the knowledge gathered, and the personnel involved could be reused in a certain way. Third, and related, the preservation of the gathered sources could be ensured and the collections eventually extended and done on a long-term basis. Fourth, researchers using the sources could be affiliated with the institute and hence linking documentation and historical research.

2.7.2 Methods

Methodological innovations and practices have, from the perspective of the project, taken place at a microlevel and a macrolevel. Innovations and practices at the latter level have been shaped, to a larger extent, by organization and theoretical approach than innovations and practices at the former level.

Even if the ensemble of methods applied was decided and fixed at roughly the same time as the project became large scale, i.e., at the beginning of 2007, there was still plenty of room for the participating research secretaries to experiment with oral history interviews and witness seminars within the given format. Thus, there are several observations on method to be made at the microlevel. The number of preparations, the skills

---

[35] This also seems to be an international trend as hinted by Rosenzweig, "Scarcity or Abundance?" 758f. There are, of course, exceptions to this trend as Marie Lennersand points out in "Historikern som arkivarie," *Arkiv, samhälle och forskning* 2008:2, 62–6.

of the interviewer (or moderator), arrangements and techniques, and the interplay between interviewer and interviewee (or moderator and witnesses) do vary from situation to situation. Each session is a unique event. It is, therefore, difficult, perhaps impossible, to recommend a best practice on how to conduct oral history. Methods have to be adapted to the aim of the oral history session, the specific circumstances, the abilities of the interviewer, and not least the subject of the interview. Recognizing this, we designed the project to be, in a sense, a methodological experiment from beginning to end.

When it comes to oral history interviews and witness seminars, my conclusions are very much in accordance with those in the literature. The following observations are attempts to generalize from the particular sources we have gathered. As always, when making generalizations, there are exceptions to be found—we simply have to acknowledge the fact that reality is more complex than the most sophisticated model or theory—but it is the overarching features that count.

There are six observations to be made on the oral history interviews conducted in the project. Firstly, trained historians or the like should, if possible, do the interviews. When the project evolved, we debated whether the senior practitioners themselves or scholars should conduct the interviews. Senior practitioners were involved as interviewers in 31 of the 166 interviews completed in the project. Unfortunately, many of those interviews proved to be of limited value for a couple of reasons. (It should be noted that I use the terms "value" or "valuable," when discussing sources here and elsewhere, in the sense of possessing unique oral qualities, i.e., qualities not possible to achieve with the help of written or other types of sources.) The interviewer was often an old colleague of the interviewee, and, since both belonged to the same social network and shared similar experiences, it became difficult for the interviewing senior practitioner to pose critical questions. Furthermore, questions and details which the historian and the posterity find interesting may often be mere truisms for them. To stretch the argument, the senior practitioners preferred to analyze, and generalize from, the past rather than create and collect sources on it.

Secondly, extensive preparations are essential for the quality of the oral history interview. Since we did not have the possibility to link our documentation efforts to an explicit research program, both the knowledge outline and the senior practitioners in the focus groups became important tools for the research secretary to become acquainted with the focus area and the interviewees.

Thirdly, "interactive" interviews are more likely to produce a better result than "passive" interviews, but only if the interviewer is well prepared and has a good knowledge of the field. An interactive interview by an interviewer not sensitive and aware of the many nuances and empirical details will, in most cases, be of limited value. In these cases, a passive interview, albeit unstructured, will most probably be a better choice. Also, an inherent danger with the interactive interview is that the questions posed may be leading. These possible flaws in the interactive interview format can (and should) be eliminated by meticulous preparations.

Fourthly, career or life-story interviews seem to be of more value (for archival purposes) compared with subject interviews, i.e., oral histories focused on certain aspects in the professional life of one individual. This has, of course, to do with the aim of the project, which is to create sources that are broad and open for as many potential uses as possible. When dealing with a specific research project, it may be justified to concentrate the interview on details of interest for a particular research question, but when creating sources for the posterity, the strategy will most probably limit the archival value. The life-story interview has another advantage. Questions about the interviewee's childhood and youth surprisingly often "open up" the interview situation. The interviewee usually does not expect, or is not used to, these kinds of questions. They may help the interviewer to get behind the official "mask" of the interviewee. Moreover, the life-story interview helps to understand why a person acted as he or she did. Early experiences in life often explain decisions later on. Therefore, I would even argue that the life-story interview, in many cases, is the best choice also when specific research details are the primary aim.

The fifth observation considers the setting of the interview. We allowed the research secretaries and the senior practitioners to experiment rather freely with the setting. Sometimes it consisted of two interviewers (usually a research secretary and a senior practitioner), sometimes two interviewees, and, in rare cases, a mix of these settings. After reviewing the transcripts, my conclusion is that a setting with only one interviewer is preferable. It makes it easier for the interviewer to remain in charge and to construct a story line. The other way around seems not to be that critical. Two subjects can be interviewed at the same time, given that they share experiences.

The last observation on oral history interviews concerns transcribing and editing. These two moments in the processing of oral histories are sometimes questioned, not least by financiers, because of their time- and resource-consuming nature. Today, it is possible to make sound and images directly available over the Internet, but I would like to emphasize that the edited transcript still has a number of advantages. It gives the scholar a good overview of the oral history since it is possible to skim through it rather quickly. Notwithstanding the possibility of indexing digital sound and image, it is difficult to survey audio files in the same manner as text files. Although painstaking, the transcribing and editing process adds value to the transcript. It increases readability, removes misspellings, and improves empirical accuracy. Perhaps this added value is even more beneficial in our digital age. With the advent of new methods such as text mining, scholars and researchers can look for patterns in large collections of oral histories, but with the prerequisite that names are correctly, at least consistently, spelled throughout the collection, which ideally should be fully searchable.

Our experience is that, above all, three factors are critical when arranging a witness seminar: the choice of subject, witnesses, and moderator. As mentioned earlier, witness seminars have been used to create general overviews, to challenge narratives, and to document and understand teamwork. A number of the seminars that we conducted early on in the project had the character of general overviews of a certain topic (such as the use of computers in the financial industries). The participating witnesses represented different competencies, different organizations, and sometimes different historical periods. Although the overviews created must be considered valuable sources, several of them tended to be superficial. It is simply difficult to cover a broad field in depth during a 4-h session. Furthermore, the dynamic that characterizes the witness seminar at its best was, by and large, absent in these sessions. One reason was that the participating witnesses had too few shared experiences. Seminars dealing with more focused themes, such as specific events, artifacts, environments, organizations, or projects, proved generally to be of more value. To conclude, the witness seminar as a method seems to be more suited for creating sources on the witnesses' shared experiences, be it a controversy or a project, than on whole industries or technological developments.

The second critical factor is the witnesses themselves. In addition to the task of identifying and inviting the "right" witnesses—i.e., people who have common experiences of the theme, are talkative, and are not senile—the composition of the panel has to be considered. Mixing people from different social groups/different positions in a hierarchy does not work very well. The rank and file of an organization are obviously not likely to be open and honest if participating on the same panel as a number of managers from the very same organization. It seems often to be the case that the social relations of the past are reestablished. Although there might be a value in itself for some scholars and researchers to get an understanding of the group dynamics, a homogeneous group made up of participants largely equal in social status, knowledge, and experience will more likely create an atmosphere of high confidence where no one feels threatened.[36]

When it comes to the moderator, he or she should, to begin with, be familiar with the theme. Ideally, the moderator should start with an introduction that contextualizes the theme and introduces a set of overarching questions. Such an introduction will help to focus the seminar. Furthermore, the moderator should have authority, which can come from age, position, or historical knowledge of the field. This last remark is linked to the question of whether a senior practitioner or a professional historian should moderate the session. Our experience is that the latter alternative, if available, is preferable. The trained historian is usually more skilled in interviewing techniques and in posing critical and historically relevant questions. However, since it was difficult to find a historian suitable for the task, senior practitioners led the majority of our seminars. I would like to emphasize that the interview is more sensitive than the witness seminar regarding the role of the interviewer, since the latter method tends to be self-regulating to a larger extent than the former. This is also a point made by E. M. Tansey on the witness seminars completed by the Wellcome Trust.[37] I believe that there are at least two contributing factors: firstly, that the sessions are moderated; and, secondly, that they are videotaped in front of an audience.

The most crucial methodological observations at the macrolevel are, first, the mutual interdependence of methods, organization, and theoretical approach as touched upon in the previous section; second, the pros and cons of different methods; and, third, the importance of collaboration between historians and practitioners. In what follows, the second and the third observation will be discussed in more detail.

---

[36] This is also the case for group interviews. Slim and Thompson, with Bennett and Cross, "Ways of Listening," 147.

[37] A commonly held belief in the literature, though, is that group interviews tend to be unstructured. Our experiences, however, juxtapose Tansey's. "Witnessing the Witnesses," 260–78.

Fig. 2.4 With the call for autobiographies, we were able to reach the "end user," who was in several cases a woman. The picture shows the office worker Ingeli Åkerberg with the word processor Wordplex at the end of the 1970s (Source: Tekniska museet)

The oral history interviews and witness seminars completed in the project paid, above all, attention to "elite" users. In that sense, we have used them in a similar manner, i.e., focusing on elite persons, as in many of the earlier mentioned documentation efforts in the history of computing. However, with the collection of autobiographies, we also reached the "end user" and, thus, acquired a more diverse picture of users of digital technology in Sweden between 1950 and 1980. Among the collected autobiographies, we find those by punch operators and secretaries. A measure of diversity is the number of participating women. In the completed interviews and seminars, the share of women was only 7%, while it was 21% in the acquired written recollections (Fig. 2.4).

The Writers' Web was not as successful as the above-mentioned "traditional" collection of autobiographies. One explanation is that we did not combine the launching of the Writers' Web with nationwide advertisements, and as a consequence, few outside the Swedish Computer Society were aware of its existence. As has been noted in the literature, finding contributors to a collection project requires "significant legwork and staff time."[38] We failed to promote the project in the digital world.

---

[38] Schrum et al., "Oral History in the Digital Age," 511f.

Fig. 2.5 The Writers' Web invited the visitors to upload digital material. However, it was difficult to reach a broader spectrum of users with the method. Quite notably, many of the postings dealt with development of hardware and software. This picture, provided by Björn Sölving, shows programming of the computer ÅNG-CENSOR constructed by the Swedish firm Standard Radio & Telefon AB (SRT)

Another contributing factor is that a Web site benefits from having material to browse when it goes public. It is therefore important to find people that are willing to contribute with stories and material when launching. And finally, there are large variations in the familiarity with the Internet among people with memories from the period between 1950 and 1980, depending on the professional, social, and cultural background. It is simply not (yet) possible to reach everybody with this kind of method. A striking illustration of the uneven distribution of Internet users in this age group is once again the number of contributing women: less than 3% (Fig. 2.5).

My third and final observation at the macrolevel deals with the active interest in the project from the communities of computer users. For reasons given below, I would argue that this interest was pivotal to the realization of the project. In order to arouse the users' interest, two things have been considered crucial: firstly, the importance of a continuous collaboration between senior practitioners and historians.[39] The senior practitioners were, in this respect, tremendously useful

---

[39] It is necessary, however, to agree upon the roles and responsibilities of the different parties. To put it simply, a successful collaboration needs well-defined rules.

for the historians in their efforts to identify important events and processes as well as historical subjects. The interaction between these two was, furthermore, decisive for shaping the outcome. The senior practitioners taking part in the focus groups had, on the one hand, a comprehensive and profound understanding of the historical events because they had been *close* to them, while they, at the same time, had difficulty contextualizing and evaluating the events precisely because of their involvement in them. The research secretaries, on the other hand, had as trained historians an ability to see the events as a part of a greater whole, precisely because of their *distance* to the past events. Secondly, the importance of creating events where the subjects are given the chance to gather for discussing and remembering their historical past and, at the same time, socialize. While witness seminars and the specially designed Writers' Web were seen as pure intellectual ventures by historians, they were actually received as social events by the senior practitioners. Also, the use of different methods gave rise to mutually reinforcing events. Witness seminars led to interviews that eventually led to the donation of archival records, artifacts, movies, pictures, or written recollections. Furthermore, many of the witness seminars had an audience mainly consisting of colleagues of the witnesses. Together with our continuous dissemination of the edited and published transcripts, this clearly raised the interest in the project. (Here is perhaps another explanation for why the Writers' Web did not succeed—we failed to make it an event.) The sheer intensity of the activities—the large number of events during a 2-year period—created a social fabric. The word was, so to say, spread, and it happened that people contacted the project because they knew something was going on. This active interest made it easier, and gave legitimate reasons, for the research secretaries to approach people otherwise inaccessible. Oral historians devoted to the study of communities have repeatedly pointed out that it takes time, Shopes even talks about years, to make contacts with community representatives, gain entrée, cultivate trust, and then set up, analyze, and present a collection of oral histories.[40] Interpreted in this light, the continuous collaboration and the event making were both parts of a social process that served to establish a trusting relationship between the historians and the community.

---

[40] Shopes, "Oral History and the Study of Communities," 269.

Chapter 3
Oral Evidence and the Swedish Historiography of Computing

The actors in history are its first interpreters.[1]

Karl Molin

In the first chapter of this book, I argued that if we want to understand how "computing has changed the world," a more user-centered historiography of computing is needed. For this purpose, we need sources of those who used digital technology and how they used it. In the following chapter, I described and analyzed how we conducted a large-scale documentation project, which aimed to collect and create sources of the use of computers in Swedish society between 1950 and 1980. In this concluding chapter, I concentrate on a discussion of how the collection of oral history interviews and witness seminars, that form the core of our documentation efforts, can contribute to the Swedish historiography of computing. However, my intention is not to make a thorough analysis of this rich and comprehensive material. That formidable task I happily leave to other scholars and researchers.[2] Here, my aim is rather to suggest how the collection can be used for addressing recent historiographical issues. I present three cases, using diverse examples from our collection, which each illustrates how oral evidence can inform us about the interaction of computing with large-scale transformations in economies, cultures, and societies. The first case deals with career patterns, social networks, and flows of knowledge,

---

[1] Karl Molin, *Den moderne patriarken: Om arbetsledarna och samhällsomvandlingen 1905–1935* (Stockholm, 1998), 5.

[2] Indeed, several scholars and researchers have used the collection for scholarly purposes. See, for instance, Isabelle Dussauge et al., "Precursors of the IT Nation: Computer Use and Control in Swedish Society, 1955–1985," in *History of Nordic Computing 3*, 425–432; Johan Gribbe, "Controlling the Battlefield: Computing and Operational Command in the Swedish Armed Forces, 1966–1989," in *ibid.*, 22–7; Anna Orrghen, "Collaborations between Engineers and Artists in the Making of Computer Art in Sweden, 1967–1986," in *ibid.*, 127–36; Gustav Sjöblom, "The Totally Integrated Management Information System in 1960s Sweden," in *ibid.*, 83–91.

the second with users and uses of technology, and the third with the materiality and geography of computing. However, I will start out with a critical discussion on the interpretation of oral evidence.

3.1   Interpreting Oral Evidence

In my analysis of the oral evidence created in the project, I will take advantage of having a rather large set of oral history interviews and witness seminars on a quite well-defined community at hand. I will give examples that demonstrate how it can be used to uncover patterns and to develop (qualitative) historical generalizations.[3] The approach is not so common as one might believe. The editors of *The Oral History Reader* (2006) note that since the 1980s, oral history interpretation has focused above all on analyzing individual interviews, and, consequently, "the issue of historical generalization, the search from patterns, has receded from view."[4] In 1983, the British historian Trevor Lummis claimed that "the problem at heart of using interview method in history still remains that of moving from the individual account to a social interpretation," and his assertion seems equally valid almost 30 years later.[5] However, since the beginning of the 1980s, a number of factors have changed. Most importantly, today, a large number of vast oral history collections are found in archives all over the world, and the number is rapidly increasing. Their accessibility has increased dramatically with the advent of digital communication technologies, above all the Internet. Many collections are now attainable online, and their availability range from catalogs presented as a list or a searchable database with metadata about oral histories available only by request or in person to transcripts, streamed audio, or video clips. Furthermore, new computer-based methods and tools such as fully searchable text files or text mining facilitate the analysis of large amounts of data and the search for anticipated and unanticipated patterns.[6]

Thus, the accumulation of oral evidence as well as the technological break-throughs gives new incentives and possibilities to generalize from large sets of oral histories. The challenge is nevertheless formidable. It is essential to show an awareness of both the interpretative limitations and possibilities when using oral evidence. To begin with, the collection must be relevant for the questions posed. It is true that an oral source, like any source, can be used and interpreted for various different purposes. Depending on the question, one single source will give us different answers.

---

[3] I would like to emphasize that this is only one of many possible ways of using the collection.

[4] Perks and Thomson, *The Oral History Reader*, 213.

[5] Trevor Lummis, "Structure and Validity in Oral Evidence," in *The Oral History Reader*, 255.

[6] See, for instance, Schrum et al., "Oral History in the Digital Age," 501f. Indeed, a Finnish research team has analyzed our interviews with the help of text mining. Petri Paju, Eric Malmi and Timo Honkela, "Text Mining and Qualitative Analysis of an IT History Interview Collection," in *History of Nordic Computing 3*, 433–43.

It speaks to us in a multiplicity of voices.[7] But to acknowledge that a source is polyphonic is not the same as to argue that it can answer *any* question. That a source has multiple meanings does not imply that the historian has unlimited power to shape interpretation.[8] In the case of an extant oral history collection, it becomes essential to know more about its provenance. In which context and for what purposes was the collection created? With knowledge of the intellectual and social setting of the collection, the historian will understand what kind of factors and considerations that shaped the oral histories and in that way find himself in a better position to assess the strengths and weaknesses of the material.[9] Thus, depending on its origin, a collection might be more or less useful for addressing a certain historical problem. Certainly, it cannot be used for any purpose.

That said, we can concentrate on the interpretative possibilities at hand. Oral histories are layered with different meanings, but even for the trained historian, these may not appear at first glance. When using extant oral history collections, Linda Shopes therefore urges historians to immerse themselves in the oral histories. Insights, she maintains, do not come from a mere scanning of the transcripts. "[O]nly occasionally does an interview provides a flash of insight that enables us to read the culture outward and make connections with broader historical concerns."[10] In the conjectural or evidential paradigm elaborated by the Italian historian Carlo Ginzburg, such flashes can be likened to traces or clues. Ginzburg pays attention to the information provided unintentionally, the marginal and seemingly irrelevant detail, the overlooked and the trivial, i.e., to information difficult or even impossible to reach with other methods. Contrary to the intentions of the sender, there may be "infinitesimal traces" in the material that permit the comprehension of deeper, otherwise unattainable, layers of meaning.[11] When searching large sets of data, these occasional flashes or infinitesimal traces multiply and eventually make up patterns. Interpretations based on indirect, scarce, and scattered evidence will always show a various degree of uncertainty, but by searching a large number of sources, they can be made more robust. Herein lies one of the great strengths of having access to a large collection of data.[12] When the oral histories are juxtaposed, patterns, similarities or differences, eventually appear—and the larger the search the clearer they appear. It should be added that the robustness of the interpretation will increase if the patterns can be verified with other types of sources.

---

[7] Ågren, "Synlighet, vikt, trovärdighet – och självkritik," 249–62; Richard Evans, *In Defence of History*, new ed. (London, 2000), 103ff.

[8] For a powerful argument against the neoskepticism expressed by some postmodernists, see Evans, *In Defence of History*, Chap. 4.

[9] See Shopes, "Oral History and the Study of Communities," 261.

[10] Ibid., 267.

[11] Carlo Ginzburg, *Clues, Myths and the Historical Method*, English trans. John and Anne Tedeschi (Baltimore, 1989), 96–125.

[12] On robust interpretations, see Hoddeson, "The Conflict of Memories and Documents," 196. For a discussion of Ginzburg's method in relation to large sets of data, see Janken Myrdal, "Source Pluralism as a Method of Historical Research," in *Historical Knowledge: In Quest of Theory, Method and Evidence*, ed. Susanna Fellman and Marjatta Rahikainen (Cambridge, 2012).

Ginzburg's sophisticated method requires a possession of almost detective-like skills. Nevertheless, I believe that it can inspire historians to novel interpretations of oral sources. My analysis of the created oral histories in the three cases has in parts been guided by a "light" version of his method.

3.2 Career Patterns, Social Networks, and Flows of Knowledge

In this first case, I discuss how the set of oral histories created in the project can help us to identify the individuals and central institutions that took part in major postwar transformations of the Swedish society such as the establishment and consolidation of the welfare state as well as its lesser known twin, the warfare state.[13] I also point out how the collection allows us to recognize social networks, i.e., the ties these individuals formed during their education, in different professional and semiprofessional organizations as well as at different institutions and workplaces.[14] Finally, I maintain that they can contribute to our understanding of the transdisciplinary, transsectorial, and transnational character of the flows of computing-related artifacts, expertise, and knowledge.

The focus on life histories when conducting oral history interviews, and the extensive footnoting including short biographies when arranging the more subject-oriented witness seminars, makes the created sources valuable for identifying career patterns. Since the biographies usually were cocreated by the research secretary and the historical subject with the help of biographical encyclopedias and provided documents such as CVs, their factual details are unusually reliable. Thus, the gathered evidence can be helpful for different kinds of analyses such as prosopography—i.e., the examination of significant number of lives in a given occupation, institution, or place—or analyses of social networks.[15]

Samples from the oral histories indicate what the career paths of the first generation of computer users could look like. Evidently, these paths varied, but some common traits stand out. A glance at the career paths of the early users of digital technology reveals that they were often educated at the Royal Institute of Technology, KTH for short, and Uppsala University as well as at the Chalmers Institute of Technology, Lund University, Stockholm University College, or the Stockholm School of Economics (Handelshögskolan i Stockholm). It can be worth mentioning that in the 1940s and 1950s, very few entered the university system. For instance, the engineering

---

[13] For an extended argument on the Janus-faced nature of the postwar Swedish state, see Per Lundin and Niklas Stenlås, "Technology, State Initiative and National Myths in Cold War Sweden: An Introduction," in *Science for Welfare and Warfare*, 1–34.

[14] On social networks, see, for instance, Ylva Hasselberg, Leos Müller and Niklas Stenlås, *History from a Network Perspective: Three Examples from Early Modern and Modern History c. 1700–1950* (Borlänge, 1997).

[15] On prosopography, see Lawrence Stone, "Prosopography," *Daedalus* 100, no. 1 (Winter, 1971), 46–79.

programs at KTH in the early 1950s consisted of about 20–30 students. The shift from elite university to mass university took place in the following decade. In many cases, they continued to the Swedish Defence Research Agency (Försvarets forskningsanstalt), FOA for short, by far the largest research institute in Sweden, universities included, during the first postwar decades, or to other directly or indirectly defense-related bodies such as the Swedish Board for Computing Machinery, MMN for short, where they usually stayed a number of years before, in the majority of the cases, they went to the trade and industry, got a position in the state bureaucracy or returned to the university.

The biography of the outstanding control theorist Karl Johan Åström (b. 1934) illustrates, in several aspects, a typical research-oriented career. He studied engineering physics at KTH during the 1950s. At KTH, he became involved in a joint project with FOA as well as the industry on missile guidance and inertial navigation. The project aroused his interest for control theory. In the beginning of the 1960s, Åström joined the newly established IBM Nordic Laboratories in Stockholm, and he visited IBM's laboratories in Yorktown Heights and San José. He developed methods for computerized process control, which were tested on a paper mill owned by the Swedish company Billerud. Åström left IBM Nordic Laboratories in the mid-1960s for a chair in automatic control at Lund Institute of Technology (Lunds tekniska högskola, LTH).[16] The fascinating career of Göran Kjellberg (b. 1920) provides a variant of this pattern (Fig. 3.1). He graduated from Stockholm University College during World War II with a degree in mathematics and physics. During the war years, he also worked at the National Defence Radio Establishment (Försvarets radioanstalt, FRA), where he monitored the German teleprinter traffic over Stockholm. After a short stay at the telecommunications company LM Ericsson, he became one of five young scholars who were sent in 1947 by the Royal Swedish Academy of Engineering Sciences (Ingenjörsvetenskapsakademien, IVA) to study computing technology at the leading centers in the USA, in Kjellberg's case the Harvard Computation Laboratory. Returning to Sweden, he joined MMN, which built the first Swedish digital computers. Kjellberg did the programming. In the mid-1950s, he returned to LM Ericsson and remained there for over a decade. Among other things, he developed software for Sweden's new and prestigious fighter aircraft Saab 37 Viggen. In the late 1960s, Kjellberg became head of computing at the grocery store chain Metrobutikerna, where he led the upgrading of the computer system and the expansion of existing routines. In 1974, a former colleague of

---

[16] Karl Johan Åström, interview from 2007 by Per Lundin, Div. of History of Science and Technology, KTH, Stockholm. Another example is the career of the electrical engineer Lars Zetterberg (b. 1925), who studied at KTH in the early 1950s, moved to FOA, where he also wrote his doctoral dissertation. After a research position at the aircraft manufacturer Saab in the early 1960s, Zetterberg returned to KTH as a professor in communication theory via short detours to Lund Institute of Technology and University of Southern California. Dávila, *Datorisering av medicinsk laboratorieverksamhet 1*, 26. For further examples, see Lundin, *Att arbeta med 1950-talets matematikmaskiner*, passim, or Olof Carlstedt, interview from 2008 by Johan Gribbe, Div. of History of Science and Technology, KTH, Stockholm.

Fig. 3.1 Göran Kjellberg
(b. 1920) (Photo: Nisse
Cronstrand, Tekniska museet)

Kjellberg's from MMN, who now headed a department at KTH, recruited him to teach the use of computers and numerical analysis.[17] Some readers may find Kjellberg's move from defense industries to retail industries surprising, but these kinds of transsectorial moves were quite typical for the early users of computing technology. There are examples of early users, who via defense industries moved on to different tasks in banks and insurance companies, but above all, they continued to the different government bodies that administered, rationalized, and served the many health and welfare reforms—including communication, transportation, and higher education—in the expanding Swedish postwar state.[18] Typical is also, as in the case of Kjellberg, how they often changed from a position as constructors, manufacturers, or salesmen of computing technology to various positions as users, or the other way around.[19] They changed arenas, functions, and positions rather frequently during their careers.

The above-mentioned sample careers illustrate several typical traits of the pioneering generation: they came from a few universities; as a rule, they worked with

---

[17] Göran Kjellberg, interview from 2008 by Gustav Sjöblom, Technology and Society, Chalmers University.

[18] See, for instance, Johan Gribbe, ed., *Att modellera slagfältet: Tidig databehandling vid FOA, 1954–66: Transkript av ett vittnesseminarium vid Tekniska museet i Stockholm den 15 oktober 2007* (Stockholm, 2007), 13f; Sofia Lindgren and Julia Peralta, eds., *Datacentralerna för högre utbildning och forskning: Transkript av ett vittnesseminarium vid Tekniska museet i Stockholm den 27 mars 2008* (Stockholm, 2008), 8f. Gert Persson, part I, interview from 2007 by Julia Peralta, Div. of History of Science and Technology, KTH, Stockholm; Gert Persson, part II, interview from 2007 by Julia Peralta, Div. of History of Science and Technology, KTH, Stockholm; Per Svenonius, interview from 2008 by Julia Peralta, Div. of History of Science and Technology, KTH, Stockholm.

[19] An illuminating example is the technician Pär Olov Sparén (b. 1928), who during the first half of the 1950s worked as a constructor in telecommunications at LM Ericsson. He then held a position as salesman at IBM Sweden for a number of years. In the late 1950s, Sparén moved to the retail and wholesale industries, where he the following three decades worked with the use of computers at the data processing department of the Cooperative Union (Kooperativa Förbundet, KF), one of the three major chains in Sweden. Gustav Sjöblom, ed., *Varuhushandelns datorisering före 1980: Transkript av ett vittnesseminarium vid Tekniska museet i Stockholm den 29 september 2008* (Stockholm, 2009), 15.

defense-related tasks; they were internationally oriented, particularly toward the USA; they moved easily and often between academia, government bodies, and trade and industry; they often changed industry or sector. It appears as if the later generation followed a similar pattern with the important exception that defense-related tasks became a less obvious part of their careers.[20] By juxtaposing the careers of the early computer users, we can also identify the central institutions that appropriated, developed, and disseminated knowledge of computing technology. Thus, during the two first postwar decades, FOA can be depicted as, to use a concept from the actor network theory, an "obligatory passage point" for elite users of digital technology.[21] Likewise, IBM Nordic Laboratories emerges as the obligatory passage point in the establishment of control theory in the Nordic countries. Judging from the oral histories, FOA in particular, but also other more specialized organizations such as IBM Nordic Laboratories, stand out as creative milieus, which, albeit for a limited time period, attracted and trained young "computer boys," who later advanced to different positions in Swedish academia, government, and business. Obviously, observations of this kind need to be confirmed by a more systematic survey of the whole set of oral histories as well as by written sources.

The career patterns of those men in charge of rationalization, i.e., the implementation of computing technology, in and of government bodies as well as trade and industry are perhaps even more intriguing. To them, computing technology promised "rationalization." Recalling, one witness said at a seminar, "Why, the potential for rationalization was enormous."[22] The collection of oral histories provides numerous similar statements from users of computing technology active in virtually all segments of society. The historiography acknowledges the computerization of the rapidly expanding public sector as one of the major computer-related undertakings in the postwar period.[23] The computerization, i.e., rationalization, in the public sector, the defense aside, was forced above all by the many welfare reforms. The comprehensive state-led reforms that led to the social and health insurance, unemployment insurance, and pension systems were funded by an increased taxation.[24] From 1950 to 1960, taxes increased from 20% of the GDP to 30%, i.e., with 50% during a 10-year period.

---

[20] See, for instance, the physicist Ragnar Nordberg (b. 1936), who studied at Uppsala University in the early 1960s and earned his PhD degree in 1968 at the same university. Thereafter, he began as head of computing at the clinical chemistry laboratory at Sahlgrenska University Hospital, where he eventually advanced to CIO. During his career, Nordberg visited or had shorter positions at several US universities and firms such as MIT, Stanford University, and Hewlett-Packard. Dávila, *Datorisering av medicinsk laboratorieverksamhet 2*, 7f.

[21] MMN probably had a similar role but for a substantially shorter period. See Gustav Sjöblom, "The Programming Priesthood Comes to Sweden: Computer Training in the 1950s" (unpublished manuscript, presented at the Division of History of Science and Technology, KTH, November 2, 2009).

[22] Julia Peralta, ed., *ADB i folkbokföring och beskattning: Transkript av ett vittnesseminarium vid Tekniska museet i Stockholm den 17 januari 2008* (Stockholm, 2008), 38.

[23] Annerstedt et al., *Datorer och politik*; De Geer, *På väg till datasamhället*.

[24] So was the construction of a national road system, the large housing programs, and hydroelectric and later nuclear power plants.

The result of this redistribution of wealth was an enormous increase in transactions. The vast quantities of information that had to be transferred from citizens and organizations, and, via a substantial number of government bodies, back to the citizens, made computerization to a central element, probably even a prerequisite, for the realization of the comprehensive reforms.[25] For instance, the social insurance offices gradually took over duties from the municipalities such as the administration of child allowance, advance payment of allowances, and housing allowance for families and low-income earners, and as the former director-general of the National Government Employee Pensions Board (Statens löne- och pensionsverk, SPV), Olof Bergvall (see further below) noted at a witness seminar, "these were heavy activities [...] that would not have been possible to handle without a powerful development of data processing."[26]

As the historian Hans De Geer concludes, government agencies and their in-house expertise had pivotal positions in the computerization of the welfare and warfare state.[27] Part of the explanation is the specific structure of the Swedish state during the postwar period. It consisted of small ministries and independent government agencies. The ministries did not have own expertise to any large extent, and therefore, delegated the task of charting the course of state action in different economic and social sectors, as well as its implementation, to agencies. The government appointed the director-general that led each agency, but otherwise, it rarely interfered in the affairs of the agencies. Consequently, the agencies established themselves as powerful and autonomous actors in postwar Sweden. De Geer assigns the Swedish Agency for Public Management (Statskontoret) a key role in the computerization of the public sector industries,[28] but bodies such as the National Social Insurance Board (Riksförsäkringsverket, RFV), the Swedish Tax Agency (Riksskatteverket, RSV), and the National Land Survey of Sweden (Lantmäteriverket) also built up their own competence in data processing and became powerful drivers.

The biography of the land surveyor Carl-Olof Ternryd (b. 1928) serves as a prime example of a career within the structure of the Swedish state (Fig. 3.2). Ternryd earned his degree from KTH in the early 1950s, and after a number of years at the National Land Survey of Sweden, he returned to KTH as a teacher and as a research assistant in photogrammetry. In 1957, Ternryd was employed at the Royal Board of Road and Waterways Building (Kungl. Väg- och vattenbyggnadsstyrelsen, VoV), where he worked with the development of data processing, photogrammetry, and metrology in the planning, design, and laying out of roads. Ten years later, he became responsible for the long-term planning at the agency. Simultaneously, he continued his teaching at KTH, and in 1971, he defended his licentiate thesis. The very same year, Ternryd

---

[25] Julia Peralta, ed., *ADB och den Allmänna försäkringen: Transkript av ett vittnesseminarium vid Tekniska museet i Stockholm den 12 februari 2008* (Stockholm, 2008), 13.

[26] Idem, ed., *Statskontoret: Transkript av ett vittnesseminarium vid Tekniska museet i Stockholm den 5 februari 2008* (Stockholm, 2008), 31.

[27] De Geer, *På väg till datasamhället*, 127–49.

[28] Ibid.

Fig. 3.2 Carl-Olof Ternryd
(Photo: Nisse Cronstrand,
Tekniska museet)

advanced to technical director of the National Road Administration (Vägverket), as the agency now was called, and in 1978, he was appointed its director-general. Only 4 years later, Ternryd abandoned the transportation industry for the defense industry, and he became director-general of the Swedish Defence Materiel Administration (Försvarets Materielverk, FMV). From 1988, he served as adjunct professor in photogrammetry at KTH.[29] Ternryd's biography indicates how expertise in the novel computing technology was considered essential for planning and administering the big infrastructural ventures that formed part of the postwar welfare (and warfare) package. The career of the policeman Olof Bergvall (b. 1926) underpins the argument. Bergvall found the patrol duty heavy and hard to combine with family life, and in the early 1960s, he started out as an investigator of insurance frauds at the Social Insurance Office in Stockholm (Försäkringskassan i Stockholm). During the 1960s, he advanced quickly in the organization, and after a couple of years as director of a large regional social insurance office, he became in 1970 responsible for the big RAFA project at the National Social Insurance Board. The project spanned over the whole decade. The aim of the RAFA project was to rationalize the administration of the general social security. After the project had been completed in 1979, Bergvall was appointed director-general of the National Government Employee Pensions Board, a position he held for 12 years.[30] Although Ternryd's and Bergvall's careers follow completely different trajectories within the structure of the Swedish state, they nevertheless display common traits. Their allegedly successful implementation of computing technology, albeit for different purposes, proved decisive of their careers. The expertise they gained and the central position in the rationalization process they acquired pushed them up the career ladder.

From the oral evidence, it seems as if the pattern was repeated in trade and business as well. One example is Rune Brandinger (b. 1931), who studied economy at the Stockholm School of Economics. During the latter part of the 1950s, he started out

---

[29] Lundin, *Databehandling vid Väg- och vattenbyggnadsstyrelsen/Vägverket 1957–1980*, 7.

[30] Another example is Karl Gustaf Scherman (b. 1938), who held both a degree in engineering from KTH and a degree in economics from the Stockholm School of Economics. After a long career he ended as director-general for the National Social Insurance Board. Peralta, *ADB och den Allmänna försäkringen*, 14f.; idem, *Statskontoret*.

at IBM Sweden (IBM Svenska AB) as a salesman, continued his education and learning, and eventually became responsible for the Custom School (Kundskolan). At IBM, Brandinger wrote and published one of the very first Swedish educational books on the use of computers. In the mid-1960s, Brandinger was headhunted to a position as data processing manager for the large Swedish insurance company Skandia. In the next 10 years, he held various top positions at different companies related to the investment trust company Ratos. In 1980, Brandinger returned to the insurance industries as CEO for the company Valand, and 6 years later, in 1986, he became CEO for the forest owners' association Södra Skogsägarna AB. Since 1993, he has been a member of numerous boards.[31]

Judging from the oral histories, it is striking how many of these participants in central reform projects later advanced to top positions in the government administration or in private firms. This observation, if correct, underscores in particular the central role of rationalization in the strong postwar state and the many reform programs it undertook. The users of computing at government bodies and firms acted as "rationalization engineers," and this competence, among others, took them in a number of cases to the top.

However, it is important to underscore that the majority of the interviewees and participants in witness seminars did not reach top positions. But, and this is perhaps even more significant since they constitute a large number, very often they occupied key positions just below the top level in government agencies or firms. The physicist Per Svenonius (b. 1926) defended in 1952 his licentiate thesis at Uppsala University, did his military service at FOA the following year, taught at KTH for a couple of years, and returned to FOA for a position as research leader in the mid-1950s. After 10 years at FOA, where he among other things designed and led the organization around the agency's mainframe computer, he got a position at the Swedish Agency for Public Management, which had a central and strategic role in the rationalization of the public administration, and stayed there until his retirement. Svenonius was the mastermind behind the establishment of a government-controlled and centralized system of data processing centers at the universities. During his time at the agency, he was also an active member of a wide range of government agencies and committees responsible for the computerization of various sectors of the Swedish welfare state.[32] The 10 year younger economist Olli Aronsson (b. 1936) graduated from the Stockholm School of Economics in the early 1960s and was employed as

---

[31] Rune Brandinger, interview from 2008 by Björn Thodenius, Center for Information Management, Stockholm School of Economics; Björn Thodenius, ed., *De viktigaste drivkrafterna för att utnyttja IT inom försäkringsbranschen mellan 1960–1985: Transkript av ett vittnesseminarium vid Tekniska museet i Stockholm den 28 november 2007* (Stockholm, 2008), 7. There are of course more examples. The outstanding career of Percy Barnevik (b. 1941), for instance, began with a successful implementation and use of computing technology. Percy Barnevik, personal communication with Rolf Berndtson, Gunnar L. Johansson and Per Lundin, November 14, 2007.

[32] Svenonius, interview. See also Sofia Lindgren and Julia Peralta, eds., *Datacentralerna för högre utbildning och forskning: Transkript av ett vittnesseminarium vid Tekniska museet i Stockholm den 27 mars 2008* (Stockholm, 2008); Peralta, *Statskontoret*, 15ff.

Fig. 3.3 Olli Aronsson
(Photo: Ellinor Algin,
Tekniska museet)

a salesman of mainframe computers at Bull General Electric (Fig. 3.3). In the late 1960s, he came to the Swedish Agency for Public Management as a project leader. For a period of 10 years, he was involved in two big projects that dealt with the computerization of the general social security and the tax administration, respectively. In the late 1970s, Aronsson moved to the insurance industries where he stayed for over 20 years as CIO for the large insurance company Trygg-Hansa and later for Skandia.[33] The collection contains multiple variants of Per Svenonius and Olli Aronsson's careers.

Based on the conducted oral histories, a tentative conclusion is that a rather limited number of people occupied many of the key positions in the small "world of computing" and that they frequently kept in touch with each other. Thus, considering the above sample careers only, Olli Aronsson was a colleague of Per Svenonius at the Swedish Agency for Public Management, and he worked with the above-mentioned Olof Bergvall with the computerization of the general social security in the RAFA project, and he held the same position at the insurance company Skandia as earlier Rune Brandinger. A meticulous reading of the whole collection would probably expose an intricate web consisting of codependent, intersecting, and parallel career paths of a limited number of people.

The oral evidence provides several examples of, and in-depth details on, the personal relationships and shared values, norms, and beliefs of the interviewed men and women, i.e., traits that ultimately make up social networks. When reading the set of oral histories side by side and searching for evidence of intended and unintended cross-references, it is fascinating to see how the paths of the narrators repeatedly crisscross each other through history. In several cases, their careers were closely intertwined and even mutually dependent. Thus, when the above-mentioned Karl Johan Åström began studying engineering physics at KTH, he had about a dozen course mates, which had no other choice but to work closely together with labs and exercises, and they quickly became friends as well as competitors. Torsten Bohlin (b. 1931) was one of them. After some years at FOA, where Bohlin among other

---

[33] Peralta, *Statskontoret*, 8. See also Thodenius, *De viktigaste drivkrafterna för att utnyttja IT inom försäkringsbranschen.*

things worked with the semiautomatic command and control system STRIL 60, he returned to KTH in order to complete a licentiate thesis. In 1963, Åström recruited Bohlin to IBM Nordic Laboratories, where they together made important contributions to the field of control theory. After working for a while with medical applications, Bohlin was appointed professor of control theory at KTH—where, by the way, another course mate eventually became vice chancellor—and found himself in a position where he now competed with Åström, who had the corresponding chair at Lund Institute of Technology.[34]

It can be hypothesized that in postwar Sweden, the relationship between the state, the academy, and the interest organizations often took the form of intricate social networks. Indeed, the British political scientist Ralph Miliband observed in his classic study of the state in capitalist society that a "new breed of 'technocrats'" had advanced and seized power in ministries, planning bodies, and committees:

> These men belong exclusively neither to the world of government nor to the world of business. They belong and are part of both, and move easily between them, the more easily in that the boundaries between these worlds are increasingly blurred and indistinct.[35]

Several, albeit far from all, of the interviewees and witness-seminar participants belonged to this "new breed of 'technocrats.'" The above-mentioned Carl-Olof Ternryd is an example of a person that sustained a close cooperation between the state, academy, and organized interests, and as the below excerpt illustrates he moved easily between the different spheres. The excerpt also gives a clear-cut illustration of how social networks could be produced and reproduced in the 1950s, 1960s, and 1970s:

> I was a teacher in photogrammetry for quite a few years at the [Royal] Institute of Technology, and during a certain period I arranged that the exercises regarding measuring instruments were located to the Royal Board of Roads and Waterways. And it meant that they knew where the Royal Board of Roads and Waterways was located. And then I went out with them on field exercises for fourteen days. There were two groups. There were forty persons in each, and then you learned what sort of person each one was, and then you picked out the best and brought them over to the Royal Board of Roads and Waterways in different positions. Of course, such things are not possible today, but then it was a great advantage since you could shape these young students by taking an active part in them when you saw what qualities they had and so forth, and you could tell them "off record" what it was all about. It is very important to bring them with you in the leadership, and I think we were quite successful in that.[36]

Ternryd's strategy was by no means unique. FOA, recalled the electrical engineer Olof Carlstedt (b. 1925) in an interview, actively recruited at Chalmers Institute of Technology (and most probably at other universities as well). A group of people led by Tord Wikland (b. 1912), who headed a department at FOA, came down to

---

[34] Åström, interview; Torsten Bohlin, interview from 2007 by Per Lundin, Div. of History of Science and Technology, KTH, Stockholm.

[35] Ralph Miliband, *The State in Capitalist Society* (London, 1969), 126.

[36] Lundin, *Databehandling vid Väg- och vattenbyggnadsstyrelsen/Vägverket 1957–1980*, 41.

Gothenburg at the end of the 1940s and headhunted students for the research agency.[37] About a decade later, Wikland was appointed CEO for Teleutredningar AB (TUAB), a consulting research organization modeled on the pattern of RAND Corporation. TUAB served as a bridge between the electronics and defense industries. Wikland quite notably recruited many of his former colleagues from FOA to the new firm.[38] Although the examples suggest how the networks spanned academy, state, and organized interests—Ternryd later became chair of the Association of Swedish Automobile Manufacturers (Bilindustriföreningen) and the Swedish Road Association (Svenska vägföreningen)—it remains to be investigated how this specific configuration in detail shaped the use and implementation of computing technologies in the expanding welfare state.

As we have seen from the career paths above, the interviewees and witness-seminar participants formed a very mobile group. They constantly crossed disciplinary, occupational, industrial or sectorial, and national borders. And their networks often spanned the same borders. Here I will concentrate on the transnational aspect and more specifically the flows of knowledge. The oral evidence hints that they read international journals regularly and frequently attended international conferences. Regarding the impact of international journals on their practice, the mathematician and FOA researcher Elsa-Karin Boestad-Nilsson (b. 1925) provided a telling anecdote at a witness seminar, "I will never forget the day when Germund Dahlquist [at MMN] comes flying out of the room, flapping a journal and shouting: 'The Wheeler Jump!'"[39] Besides illustrating the importance of having access to the latest issues of the key journals, the anecdote also hints that during the first postwar decades, it was government bodies such as MMN (and later large firms such as IBM Sweden) that had access to the latest literature, not the universities, which in the 1950s were far from the full-fledged research organizations they are today.[40] Meetings such as the early pan-Nordic NordSAM conferences, succeeded by the NordDATA conferences, which gathered the majority of the active constructors and users in the Nordic countries play a prominent part in the oral histories.[41] Also the international IFIP conferences were important for the circulation of knowledge. The participants in a witness seminar on systems development dwelled particularly upon

---

[37] Carlstedt, interview.

[38] See Johan Gribbe, ed., *NIBS: Utvecklingen av Näckens informationsbehandlingssystem, 1966–82: Transkript av ett vittnesseminarium vid Tekniska museet i Stockholm den 14 januari 2008* (Stockholm, 2008), passim.

[39] Lundin, *Att arbeta med 1950-talets matematikmaskiner*, 16. David John Wheeler, who was part of the EDSAC team, suggested a way of storing the addresses in the main program that these sequences would have to jump to and from each time they were executed. This "Wheeler Jump" was the predecessor of the modern subroutine call. Paul E. Ceruzzi, *A History of Modern Computing*, 2nd ed. (Cambridge, MA, 2003), 84.

[40] Svante Lindqvist, "A Cost-Benefit Analysis of Science: The Dilemma of Engineering Schools in the Twentieth Century," in *Science, Technology and Society: University Leadership Today and for the Twenty-First Century*, ed. Ingemar Grenthe et al. (Stockholm, 1998), 105–16.

[41] Hallberg, *IT-gryning*, 259f.

the importance of the IFIP conference FILE 68 as well as the NATO Software Engineering Conferences in 1968 and 1969.[42]

Furthermore, shorter or longer study trips or job positions abroad were common. Especially US firms or universities were found attractive. Well-known from the literature are the study trips by five young scholars sent in 1947 by the Royal Academy of Engineering Sciences to study computing technology at the leading centers in the USA. A key figure was Edy Velander (1894–1961), the CEO of the academy, who eventually turned out to be one of the most important individuals in the establishment of a domestic computer industry, especially in his role as an intermediary, both for the transfer of information between the USA and Sweden and in balancing public and private interests in Sweden. He had already in the early interwar period spent a couple of years at the Massachusetts Institute of Technology (MIT), where he became acquainted with Vannevar Bush. In 1943, he was appointed technical attaché at the Swedish legation in Washington, and he frequently reported back home about the developments concerning computing technology. Velander was the mastermind behind the decision in 1946 by the Royal Navy Board (Kungl. Marinförvaltningen), FOA, and the Royal Academy of Engineering Sciences to send Stig Ekelöf (1904–1993), professor in theoretical electricity at Chalmers Institute of Technology, on a 3-month-long mission to obtain information about the latest developments in the USA. Velander contacted Bush, who promised to help Ekelöf make the right connections. Ekelöf was followed by the five above-mentioned young mathematicians and physicists, who were sent to the USA on a similar mission. They stayed for 6 months and worked with the most advanced technology at that time.[43] The knowledge they gathered was probably decisive for the construction of the first Swedish digital computers at MMN. The conducted oral histories together with donated archival records and pictures reveal new and fascinating details about these rather well-known early missions,[44] but first and foremost, they serve to expose the sheer scale and scope of the US influence during the following decades. Users from different industries and societal sectors frequently went abroad and above all to the USA. Judging from the oral histories, the US developments in computing technology often served as a point of reference when Swedish solutions were discussed and developed.

The intense contacts with the USA were perhaps most conspicuous when it came to defense matters since Sweden had declared a policy of nonalignment in peace and neutrality in war. However, as underscored by recent research as well as numerous voices in the collection of oral histories, Sweden had an intimate and long-lasting exchange of defense matters with above all Great Britain and the USA, but

---

[42] Per Lundin, ed., *Administrativ systemutveckling i teori och praktik: Transkript av ett vittnesseminarium vid Tekniska museet i Stockholm den 26 november 2007* (Stockholm, 2008), 41ff.

[43] Petersson, "Private and Public Interests in the Development of the Early Swedish Computer Industry," 113f.

[44] See, for instance, Kjellberg, interview; Lundin, *Att arbeta med 1950-talets matematikmaskiner*, passim.

also with other NATO countries.[45] The Swedish historian of technology Johan Gribbe argues that collaboration was most intensive at the "operative" level. As he demonstrates in his examination of the development of the semiautomatic command and control system STRIL 60, it is also at this level computing technology comes into play. Several engineers and scientists earlier active in the defense sector witness in the oral testimonies how far-reaching, important, and even "natural" the contacts were with their US counterparts. They were well aware of advances in US technology, and more importantly, they often got access to it. The mathematician and operations analyst Mårten Lagergren (b. 1935), who headed the operations research teams at FOA during the 1960s, emphasized especially the close contacts with the think-tank RAND Corporation, which sorted under the US Air Force. "We were really inspired by the development, above all in the USA. RAND Corporation was a Mecca, where you went to learn things."[46] That the US contacts were close and long-lasting is also indicated by the fact that Albert Wohlstetter, one of RAND's more acknowledged researchers, visited FOA and discussed the agency's operations research activities already in the late 1950s.[47] Likewise, the electrical engineer Ingemar Carlsson (b. 1933) at the Royal Swedish Air Force Board (Kungl. Flygförvaltningen) admitted during a witness seminar that the collaboration with foreign nations was decisive in the development of real-time control systems for the military fighter aircraft Saab JA 37, known under the name Viggen. One of the engineers that participated in the development of the Pulse-Doppler radar, named PS-46/A, for the JA 37 project remembered how they were in "constant contact" with the Hughes Aircraft Company. Moreover, Carlsson dwelled upon the quite notable fact that the whole managerial group of the US Army-Navy Instrumentation Program, "the ANIP-people," visited the Swedish project and flew around in a Pembroke "some time" in the end of the 1960s.[48]

The US missions and contacts often proved valuable for their careers. For instance, the above-mentioned Olof Carlstedt, who was employed as researcher at FOA, was

---

[45] Johan Gribbe, *Stril 60: Teknik, vetenskap och svensk säkerhetspolitik under det kalla kriget* (Hedemora, 2011); Per Lundin, Niklas Stenlås and Johan Gribbe, eds., *Science for Welfare and Warfare: Technology and State Initiative in Cold War Sweden* (Sagamore Beach, 2010); Mikael Nilsson, *Tools of Hegemony: Military Technology and Swedish-American Security Relations 1945–1962* (Stockholm, 2007).

[46] The biography of Lagergren underscores my above argument on transsectorial mobility. He went from the defense industries to the healthcare industries, where he had positions at the Swedish Planning and Rationalization Institute for Health and Social Services (Sjukvårdens planerings- och rationaliseringsinstitut, SPRI) and the Ministry of Health and Social Affairs (Social departementet), where he contributed to the computerization of the healthcare sector. Gribbe, *Att modellera slagfältet*, 13, 30.

[47] See David Hounshell, "The Medium is the Message, or How Context Matters: The RAND Corporation Builds an Economics of Innovation, 1946–62," in *Systems, Experts and Computers: The Systems Approach in Management and Engineering, World War II and After*, ed. Thomas P. Hughes and Agatha C. Hughes (Cambridge, MA, 2000).

[48] Johan Gribbe, ed., *JA 37: Pilot och system: Transkript av ett vittnesseminarium vid Tekniska museet i Stockholm den 11 december 2007* (Stockholm, 2008), 20, 22, 44.

awarded a scholarship by the Sweden-America Foundation (Sverige-Amerika Stiftelsen) to study control theory at MIT, and after his return to Sweden in 1958, he was appointed head of a new division for information theory, which dealt with radar information, and command and control systems, at FOA. He participated in the evaluation and negotiation of the proposed semiautomatic data handling system for the Royal Swedish Air Force Board by the British company Marconi Wireless & Telegraph and also in the initial development of the command and control system for the Swedish-built Näcken-class submarines at the late 1960s.[49]

The transnational flow of knowledge, in particular from the USA, played an influential role also in other segments of society.[50] The overwhelming majority of trade and business, in particular banking, insurance, manufacturing, retail and wholesale, and transportation industries as well as agricultural and forest industries, were part of the internationally oriented IBM world. In particular, data processing managers went to IBM in Brussels for training courses in technology as well as management and at least once a year to conferences in the USA. At conferences and seminars overseas or in Brussels, they met with representatives from US firms and other firms from all over the world and "got a clear idea of what was going on."[51] An important node for data processing managers from different industries was the Swedish Computer Association (Svenska Dataföreningen, SDF).[52] Originally named the Hollerith Club (Hollerithklubben), it turned exclusively to IBM users, but later users of other brands were also allowed as members. Study trips were organized regularly by the association, and as one participant in a witness seminar on computer societies in Sweden mentioned, "they went almost always to the US, of course." And he later added, "IBM was a supplier that you always had to visit." About 60 people participated in each trip, and they were often organized in four groups depending on the industry they belonged to. Ingemar Svensson (b. 1939), who during the 1970s and 1980s was data processing manager

---

[49] Gribbe, *NIBS*, 13; Carlstedt, interview.

[50] An example from the public sector industries is the development of online databases and information retrieval systems at Swedish research libraries and information science in general. Marie-Louise Bachman, interview from 2007 by Anna Orrghen, School of Culture and Communication, Södertörn University, Stockholm; Roland Hjerppe, interview from 2008 by Anna Orrghen, School of Culture and Communication, Södertörn University, Stockholm; Mats Lindquist, interview from 2008 by Anna Orrghen, School of Culture and Communication, Södertörn University, Stockholm; Anna Orrghen, ed., *Tidiga söksystem: Transkript av ett vittnesseminarium vid Tekniska museet i Stockholm den 21 januari 2008* (Stockholm, 2008), passim.

[51] Thodenius, *De viktigaste drivkrafterna för att utnyttja IT inom försäkringsbranschen*, 17. See also Esbjörn Hillberg, interview from 2008 by Gustav Sjöblom, Technology and Society, Chalmers University; Bernt Malmkvist, interview from 2007 by Kurt Gladh, Stockholm, and PhD Jan af Geijerstam, Stockholm; Gustav Sjöblom, ed., *Införandet av streckkoder i Sverige: Transkript av ett vittnesseminarium vid Tekniska museet i Stockholm den 22 oktober 2008* (Stockholm, 2009), 7ff., 13f., 21f. 38f.; idem, *Varuhushandelns datorisering före 1980*.

[52] Svenska Dataföreningen eventually merged into Dataföreningen i Sverige but kept its English name.

for the large food producers' cooperative Lantmännen, recalled how he during these trips made several long-lasting acquaintances with other persons from the retail and wholesale industry:

> Then we met, there were fifteen of us from firms within trade and distribution, and we met outside the scheduled meetings, and we were talking in the evenings or when travelling in the bus and we got to know each other. And when we were back home, we had a fantastic exchange [of knowledge] now that you had got to know fourteen new persons, whom I may not have known before going on this trip.[53]

These kinds of recurrent activities contributed to create and sustain social bonds between data processing managers within respective industry.

To sum up, the created oral histories that I have paid attention to in this section supply evidence of career patterns, the form and content of social networks, and flows of knowledge, i.e., how local participants acted transnationally and transdisciplinarily and transsectorially. The conclusions I have presented are of course uncertain, but a more systematic search of the oral history collection would probably make them more robust.

3.3   Users and Uses of Technology

This second case exemplifies how the created oral evidence can contribute to our understanding of how, during the first postwar decades, users at various levels in different organizations adapted, modified, reconfigured, and resisted computing technology in order to fit their purposes and the intentions of their organizations. Thus, the collection of oral histories allows us to counter the simplistic, but widely held assumption, of wholesale appropriation of technology. It provides numerous examples of multiple processes of coconstruction in virtually all segments of society. It also exposes the technological, institutional, social, and cultural configuration that the digital technology had to be embedded in, and that, to a large extent, forced adaptation, modification, and reconfiguration of the technology in question. Furthermore, it suggests, what we tentatively can call, the codependence of the computerization of different industries and sectors. The rapid rationalization of banks and insurance companies, to mention one example, depended on a number of key features of the welfare state such as the introduction of social security numbers, the national automobile register, and the land and property registers—and not least their computerization.[54]

---

[53] Sofia Lindgren, ed., *Dataföreningar i Sverige: 1949–1990: Framväxt och förändringsmönster: Transkript av ett vittnesseminarium vid Tekniska museet i Stockholm den 26 september 2008* (Stockholm, 2008), 45ff.

[54] Thodenius, *De viktigaste drivkrafterna för att utnyttja IT inom försäkringsbranschen*, 9f., 15. See also Ebba Larsson, ed., *Fastighetsdatasystemet: Transkript av ett vittnesseminarium vid Tekniska museet i Stockholm den 30 september 2008* (Stockholm, 2008).

Although, as the examples in the previous section have shown, a transnational flow of artifacts, expertise, and knowledge was a prominent feature in the computerization of Swedish industries and societal sectors—in particular American role models and technology were important—they do not imply that the users at Swedish agencies and firms simply adopted foreign, mainly US, solutions. A study trip to the USA by 3 civil engineers who traveled 30 states during 9 weeks in 1958 proved formative when the Royal Board of Roads and Waterways, the government agency responsible for building and maintaining roads, established a data processing department.[55] However, it did not mean that the agency copied US methods and practices. As the above-mentioned Carl-Olof Ternryd later recalled during a witness seminar dealing with data processing at the agency, "We learned quite a lot over there, and we also learned how not to do it."[56] The collected oral evidence reveals that the process of adapting computing technology was complex and that it varied between agencies and between companies. The Royal Board of Roads and Waterways is a case in point. During the postwar period, the agency, the second largest in Sweden after the Defense due to extensive road planning, construction, and maintenance programs, underwent a dramatic professionalization. Up to 75% of the technical tasks at a regional road administration could be planning-related tasks.[57] In the light of this, the data processing department (Vägbyråns elektroniska räknebyrå, VERA), headed by Ternryd, was established and quickly gained a position as an indispensable intermediary. The data processing department worked in close collaboration with the different parts of the organization. According to the oral histories, the people of this department went on information and study trips to the 24 regional road administrations in order to reach an understanding of the need for computing power. One man from each regional administration was in turn invited to work at the centrally located data processing department for about 2 weeks. Tasks such as road planning and traffic counts for the road department, statistical processing for the department of human resources, as well as for the department for supplies and workshops were conducted in close cooperation with the "end users" at the respective department. This, as it seems, far-reaching user adaptation may partly explain why the agency chose to configure the technology in a radically different manner than other government bodies. While these mostly worked with IBM solutions and punched cards, the Royal Board of Roads and Waterways, on the other hand, purchased Swedish-built mainframe computers from the company Saab and used punch tape-based systems.[58] Saab, a manufacturer of aircraft, originally started to develop

---

[55] On the study trip, see Carl-Olof Ternryd, Bo Hallmén and Göran Waernér, *Fotogrammetri och datamaskiner i vägplaneringen i USA och Kanada: Erfarenheter från studieresa 3.8.–5.10. 1958* (Stockholm, 1958).

[56] Lundin, *Databehandling vid Väg- och vattenbyggnadsstyrelsen/Vägverket 1957–1980*, 9.

[57] Per Lundin, *Bilsamhället: Ideologi, expertis och regelskapande i efterkrigstidens Sverige* (Stockholm, 2008), 22; Ove Pettersson, *Byråkratisering eller avbyråkratisering: Administrativ och samhällsorganisatorisk strukturomvandling inom svenskt vägväsende 1885–1985* (Uppsala, 1988), 58ff.

[58] Lundin, *Databehandling vid Väg- och vattenbyggnadsstyrelsen/Vägverket 1957–1980*, passim; Peralta, *Statskontoret*, 19.

computers for handling the heavy calculations that were part of the design process of the planes. As programming language, the agency chose ALGOL-GENIUS, a derivative of ALGOL 60 with elements of COBOL. The language had been developed at the early 1960s by engineers at Saab for the company's mainframe computers.[59] Although colleagues from other agencies considered it "rather odd," the Royal Board of Roads and Waterways even used the language for programming administrative routines. However, the systems bought from Saab also underwent considerable adaptation, modification, and reconfiguration in order to fit the complex and multifaceted character of the agency. Regarding the administrative systems, one of the persons responsible at the data processing department mentioned that

> Originally, you bought an accounting system from Datasaab with indata as a punch tape. [...] This was one of very few accounting systems with punch tape as indata. And there must have been quite a lot of work to adapt the Datasaab system to the needs of the Board of Roads and Waterways.

As a consequence, the data processing department decided in the mid-1960s to develop their own administrative system specifically tailored to the demands of the agency. To give an idea of the complexity the administrative system had to manage, there were about 100 different professions and occupations employed by the agency. On top of that, the three different agreements that regulated the conditions of the road workers had to be dealt with[60] (Fig. 3.4).

Firms in the shipbuilding industry also collaborated with Saab's computer division, which later became a subsidiary company named Datasaab. Until its sudden collapse in the mid-1970s—the immediate cause was the opening of the Suez Canal, but signs of structural problems had been visible already by the end of the previous decade—the Swedish shipbuilding industry was among the largest in the world, and Kockums one of its major players. During the 1960s and 1970s, Kockums developed Styrbjörn (Steerbear), a computer-based system for the construction and production of ships. The task as formulated by the mastermind behind Styrbjörn, the physicist Kai Holmgren (b. 1930), was to investigate "a shipyard as an object for rationalization with computing technology." In other words, the aim was to computerize a process that went from one unity (the ship at the conceptual stage) via hundreds of thousands single details back to one unity (a ship ready for delivery).[61] Originally, Styrbjörn was a numerical system for construction of body details, but it soon developed into an integrated system for both construction and production of ships. When developing Styrbjörn, Kockums used the computer D21 manufactured by Saab as well as the above-mentioned programming language ALGOL-GENIUS.

---

[59] For Saab's main frame computers, see Hallberg, *IT-gryning*, Chap. 13. For the programming language ALGOL-GENIUS, see Bengt Asker, "ALGOL-GENIUS: An Early Success for High-level Languages," in *History of Nordic Computing: IFIP WG9.7 First Working Conference on the History of Nordic Computing (HiNC1), June 16–18, 2003, Trondheim, Norway*, ed. Janis Bubenko, Jr., John Impagliazzo and Arne Sølvberg (New York, 2005), 251–60.

[60] Lundin, *Databehandling vid Väg- och vattenbyggnadsstyrelsen/Vägverket 1957–1980*, 27f.

[61] Kai Holmgren, "Datorverksamheten vid Kockums under efterkrigstiden," in *Vårt Kockums* (Malmö, 2010), 279–310.

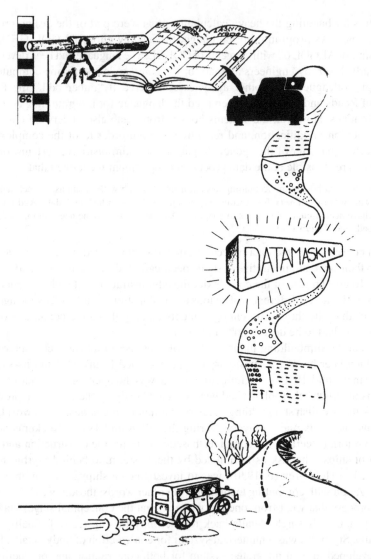

Fig. 3.4 The illustration shows a document dated June 1, 1960, from the Royal Board of Roads and Waterways, which describes the role of computing machinery in the planning and construction of roads. The document was donated by a witness-seminar participant (Source: Tekniska museets arkiv)

Engineers at the two companies collaborated closely when elaborating the software. They developed KOCK, a derivative of ALGOL-GENIUS specially designed for shipbuilding. Updated versions of this specific hardware and software configuration were in fact in use until the mid-1980s, when the production of the D20 mainframe computer series came to an end and Kockums were forced to change to an IBM and

PL/I configuration.[62] The oral evidence suggests that detailed and intimate knowledge of different aspects of shipbuilding and shipyards ranging from the workshop floor to the administration and management was a prerequisite when developing the Styrbjörn system. At a witness seminar that dealt with the development and use of the system, Kai Holmgren emphasized the importance of being close to the users throughout the design process:

> Then we had the shipyard and I would like to say that without the shipyard we would never have been able to develop this system. It is quite clear. We could just walk down to the workshop and up to the drawing office, and so forth. And I can say that when I started there, the first I asked to do was to visit all the functions in the shipyard. I was at the administrative function also, so you got to know how this was working. And then you got to know lots of people. And it meant that later you could get in touch when you needed to know something. For example, when we had to develop the program for double-curved sheet metal... It is not an easy problem. You know the shape in space, but you should produce it from a flat sheet. How do you cut it out? And then Saab had developed some methods that you knew in theory, but no one had really thought of how to do it in the workshop. How do you handle that? So I went out to talk with the guys. One was called Lomma and another Kanada, and I stood watching when they were working with sheet metal. How they put them up on sawhorses, how they heated them up and such things. And I saw it as my task to translate this into a method that could be programmed. And we succeeded. You saw that they intuitively chose a line where it was minimum curvature on the double-curved sheet metal. If it was an ordinary double-curved, you made wedges from the edge and inwards that you heated up so there was a compression and the sheet collapsed. Or if it was saddle shaped you had to do the same thing but in the middle of the sheet. You could see that's what they did. They could handle this method. If you then could put it in the program, well, then you knew that the guys could follow it.[63]

The above examples of the Royal Board of Roads and Waterways Building and Kockums both indicate that the initiative came from the data processing departments rather than from the management (although the management in both cases decided to support the ventures at an early stage). They reveal that the computing technology was substantially adapted and modified to meet the specific demands of the respective organization. They also give at hand that "end users" were involved in the processes and that the technological solutions were designed with them in mind, although they tended to be viewed as objects rather than subjects, and perhaps particularly so at Kockums. This in-depth knowledge of the object and the environment to be computerized proved to be an indispensable competence for adapting the system to fit the organization and its needs.

Also in healthcare, the technological solutions had to be modified to meet the needs of the users. The main reason to computerize laboratory work, the physician

---

[62] In fact, Kockums and IBM had already in the 1970s made a conversion of the ALGOL-GENIUS code into PL/I code since Kockums wanted to sell Styrbjörn on the international IBM-dominated market. Sten Kallin, interview from 2007 by Anna Orrghen, School of Culture and Communication, Södertörn University, Stockholm.

[63] Per Lundin, ed., *Styrbjörn: Utvecklingen och användningen av ett konstruktions- och produktionssystem för skeppsbyggnad vid Kockums under 1960- och 1970-talen: Transkript av ett vittnesseminarium vid AVEVA AB i Malmö den 2 oktober 2007* (Stockholm, 2008), 33f.

Sven Lindstedt (b. 1927), who headed the department of clinical chemistry at the Sahlgrenska University Hospital in Gothenburg, recalled at a witness seminar, was above all "a matter of putting things right in the utter confusion—to put it mildly—prevailing at that time and which suddenly came to be my responsibility." At the laboratory, he remembered, a nurse took the blood sample:

> At the best, she would write the patient's name on the tube. If it came to the worst, she would just grab a referral, wrap it around the tube and send it down to the lab. Thus, by the end of the day there were twenty tubes without referral and twenty referrals without a tube and you wouldn't know what to do with them.[64]

One of the first measures was to get rid of the referral and simply put a flag on the tube. The next step was to computerize the process. At the department of clinical chemistry at the Sahlgrenska, Ragnar Nordberg (b. 1936), who had a doctoral degree in physics from Uppsala University and had held positions at US universities and firms such as MIT, Stanford University, and Hewlett-Packard, came into the picture. This was in 1970. As a physicist specialized in analytical chemistry, he entered another world. "[A]t the Chem-Lab quality was kept on an entirely different level [than in research]. The challenge was to keep quality and to repeat the same thing over and over again in long sequences." Nordberg underscored that in the laboratory, it was an explicit demand to quickly adapt to different situations. It was a constant pressure to "reprogram" as he phrased it. He remembered that it was almost impossible to achieve the flexibility needed with purchased software. "Then it took ages to get it done and implemented." As a consequence, they decided to do the programming in-house.[65] They hired programmers, but at the witness seminar, which more specifically dealt with computerization of blood analysis and health screenings, the participants repeatedly stressed the difficulties of the programmers to adapt their methods and themselves to the demands of the laboratory. Lindstedt summoned:

> I and Ragnar [Nordberg], who is a physicist, hired some programmers. It was kind of hard because the programmers had a conventional training. They asked for a systems analysis, and I answered, "I can't tell you what this lab looks like in one week or in one month. Hopefully it does not look like today in any case." Both Ragnar and I realized that we had to use the computer as full control of this machine was a must, and we had to use it as a tool for improving the situation. Then it was actually simpler to learn basic programming rather than to try to teach a professional programmer to understand what a lab was. It was almost impossible, because they believed there were rules when there were none.[66]

So rather than trying to get the programmers to learn the environment, the chemists and physicians at the lab decided to do the programming by themselves. Nordberg recalled: "This meant that our programming developed from binary systems, through assembler to FORTRAN. Everybody was programming. Sven programmed during nights. I programmed. We had physicians that programmed."[67]

---

[64] Dávila, *Datorisering av medicinsk laboratorieverksamhet 2*, 7f.

[65] Idem, *Datorisering av medicinsk laboratorieverksamhet 1*, 10ff.; idem, *Datorisering av medicinsk laboratorieverksamhet 2*, 9, 20.

[66] Idem, *Datorisering av medicinsk laboratorieverksamhet 2*, 7f.

[67] Ibid., 20.

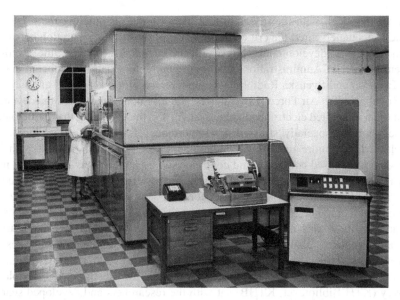

Fig. 3.5 The prototype of the automatic blood analysis equipment AutoChemist from 1965 developed by the brothers and physicians Gunnar and Ingmar Jungner. In the foreground, the computer Eurocomps LGP 21 and the printer FlexoWriter (Source: Ingmar Jungner, "Berättelsen om AutoChemist," http://www.tekniskamuseet.se/it-minnen)

As in the previous cases, this example from the healthcare sector indicates a user-driven, bottom-up process, in which the clinical departments at the hospitals rather than the Royal Board of Health and Welfare (Kungl. Socialstyrelsen), the government body in charge, were instrumental in the introduction, implementation, and use of digital technology. Lindstedt, for instance, claimed at the seminar that he had to call DEC, HP, and other manufacturers by himself in order to find out what kind of systems was available, how they worked, and then he took the decision to purchase a computer.[68] The example also suggests that it was easier to teach the users to program than to teach the programmers the environment. It should be noted, however, that the "users" in all the above cases are good examples of "elite users" (for a discussion of the concept, see Chap. 1 of this book). "End users," perhaps with the exception of the Royal Board of Roads and Waterways Building, did not have much influence over the adaptation, modification, reconfiguration, and use of the digital technology. To put it simply, they were looked upon as objects rather than subjects (Fig. 3.5).

There are, though, examples in the collection which show that also "end users" were directly involved as coconstructors of the technological solutions. A prime example of user collaboration in the defense sector is the development of the real-time control system for the fighter version of the aircraft Viggen (JA 37). At a witness

---

[68] Ibid., 7f.

seminar that dealt with the integration of the systems surrounding the pilot, the participants underscored the critical importance of the close cooperation between, on the one hand, development engineers at the customer FMV (i.e., the Swedish Defence Materiel Administration), the main contractor Saab, the subcontractors LM Ericsson and Svenska Radiobolaget, and, on the other, test pilots at Saab and the Royal Swedish Air Force (Flygvapnet). A major undertaking was the development of an integrated electronic display system, and the test pilots that participated at the seminar especially stressed the importance of a novel tactical indicator, which facilitated more autonomous fighter tactics than had been possible with the previous radar-based command and control systems.[69] "End users" also came into play in wholly different segments of society. In the sector consisting of museums, libraries, and archives, the MLA sector for short, the research libraries were the first ones to computerize. When librarians at the university libraries as well as at research institutes such as FOA developed information retrieval systems, researchers, and sometimes also students, were involved at an early stage in the design process. To mention one example, the librarian Malin Edström (b. 1942) admitted in an interview how she and her colleagues at the Royal Institute of Technology Library (KTH Biblioteket, KTHB) sat with the researchers and developed search profiles. "It was really like, 'I don't understand why I cannot retrieve anything.' Then you could sit down together and discuss the profile and say, 'but your question is far too narrow,' 'yes, but it is this they want,' 'yes, but this is not how they write.'" Edström also remembered that the researchers were not always keen to cooperate and that they had to be persuaded in order to participate.[70] Her last statement underscores that the "end users" in the two examples above—fighter pilots respectively researchers—differed radically from the "end users" in my earlier examples since both groups were in occupations with a high social status and were considered as highly skilled professionals.

The many examples provided by the oral evidence show that it was not a straightforward task to appropriate the new technology. It was not simply enough to purchase a computer, a system, or software—or to hire programmers for that sake. The introduction of bar codes in the Swedish retail and wholesale industries provides an illustrative example. Initially, the development of the American Unified Product Code (UPC) in the USA served as a role model for Europeans, but the Swedish retail and wholesale industry acted in a very different state-market-civil society configuration, and the standardization of bar codes had to be negotiated with stakeholders such as the National Swedish Price and Cartel Office (Statens pris- och kartellnämnd, SPK), the National Swedish Board for Consumer Policies (Konsumentverket), and the Swedish Commercials Employees' Union

---

[69] Gribbe, *JA 37*, passim. Another example of close user collaboration in the defense sector is the development of NIBS, a computerized information handling system for the Näcken-class submarines. Idem, *NIBS*, passim, but especially 17.

[70] Malin Edström, interview from 2008 by Anna Orrghen, School of Culture and Communication, Södertörn University, Stockholm, 18; Hjerppe, interview; Orrghen, *Tidiga söksystem*.

(Handelsanställdas förbund). These negotiations were often frustrating from the perspective of the data processing departments in the industry, which, at a witness seminar on the introduction and use of bar codes, claimed that the National Swedish Price and Cartel Office and the National Swedish Board for Consumer Policies "did their best to slow down the development." The result, however, was a very different system.[71]

In many cases, the coconstruction of users and technology created a path dependence from which it became increasingly difficult to deviate. The (elite) users shaped the systems and the systems shaped (all) users. The old practice of laying out roads by rule of thumb at the regional road administrations had to give away to the new, computerized practices and methods. The cutting of sheet metal at Kockums' shipyards was carried out by numerically controlled machine tools, and the highly qualified blue-collar workers, who earlier had done the job manually, had to find new tasks. And it did not take long before the nurses and physicians at the laboratory were wholly dependent of the new, computerized routines when making blood tests. Once embedded, the technology quickly became indispensable. A striking example of the central role of data processing that was touched upon in the oral histories is the failed attempt in the mid-1980s to merge four medium-sized insurance companies (Valand, Skånska Brand, Allmänna Brand, and Vegete). All four companies had developed their own technical platforms for data processing based, quite remarkably, on four different types of mainframe computer systems. And all four companies had powerful data processing managers who refused to give up their own system, i.e., their own (central) position. Rune Brandinger, CEO of Valand at that time, disparagingly described it as a situation where the "IT mafia" ruled. He continued:

> Four IT managers, all of them proud as game cocks and each one convinced that his system was the only sensible one and thus would be the system of the group. That was the starting point. Then you have the executive management with just enough knowledge of IT, but loaded with thousands of other concerns and then these four game cocks with quite a lot of power, since IT still is the central laboratory of an insurance company.

Eventually, the merger into the new company WASA took place, but according to Brandinger, "the only thing that actually happened in this merger was that the offices all over the country carried a WASA-sign on the outside, but inside they were still four companies."[72]

Judging from the oral evidence on the early computerization of different societal sectors in Sweden, it seems as if the early computing technology often was adapted in close collaboration with users in respective sector. However, the evidence also suggests that this gradually began to change with the introduction of systems thinking, the professionalization of programming, and an expansion of the consulting

---

[71] Sjöblom, *Införandet av streckkoder i Sverige*, 15, 28ff.

[72] Brandinger, interview; Thodenius, *De viktigaste drivkrafterna för att utnyttja IT inom försäkrings-branschen*, 13, 49f.

industry.[73] The user, it seems, was gradually "disengaged." The idea of management information systems (MIS) attracted a lot of attention in the 1960s, and although the totally integrated management information system in practice was a rare phenomenon in Sweden, the impact of the idea and the few examples help shed light on the changing role of the user in processes of computerization. As the historian of technology Gustav Sjöblom notes, the MIS concept derived largely from the USA, and it was transferred to Sweden through "the written work of management scientists and the activities in Sweden of computer suppliers and management consultants." In the few Swedish MIS implementations that were realized consultants from the Stanford Research Institute (SRI) had a decisive role.[74] A qualified guess is that the consultants had a rather limited understanding of, and perhaps also a limited interest in, the particularities of the Swedish firms and users. An intriguing case of the disengagement of the user is the development of the computerized command and control system, later known as the LEO system, which was initiated in the late 1960s by the Swedish Defence Staff (Försvarsstaben). According to Johan Gribbe, the LEO command system had several similarities with the MIS implementations in the private sector. Only a small part of the LEO system eventually materialized. Gribbe claims that one reason behind its failure was "the considerable passive resistance which the system encountered from both end users and senior commanders when new computing technology was to be introduced in old organizational structures." The systems men—to borrow the US-based British historian of computing Thomas Haigh's term—never accepted that the idea of an integrated and computerized command system, where highly classified information about war plans, communications, and intelligence was concentrated in a single computer system, ran counter to "the fundamental military principle that an officer should know no more than absolutely necessary to execute the task assigned to him."[75]

Of course, the role of users and the technology in use can be examined with the help of other sources. It will in fact strengthen the case. Nevertheless, I would like to argue that oral histories are an apt starting point for examining the coconstruction of users and technology since the accounts often are rich in detailed descriptions that, sometimes contrary to the narrator's intentions, exposes a complexity and

---

[73] See Jan af Geijerstam, ed., "VIS/MIS – visionen om den kompletta informationen: Transkript av ett vittnesseminarium vid Chalmers tekniska högskola i Göteborg den 8 maj 2008" (unpublished report, 2008); Lundin, *Administrativ systemutveckling i teori och praktik*; Gustav Sjöblom, *IT-konsultbranschens uppkomst och tillväxt, 1964–1985: Transkript av ett vittnesseminarium vid Tekniska museet i Stockholm den 1 april 2008* (Stockholm, 2008).

[74] Sjöblom, "The Totally Integrated Management Information System in 1960s Sweden." See also Mirko Ernkvist, ed., "Införandet av EDB som stöd för logistikprocessen inom Volvo 1958–1973, skildrad utifrån användarnas perspektiv: Rapport bearbetad utifrån ett vittnesseminarium på Volvo IT den 29 maj 2006" (unpublished report, 2007).

[75] Johan Gribbe, ed., *LEO: Databehandling och operativ ledning inom försvaret, 1972–89: Transkript av ett vittnesseminarium vid Högkvarteret i Stockholm den 15 januari 2008* (Stockholm, 2008); idem, "Controlling the Battlefield," 22f. On the "systems men," see Haigh, "Inventing Information Systems."

messiness of events and processes, artifacts, and milieus that rarely are documented in text. Especially the witness seminar appears as a promising method since, if properly used, it can produce a well-confined narrative that covers different aspects of a particular project.

3.4 The Materiality and Geography of Computing

In this final case study, I will exemplify how the collection of oral histories can inform us of the materiality and geography of computing and thereby provide a counter-narrative to the popular assumption, sustained not least by the Spanish sociologist Manuel Castells' scholarship, of the immateriality and placelessness of computing and information technology. To mention one example, the Swedish computing magazine *Computer Sweden* boasted recently that Internet weighs a mere 50 g. The magazine referred to the YouTube science channel Vsauce, which had estimated that 50 g is the total weight of all electrons in motion circulating in the 75–100 million servers that make up the Internet.[76] These electrons are of course only part of a much larger picture that among other material things includes huge server halls, with a vast energy consumption, dispersed all over the world.[77] Only recently, scholars in the history of computing have begun to show an interest in the material and geographical aspects of the information technology. In his book *The Vast Machine* (2010), the American historian of technology, Paul Edwards, recognizes the friction caused by computing,[78] and his peer Paul E. Ceruzzi describes in turn the physical concentration of much of the world's Internet management and governance to a single urban corridor in the outskirts of Washington, DC, the Internet Alley.[79]

Technology in use provides a starting point for examining the issues of materiality and geography. However, in most cases, the interviewees and witness-seminar participants only mentioned technology in use en passant on the way to what they considered more pressing and urgent matters. Nevertheless, these small glimpses serve as clues, to use Carlo Ginzburg's terminology, to the materiality and geography of computing. For instance, when discussing the theory of administrative systems, Janis

---

[76] I am grateful to Gustav Sjöblom for providing me with this example. See his blog post "Informationsteknikens materialitet," http://gustavsjoblom.blogspot.com/2011/11/informations-teknikens-materialitet.html (accessed November 20, 2011) for a more elaborated discussion. See also Karin Lindström, "50 gram fattas mig i Berlin," http://computersweden.idg.se/2.2683/1.414848/50-gram-fattas-mig-i-berlin (accessed November 20, 2011).

[77] It has been estimated recently that the use of information technology make up 1.75% of the carbon dioxide emissions in Europe. Sjöblom, "Informationsteknikens materialitet."

[78] Paul N. Edwards, *A Vast Machine: Computer Models, Climate Data, and the Politics of Global Warming* (Cambridge, MA, 2010).

[79] See, for instance, Paul E. Ceruzzi, *Internet Alley: High Technology in Tysons Corner, 1945–2005* (Cambridge, MA, 2008).

Bubenko, Jr. (b. 1935), unexpectedly added an anecdote on how physically demanding data processing could be in the era of mainframe computers:

> But actually I would like to go back fifteen years in time, to the beginning of the 1960s, to that which we may not remember all of it, that sometimes computing was very heavy work. Physically heavy. I worked with Univac Scandinavia during the first half of the 1960s. We tried to get our foot in this world of IBM which was filled with IBM-machines. At that time, 75 percent of all computers were IBM. In any case we sold a machine to Götaverken, a UNIVAC III. The problem was that there was no number III in this country. There was hardly anything like it in the whole of Europe. Finally, we found one that was more or less similar to what Götaverken wanted. Well, Götaverken is no longer there, which makes this historical in a double sense. We found one in the Kantonalbank in Bern [BEKB], in Switzerland. Our boss at Univac had promised the people at Götaverken that we would quickly develop a system to be delivered along with the UNIVAC III. And so he said that "well, it takes about a month," like every sales oriented person would say. This lead to me having to get hold of five persons, including myself, and we settled down at a hotel in Bern. And it was a magnetic tape-oriented solution, so we kept lots of magnetic tapes in tins. And these tins were kept in two big suitcases. And we were given computer time between midnight and six in the morning. Every night we passed the hotel reception carrying these big, rattling suitcases. Finally, the receptionist couldn't control himself any longer, "where are you going, gentlemen?" he asked. "To the Kantonalbank," we answered.[80]

Although the above extract can too easily be read (and dismissed) as a historical anecdote only, it can also be seen as a clue to the materiality and geography of computing. The extract suggests that users were in constant, sometimes even desperate, search of cheap computing power, and furthermore, that they were dependent on specific computers. Thus, Bubenko's team had to search over whole Western Europe for a UNIVAC III computer. Users had to physically move the punch cards, punch tapes, and later on magnetic tapes to the data processing centers. Of course, one has to be careful not to make too much out of one testimony, but as more oral histories are searched and traces of information are gathered here and there, the interpretation will eventually become more robust (or the other way around). The collection of oral evidence contains in fact numerous stories of delivery vans, lorries, airplanes, and even trains loaded with punched cards. It contains stories of punch cards dispersed all over the street from an open tailgate of a delivery van and of boxes of punch cards come tumbling on to the floor covered with ice-slush.[81] "Small insights" of this kind are scattered in the large set of oral histories, and when gathered it becomes possible to expose patterns in the large set of data.

The stories around the first Swedish digital computers BARK and BESK, the IBM-based data processing centers all over Europe, and the mini-, micro-, and personal computers of the 1970s and 1980s expose the material and geographical realities that constructors, operators, and users had to cope with—often on a daily basis. Ad hoc solutions and tinkering, heavy lifts and transportation, and nightshifts

---

[80] Lundin, *Administrativ systemutveckling i teori och praktik*, 25.

[81] See, for instance, Kent Björkegren and Bengt Risén, interview from 2008 by Gustav Sjöblom, Technology and Society, Chalmers University; Lars Irstad, interview from 2008 by Gustav Sjöblom, Technology and Society, Chalmers University; Lundin, *Tidig programmering*, 32.

and waiting time were experiences that many of them shared. The testimonies at the witness seminar "Working with the Computing Machines of the 1950s" illustrate how the constructors, operators, and users of BESK, inaugurated in early 1954 as the first Swedish electronic computer, constantly had to improvise. The operators Gert Persson (b. 1932) and Gunnar Stenudd (b. 1923) recapitulated how ad hoc solutions were repeatedly used for the construction, maintenance, and operation of BESK. For instance, Stenudd had to manually gold-plate the entire set of 2,000 electron tubes in order to get BESK to function properly. And as part of the maintenance, 100 of the electron tubes were removed and tested manually every morning before they began to use the machine. They discarded the defect tubes and put the remaining back again. Later, they developed complementary methods for making this time-consuming daily service period more efficient. The memory of the computer consisted originally of Williams Tubes, but these were soon replaced by a magnetic core memory. The electrical engineer Carl-Ivar Bergman (b. 1925) who led the development of the subsequent core memory remembered how tricky it was to test all of the approximately 40,000 small cores, each one with a diameter of 2 mm. The problem was finally solved by Persson who constructed test equipment consisting of simple tin cans, and after a month or two, all cores had been tested. "Then it was, of course, carpentry work to make the matrices, and we hired a number of housewives who had deft fingers. They sewed and soldered, and after a couple of months they had completed the 40 matrices."[82] Furthermore, the BESK operators struggled constantly with reliability. The machine stopped now and then, and the stops were very time consuming since they often had to rerun the program. Although the core memory was more reliable than the Williams Tubes, it was still very sensitive to vibrations. BESK was installed at MMN, which was located in an old nineteenth-century building at Drottninggatan, the main street of Stockholm at that time. Bergman recalled:

> And I know that we were almost walking around in felt slippers, because we didn't have concrete floor at that time but a wooden floor, so it was vibrating. And we had an observer who watched the traffic at Drottninggatan from the window, and when a truck was approaching he raised his hand. Yes, then you had to stop Bert [Bolin]'s program and wait for one minute until the truck had passed by. And when all the small grids of the electron tubes had stopped rattling, then you could push the button and so we continued.[83]

That specific contextual circumstance, such as wooden floors and heavy traffic, had an impact on the reliability of early computing would probably be very hard to grasp from documentary sources. If we immerse ourselves in the oral evidence, there are several similar anecdotes and small stories of technology in use waiting to be discovered. Like the quote above, they will probably reveal intriguing details that can help us to question the alleged immateriality and placelessness of computing (Fig. 3.6).

---

[82] Lundin, *Att arbeta med 1950-talets matematikmaskiner*, 12, 27ff.
[83] Ibid., 28.

Fig. 3.6 Carl-Ivar Bergman in the computing hall for BESK (Source: *Industria* 50, no. 10 (1954))

If we concentrate on the users, who generally wrote their own programs in the 1950s, the oral histories provide traces of a messy practice full of uncertainties. The actual programming was rather trivial in the beginning, witnesses the above-mentioned Göran Kjellberg, who programmed BESK's predecessor at MMN, the relay-based BARK, which had been inaugurated in April 1950. In fact, according to Kjellberg, the general opinion in the early 1950s was that the man in the street could learn to program after a 2-week course. However, he had much more vivid and detailed recollections of the material realities they had to cope with. "The physical difficulties to connect the wires were tedious and time-consuming." But above all, Kjellberg nurtured a "fear that the machine [which consisted of 5,200 relays] would miscalculate, because so it did. Relays can make occasional mistakes and they don't last as long as the electron tubes, which mean that occasional mistakes actually happened rather often (Fig. 3.7)."[84] As an employee at MMN, Kjellberg had almost unlimited access to the machines. This was not the case for other users, who were debited for the computing time. Soon they developed methods for using the allotted time as efficiently as possible. The civil engineer Göran Waernér (b. 1932), who worked at the data processing department at the Royal Board of Roads and Water Building, made software for road construction. At a witness seminar on early programming practices, he recalled how they were allotted two slots, 3:30 a.m. and 12:30 p.m., at BESK, and these were their chances to test their program. In order to maximize the

[84] Kjellberg, interview; Lundin, *Tidig programmering*, 9f.

Fig. 3.7 Göran Kjellberg at his desk at MMN (see also Fig. 3.1) (Source: *Industria* 50, no. 10 (1954))

time they had at their disposal, he remembered how they quickly developed practices of correcting the punch tapes on the spot:

> It certainly took a long time to correct such a big punch tape roll, but we learned to find clever methods by adding a number of blind operations, 0 0 0 0 5, shift zero, and arrow right. Then you could add operations manually with a small punch tape machine to avoid recopying the entire roll.[85]

After one year of painstaking tests, they had completed the system, which could calculate 3 km of road in approximately 10 min. If we trust Waernér's reminiscences, a road engineer needed approximately one month for performing the same calculations manually. Although we have to be careful to take such figures literally, we can probably believe him when he claimed that the "rationalization potential" was substantial.[86]

As it seems, this practice of correcting punch tapes and punch cards was rather widely spread, although it took different forms depending on the I/O devices.

---

[85] Lundin, *Tidig programmering*, 22f. For a similar example, see Elsa-Karin Boestad-Nilsson, who found this kind of tinkering "depressing," in Lundin, *Att arbeta med 1950-talets matematikmaskiner*, 29.

[86] Lundin, *Tidig programmering*, 22f.

Still in the mid-1970s members of the academic computing club Lysator used similar ad hoc methods when programming. Lysator had been established a couple of years earlier as the first Swedish computing club by students at Linköping University. The company Datasaab had donated an old mainframe computer from the early 1960s, a D21, to the club. Lysator's members maintained, operated, repaired, and remade the computer, and they used it for widely different purposes such as member registers and the making of music. At a seminar that dealt with the computing club, the witness Bo Kleve (b. 1946) admitted that handling the punch tapes was a messy business:

> If you made an error somewhere in the program you could actually cut the tape in two, add another small piece and then you started to punch null signs all over it. [---] Then you had this piece of tape that you put in and there you punched it manually, a manual punching machine, punch hole by hole, lots of fun. Many times you have corrected tapes, those tapes that went completely wrong and, as Mats [Lenngren] said at that time, this was not anything lasting and then there is mylar plastic, mylar tapes instead and they lasted a little longer.[87]

The problem with the mylar was that the tapes were static, Mats Lenngren (b. 1955) added, "so when they slipped onto the floor they became full of hair and dirt, so that was the drawback with the plastic tape."[88] All in all, the oral histories mentioned allow us to challenge the notion of computing as an abstract, clean, and neat business.

The example with Lysator also demonstrates how the introduction of mainframe computers often resulted in organizational innovations, like computer clubs. They made up physical milieus, which in the case of the D21 at Lysator attracted young enthusiasts that tinkered with the machine. The corridor at Linköping University where the computer was located became a meeting place and a workshop for experimenting with hardware and software. The experiences made by the students led eventually to the construction of the minicomputer LYS 16.[89] The large computing halls during the era of mainframe computing were very specific milieus that shaped the users and the uses of technology. The first years after its inauguration, BESK had no, and later few, competing machines, and the demand for computing time was high. Users queued at MMN for their allotted slot. Since they were not allowed to enter the computing hall, they had to patiently wait outside. Elsa-Karin Boestad-Nilsson remembered vividly and perhaps with some nostalgia the atmosphere in the waiting room. The users were drinking tea and shared experiences and programming tips. But as pointed out by another participant in the seminar, the milieu was also important in another aspect, since it—contrary to the universities—had the latest issues of the key journals in the shelves.[90] With time BESK lost its dominant position, routines became more informal, and the users were allowed to enter the computing hall and run the program themselves. Karl Johan Åström, then a young

---

[87] Sofia Lindgren and Julia Peralta, eds., *Lysator: Transkript av ett vittnesseminarium vid Linköpings universitet den 21 februari 2008* (Stockholm, 2008), 20f.

[88] Ibid.

[89] Ibid., passim.

[90] Lundin, *Att arbeta med 1950-talets matematikmaskiner*, 15, 18f.

assistant at KTH, recalled how they just went down to the board with tapes written in machine code:

> When it was your time, then you went in there. The machine was on. And then you put in your tapes and ran [the program]. And if the loudspeakers began to howl, something was wrong. Then you had to shut it off immediately and the next man entered. So you sat in a queue outside, waiting. And there was often time left over and things like that.[91]

As the introductory example to this section suggests, users were constantly looking for more capacity and struggling for the purchase of larger, more powerful computers. In doing so, they had to adapt to what can be denoted the web of computing. Users flocked around the data processing centrals, which made up nodes in the web. The result was lots of traveling and working hours during late nights, weekends, and holidays. FOA was a large user of BESK, but during the 1950s, the agency bought time at an IBM 709 in Paris as well, and the researcher traveled back and forth.[92] The agency also had access to an IBM 650 located in Arboga, a small town about 150 km west of Stockholm. The Royal Swedish Air Force Board had originally purchased the IBM 650 for spare parts managements and logistics. The mathematician Ulla Jismark (b. 1932), who was employed at the division for computing at FOA, mentioned that they worked quite much on this machine:

> You made the programs here in Stockholm and then you wished everything would be right when you came to Arboga. Of course, sometimes we had to re-write them, but it was quite easy to find the bugs. The worst of it was probably that we couldn't run the programs in the daytime, but that we had to run nights and Saturdays and holidays. On some occasions during this period, 1958–59, we went to Arboga, it was rather convenient, and we brought air mattresses and slept for a couple of hours each while the other person watched the machine. Then you went home again Monday morning, possibly Sunday evening.[93]

As the excerpt reveals, the geography of computing dictated not only their working hours but also their working life. Later, when FOA purchased an IBM 7090 and conveniently located it to its own facilities in Stockholm, the working conditions improved of course. Also private enterprises such as the small consulting firm Nordisk ADB, which provided the Royal Board of Roads and Waterways with software during the early 1960s, were looking for cheap computing power. Göran Waernér from the data processing department at the Royal Board of Roads and Waterways was one of the cofounders of Nordisk ADB. In order to lower the costs, he and his colleagues traveled several times per day to the company Asea in Västerås, some 100 km west of Stockholm, and sometimes also by air to Oslo or Zürich.[94] And so did several of the large insurance companies which had to handle vast quantities of information. The economist Jan-Erik Erenius (b. 1937) remembered when

---

[91] Åström, interview.

[92] Lundin, *Att arbeta med 1950-talets matematikmaskiner*, 17; idem, *Tidig programmering*, 11f.

[93] Gribbe, *Att modellera slagfältet*, 11.

[94] Lundin, *Databehandling vid Väg- och vattenbyggnadsstyrelsen/Vägverket 1957–1980*, 23; idem, *Tidig programmering*, 22ff.

SPP (Sveriges Privatanställdas Pensionskassa) was forced to retariff in the late 1950s because of the comprehensive pension reforms that had taken place:

> At this time, SPP was a downright punch card environment and they should retariff. What did they do? They had lots and lots and lots of punch cards. Well, they decided to fly them down to Paris where the only IBM 650 in Europe was puffing. So they chartered a plane. [...] I think it was an old two-propeller-driven aircraft. They loaded it with punch cards, flew down to Paris with three guys who were about to learn how to handle this fantastic novelty IBM 650. They spent three weeks there, chewed [punch cards] night and day and at the end, they got new punch cards that they loaded in an aircraft, or if it was the same aircraft, and they flew them back home and sorted them out.[95]

Interviewees and witness-seminar participants repeatedly pointed out the physical distance to the computer and that they had to adapt and adjust their working life to the available technology. Looking back at his first years as a programmer, Bjarne Däcker (b. 1942) at the telecommunications company LM Ericsson observed:

> My most vivid memory of this time is precisely how far away the computing machine was. Now you have it in your lap, literally speaking. But then you rarely saw it, and especially when it came to programming telephone exchanges. It was about writing some program that should be punched, send it away and then the program should be compiled on an ORION machine. It was a machine developed by Ferranti in Great Britain. And the result should in turn be sent to the computer that controlled the telephone exchange, and then it was mostly about program tests on a facility in Västberga. You went to someone called Niklasson who ran the program. And the whole procedure was so tiresome that there was only one way to do it, and it was to sit down and meticulously read through your program so there wouldn't be any errors left. It simply was such hard, hard work.[96]

This distance to the computer was not only geographical. To many, it also had a social dimension. For radical computer scientists in the late 1960s and the early 1970s, it became a matter of power and democracy, and almost 40 years later, one of them still characterized the era of mainframe computing as a "long dark period when the programmers were prevented from entering the machine hall."[97] Contemporary voices criticized the limited access to computing power and feared the monopolistic tendencies that they argued lied inherent in the mainframe computing technology. The concentration of computing power to FOA that began with the purchase in 1960 of the large mainframe computer IBM 7090 led to a heated debate during the latter half of the decade. It was spurred by the decision in 1965 by the Swedish Agency for Public Management, which purchased computers for the

---

[95] Thodenius, *De viktigaste drivkrafterna för att utnyttja IT inom försäkringsbranschen*, 22; SPP/ AMF, group interview with Perolof Axelson, Jan-Erik Erenius, Birger Fernström and Göran Krantz from 2008 by Björn Thodenius, Center for Information Management, Stockholm School of Economics. See also Lundin, *Administrativ systemutveckling i teori och praktik*, 25f.

[96] Lundin, *Tidig programmering*, 32.

[97] Sten Henriksson (b. 1938) in Lundin, *Att arbeta med 1950-talets matematikmaskiner*, 37; Sofia Lindgren and Julia Peralta, eds., *Högre datautbildningar i Sverige i ett historiskt perspektiv: Transkript av ett vittnesseminarium vid Tekniska museet i Stockholm den 24 januari 2008* (Stockholm, 2008), 33f.

Fig. 3.8   The data processing central QZ was located to the main buildings of FOA at Linnégatan 89 in central Stockholm (Source: FOA veteranförening)

public sector industries, that FOA and the universities in Stockholm should establish a jointly owned data processing central. A couple of years later, an IBM 360/75 was acquired and installed in the facilities of FOA (Fig. 3.8).[98] Teachers and researchers at the universities were upset that the data processing central, with the conspicuous name QZ, had been located to the defense agency, and they feared that this decision would limit the access to the computer. The above-mentioned Janis Bubenko, Jr., who later became professor in computer and systems sciences at KTH/Stockholm University, was one of them. At a witness seminar, he claimed that the decision by the Swedish Agency for Public Management to centralize the computing power for the university sector delayed the introduction of time-sharing with about 5–7 years.[99] Although statements like Bubenko's obviously need to be confirmed by other sources, they do expose a clash between two ideologically opposed systems: the "closed world" of the defense sector and the "open world" of the universities.

---

[98] See, for instance, Annerstedt et al., *Datorer och politik*, Chap. 8.

[99] See Lindgren and Peralta, *Datacentralerna för högre utbildning och forskning*; idem, *Högre datautbildningar i Sverige i ett historiskt perspektiv*, 33ff.

Also those who did not explicitly politicize the computer found it nevertheless frustrating to be so far away. As became clear at the witness seminar on Lysator, the main incentive for the students to establish the academic computing club in the early 1970s was to have their own computing power. Mats Lenngren, who by that time was an engineering student at Linköping University, explained:

> You have to remember that computers at that time, or mainframe computers, why they were not really accessible to ordinary people, there simply were no computers. You could find them at the data processing centrals, the universities, the institutes, the municipalities and the county councils and with the big companies. When you used the word computer, it felt like something abstract, it was something that existed, but still you couldn't touch it.[100]

In fact, the only contact the engineering students at Linköping University had with computers was through punch cards, and this information was sent, via a modem, to a UNIVAC 1108 at the data processing central at Lund University some 400 km south of Linköping. However, as one of the participants pointed out at the seminar, a visit to Stanford University in the summer of 1972 turned out to be an eye-opener. There the students had started a club, which operated an old mainframe computer with peripherals that they had got hold of. "Really, the students [at Stanford] have their own computing power, and we were connected to Lund through a line, of punch cards, that is."[101]

In particular, data processing centrals became nodes in the web of computing. Most users had but to adapt to this geographical and social reality. Exceptionally, they could, like the engineering students in Lysator, get hold of their own computer or, like Lysator later did, construct their own computer. The majority, however, was left with few other choices. To mention one example, the only way for artists and musicians interested in exploring the novel technology was to approach the few available computers like the UNIVAC 1108 at Lund University or Saab's D21 at Skandinaviska Elverk AB in Stockholm. Thus, the artist Sture Johannesson (b. 1935) began in 1969 to cooperate with the IBM employed programmer and instructor Sten Kallin (b. 1928). Johannesson and Kallin worked with their art at IBM in Solna north of Stockholm, where they used an IBM 1130 for elaborating different kinds of patterns (Fig. 3.9). Eventually, Johannesson became a trusted person. He recalled in an interview: "I borrowed a key to IBM's laboratory in Solna and went there by myself and unlocked and locked when I left."[102] The example illustrates how the only way to get access to the computing technology was to collaborate with people who had access to it.

---

[100] Idem, *Lysator*, 18.

[101] Ibid., 14, 17f.

[102] Sture Johannesson and Ann-Charlotte Johannesson, interview from 2007 by Anna Orrghen, School of Culture and Communication, Södertörn University, Stockholm; Kallin, interview; Orrghen, "Collaborations between Engineers and Artists in the Making of Computer Art in Sweden, 1967–1986," in particular 132f.

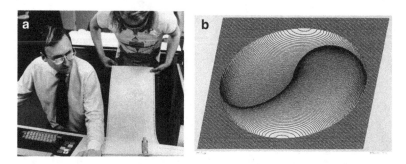

Fig. 3.9 Picture (**a**) shows Sten Kallin (*left*) and Sture Johannesson (*right*) during their work with the exhibition Intra at IBM Stockholm in the early 1970s, and picture (**b**) the computer generated graphic Spirals 106 from Intra 1969/70–74 (Photo: Courtesy of Sture Johannesson)

3.5 Conclusions

In this final chapter of the book, I have given examples of how the oral histories created in the project can be used for analyzing the interaction of computing with large-scale transformations in economies, cultures, and societies. By examining the career paths and social networks of professional elites as well as the flows of knowledge, I have pointed out the pivotal role of computing technology in the expanding postwar state. It was seen as a tool for rationalization, and it was an indispensable part of the implementation of the many state-led welfare and warfare reforms. Actors with knowledge of how to implement the new technology in public and private organizations often occupied key positions in the state apparatus or in firms. Although a transnational flow of artifacts, expertise, and knowledge—in particular from the USA—was important for the rapid computerization of Swedish industries and societal sectors, the oral histories supply evidence of how the computing technology had to be adapted, modified, and reconfigured in order to fit the new context and the demands of the users. However, the users soon became wholly dependent on the new technology. In Oudshoorn and Pinch's terminology, the users and the technology were coconstructed. The oral histories also indicate that the use of computing technology was constrained by material and geographical realities. In particular, during the era of mainframe computers, the working conditions and working life of users were shaped by the materiality and geography of computing. For practical reasons, I have limited my analysis to the created oral sources, but the created and collected autobiographies would probably be equally apt to examine similar historical problems. As I have repeatedly stressed in this final chapter, my conclusions are based on samples from the oral histories and are therefore tentative. A more systematic search of the collection would increase the robustness of the interpretations.

Appendices

Appendix I: List of Created and Collected Sources

This appendix lists the sources (oral history interviews; witness seminars; autobiographies; Writers' Web entries; and archives, artifacts, pictures, etc.) created and collected in the project.

Oral History Interviews (Recorded, Edited)

In total, 166 interviews were created and collected in the project (collected since 11 of the interviews—nos. 141–151 in the list below—were originally conducted in the 1990s and later donated to the project). The resulting recordings and transcripts are all deposited in the National Museum of Science and Technology's archival collections. Of the interviews, 153 were recorded, transcribed, and edited. The edited transcripts consist of 3,905 pages of text in total. They are listed below. Of the edited transcripts, 137 are available on the museum's Web page: http://www.tekniskamuseet.se/it-intervjuer. They are italicized below. The remaining edited transcripts are deposited in the museum's archival collections.

No. 1: *Ingemar Ringström, interview from 2007 by Per Lundin, Div. of History of Science and Technology, KTH, Stockholm, 22pp.*

No. 2: *Gunnar Wedell, interview from 2007 by Per Lundin, Div. of History of Science and Technology, KTH, Stockholm, 19pp.*

No. 3: *Karl Johan Åström, interview from 2007 by Per Lundin, Div. of History of Science and Technology, KTH, Stockholm, 33pp.*

No. 4: *Sture Johannesson and Ann-Charlotte Johannesson, interview from 2007 by Anna Orrghen, School of Culture and Communication, Södertörn University, Stockholm, 30pp.*

P. Lundin, *Computers in Swedish Society: Documenting Early Use and Trends*,
History of Computing, DOI 10.1007/978-1-4471-2933-2, © Springer-Verlag London 2012

No. 5:   Göran Sundqvist, interview from 2007 by Anna Orrghen, School of
          Culture and Communication, Södertörn University, Stockholm, 28pp.

No. 6:   Jan W Morthenson, interview from 2007 by Anna Orrghen, School of
          Culture and Communication, Södertörn University, Stockholm, 30pp.

No. 7:   Sten Kallin, interview from 2007 by Anna Orrghen, School of Culture and
          Communication, Södertörn University, Stockholm, 48pp.

No. 8:   Birgitta Frejhagen, interview from 2007 by Per Lundin, Div. of History of
          Science and Technology, KTH, Stockholm, 28pp.

No. 9:   Bengt Gällmo, interview from 2008 by Per Lundin, Div. of History of
          Science and Technology, KTH, Stockholm, 20pp.

No. 10:   Torsten Ridell, interview from 2007 by Anna Orrghen, School of Culture
          and Communication, Södertörn University, Stockholm, 25pp.

No. 11:   Björn Tell, interview from 2007 by Anna Orrghen, School of Culture and
          Communication, Södertörn University, Stockholm, 18pp.

No. 12:   Mikael Jern, interview from 2007 by Anna Orrghen, School of Culture
          and Communication, Södertörn University, Stockholm, 23pp.

No. 13:   Bodil Gustavsson, interview from 2007 by Anna Orrghen, School of
          Culture and Communication, Södertörn University, Stockholm, 17pp.

No. 14:   Lars Kjelldahl, interview from 2007 by Anna Orrghen, School of Culture
          and Communication, Södertörn University, Stockholm, 18pp.

No. 15:   Marie-Louise Bachman, interview from 2007 by Anna Orrghen, School of
          Culture and Communication, Södertörn University, Stockholm, 24pp.

No. 16:   Mats Lindquist, interview from 2008 by Anna Orrghen, School of Culture
          and Communication, Södertörn University, Stockholm, 20pp.

No. 17:   Torsten Bergner, interview from 2007 by Gustav Sjöblom, Technology and
          Society, Chalmers University, 35pp.

No. 18:   Sven-Olof Öhrvik, interview from 2008 by Mikael Nilsson, Div. of History
          of Science and Technology, KTH, Stockholm, 13pp.

No. 19:   Jacob Palme, interview from 2007 by Kajsa Klein, Dept. of Journalism,
          Media and Communication, Stockholm University, 34pp.

No. 20:   Thomas Osvald, interview from 2007 by Kajsa Klein, Dept. of Journalism,
          Media and Communication, Stockholm University, 29pp.

No. 21:   Eva Runefelt, interview from 2007 by Kajsa Klein, Dept. of Journalism,
          Media and Communication, Stockholm University, 13pp.

No. 22:   Tage Frisk, interview from 2007 by Per Lundin, Div. of History of Science
          and Technology, KTH, Stockholm, 25pp.

No. 23:   Anders Noaksson, interview from 2007 by Anna Orrghen, School of
          Culture and Communication, Södertörn University, Stockholm, 25pp.

No. 24:   Monica Bratt, interview from 2007 by Anna Orrghen, School of Culture
          and Communication, Södertörn University, Stockholm, 20pp.

No. 25:   Roland Hjerppe, interview from 2008 by Anna Orrghen, School of Culture
          and Communication, Södertörn University, Stockholm, 27pp.

No. 26:   Lars-Gunnar Bodin, interview from 2007 by Anna Orrghen, School of
          Culture and Communication, Södertörn University, Stockholm, 36pp.

No. 27: Östen Mäkitalo, interview from 2008 by Mikael Nilsson, Div. of History of Science and Technology, KTH, Stockholm, 15pp.

No. 28: Arne Sträng, interview from 2007 by Anna Orrghen, School of Culture and Communication, Södertörn University, Stockholm, 16pp.

No. 29: Per-Erik Danielsson, interview from 2008 by Sofia Lindgren, The Swedish Computer Society, 23pp.

No. 30: Rune Nilsson, interview from 2007 by Gustav Sjöblom, Technology and Society, Chalmers University, 32pp.

No. 31: Malin Edström, interview from 2008 by Anna Orrghen, School of Culture and Communication, Södertörn University, Stockholm, 25pp.

No. 32: Carl-Erik Franke-Blom, interview from 2007 by Julia Peralta, Div. of History of Science and Technology, KTH, Stockholm, 22pp.

No. 33: Lars-Erik Sanner, interview from 2007 by Anna Orrghen, School of Culture and Communication, Södertörn University, Stockholm, 20pp.

No. 34: Olof Carlstedt, interview from 2008 by Johan Gribbe, Div. of History of Science and Technology, KTH, Stockholm, 26pp.

No. 35: Lennart Olausson, interview from 2007 by Julia Peralta, Div. of History of Science and Technology, KTH, Stockholm, 26pp.

No. 36: Alf Brandtieng, interview from 2007 by Julia Peralta, Div. of History of Science and Technology, KTH, Stockholm, 24pp.

No. 37: Ingrid Strandgård, interview from 2007 by Julia Peralta, Div. of History of Science and Technology, KTH, Stockholm, 19pp.

No. 38: Nils Knutsson, interview from 2007 by Julia Peralta, Div. of History of Science and Technology, KTH, Stockholm, 23pp.

No. 39: Nils Qwerin, interview from 2007 by Julia Peralta, Div. of History of Science and Technology, KTH, Stockholm, 17pp.

No. 40: Sture Allén, interview from 2008 by Julia Peralta, Div. of History of Science and Technology, KTH, Stockholm, 11pp.

No. 41: Stig Larsson, interview from 2007 by Julia Peralta, Div. of History of Science and Technology, KTH, Stockholm, 21pp.

No. 42: Stellan Bladh, interview from 2007 by Julia Peralta, Div. of History of Science and Technology, KTH, Stockholm, 14pp.

No. 43: Björn Lundkvist, interview from 2007 by Julia Peralta, Div. of History of Science and Technology, KTH, Stockholm, 28pp.

No. 44: Björn Nilsson, interview from 2007 by Julia Peralta, Div. of History of Science and Technology, KTH, Stockholm, 20pp.

No. 45: Sven Inge, interview from 2007 by Anna Orrghen, School of Culture and Communication, Södertörn University, Stockholm, 24pp.

No. 46: Kerstin Sjöberg, interview from 2007 by Isabelle Dussauge, Div. of History of Science and Technology, KTH, Stockholm, 17pp.

No. 47: Hans Peterson, interview from 2007 by Isabelle Dussauge, Div. of History of Science and Technology, KTH, Stockholm, 49pp.

No. 48: Folke Karling, interview from 2007 by Gustav Sjöblom, Technology and Society, Chalmers University, 40pp.

No. 49: *Ove Wigertz, interview from 2007 by Isabelle Dussauge, Div. of History of Science and Technology, KTH, Stockholm, 20pp.*

No. 50: *Bengt Olsen, interview from 2006 by Urban Rosenqvist and Isabelle Dussauge, Div. of History of Science and Technology, KTH, Stockholm, 20pp.*

No. 51: *Gert Persson, part I, interview from 2007 by Julia Peralta, Div. of History of Science and Technology, KTH, Stockholm, 21pp.*

No. 52: *Martin Fahlén, interview from 2007 by Isabelle Dussauge, Div. of History of Science and Technology, KTH, Stockholm, Urban Rosenqvist, and Hans Peterson, 18pp.*

No. 53: *Ulla Gerdin, interview from 2005 by Hans Peterson, 13pp.*

No. 54: *Paul Hall, interview from 2005 by Hans Peterson, 15pp.*

No. 55: *Sven Tafvelin, interview from 2008 by Sofia Lindgren, The Swedish Computer Society, 46pp.*

No. 56: *Gunhild Agnér Sigbo, interview from 2008 by Sofia Lindgren, The Swedish Computer Society, 29pp.*

No. 57: *Gert Persson, part II, interview from 2007 by Julia Peralta, Div. of History of Science and Technology, KTH, Stockholm, 19pp.*

No. 58: *Per Svenonius, interview from 2008 by Julia Peralta, Div. of History of Science and Technology, KTH, Stockholm, 19pp.*

No. 59: *Jan Nordling, interview from 2008 by Sofia Lindgren, The Swedish Computer Society, 17pp.*

No. 60: *Anna Sågvall Hein, interview from 2008 by Sofia Lindgren, The Swedish Computer Society, 26pp.*

No. 61: *Torsten Seeman, interview from 2007 by Isabelle Dussauge, Div. of History of Science and Technology, KTH, Stockholm, Urban Rosenqvist, and Hans Peterson, 17pp.*

No. 62: Seth Myrby, interview from 2008 by Mikael Nilsson, Div. of History of Science and Technology, KTH, Stockholm, 14pp.

No. 63: *Esbjörn Hillberg, interview from 2008 by Gustav Sjöblom, Technology and Society, Chalmers University, 41pp.*

No. 64: *Jöran Hoff, interview from 2008 by Mikael Nilsson, Div. of History of Science and Technology, KTH, Stockholm, 16pp.*

No. 65: *Rolf Wedberg, interview from 2008 by Mikael Nilsson, Div. of History of Science and Technology, KTH, Stockholm, 14pp.*

No. 66: *Gösta Carlson, Nils-Erik Vall and Carl-Henrik Wallde, interview from 2008 by Göran Kihlström, Per Lundgren and Mikael Nilsson, Div. of History of Science and Technology, KTH, Stockholm, 43pp.*

No. 67: *Börje Langefors, interview from 2005 by Janis Bubenko, Anita Kollerbaur and Tomas Ohlin, 13pp.*

No. 68: Olle Lenneman, interview from 2008 by Mikael Nilsson, Div. of History of Science and Technology, KTH, Stockholm, 16pp.

No. 69: *Weiny Silander, interview from 2008 by Gustav Sjöblom, Technology and Society, Chalmers University, 34pp.*

No. 70: Crister Stjernfelt, interview from 2007 by Gustav Sjöblom, Technology
         and Society, Chalmers University, 31pp.

No. 71: Per Olof Persson, interview from 2007 by Gustav Sjöblom, Technology
         and Society, Chalmers University, 23pp.

No. 72: Lars Irstad, interview from 2008 by Gustav Sjöblom, Technology and
         Society, Chalmers University, 42pp.

No. 73: Torsten Bohlin, interview from 2007 by Per Lundin, Div. of History of
         Science and Technology, KTH, Stockholm, 27pp.

No. 74: Wigar Bartholdson, interview from 2008 by Gustav Sjöblom, Technology
         and Society, Chalmers University, 22pp.

No. 75: Kurt Fredriksson, interview from 2008 by Gustav Sjöblom, Technology
         and Society, Chalmers University, 31pp.

No. 76: Yngve Sundblad, interview from 2008 by Per Lundin, Div. of History of
         Science and Technology, KTH, Stockholm, 26pp.

No. 77: Thord Wilkne and Hans Mellström, interview from 2008 by Gustav
         Sjöblom, Technology and Society, Chalmers University, 32pp.

No. 78: Gunnar Rylander and Staffan Ahlberg, interview from 2007 by Gustav
         Sjöblom, Technology and Society, Chalmers University, 39pp.

No. 79: Gunnar Falck, interview from 2008 by Gustav Sjöblom, Technology and
         Society, Chalmers University, 30pp.

No. 80: Claes G. Nilsson, interview from 2008 by Gustav Sjöblom, Technology
         and Society, Chalmers University, 29pp.

No. 81: Anita Kollerbaur, interview from 2008 by Sofia Lindgren, The Swedish
         Computer Society, and Julia Peralta, Div. of History of Science and
         Technology, KTH, Stockholm, 31pp.

No. 82: Kent Björkegren and Bengt Risén, interview from 2008 by Gustav
         Sjöblom, Technology and Society, Chalmers University, 33pp.

No. 83: Claes Schenatz and Anders Svensson, interview from 2008 by Gustav
         Sjöblom, Technology and Society, Chalmers University, 39pp.

No. 84: Palle Fredriksson, interview from 2007 by Isabelle Dussauge, Div. of
         History of Science and Technology, KTH, Stockholm, 21pp.

No. 85: Gunnar Eriksson, interview from 2007 by PhD Jan af Geijerstam,
         Stockholm, 24pp.

No. 86: Bernt Malmkvist, interview from 2007 by Kurt Gladh, Stockholm, and
         PhD Jan af Geijerstam, Stockholm, 51pp.

No. 87: Göte Håkanson and Lars Sjögren, interview from 2008 by Gustav
         Sjöblom, Technology and Society, Chalmers University, 33pp.

No. 88: Ingemar Claesson, interview from 2008 by Gustav Sjöblom, Technology
         and Society, Chalmers University, 25pp.

No. 89: Gunnar Wedell, interview from 2008 by Gustav Sjöblom, Technology and
         Society, Chalmers University, 37pp.

No. 90: Sven Gunnar Ericsson, interview from 2007 by Gustav Sjöblom,
         Technology and Society, Chalmers University, 28pp.

No. 91: Jerry Lundqvist, interview from 2008 by Gustav Sjöblom, Technology and
         Society, Chalmers University, 33pp.

No. 92: Mats Schedin, interview from 2007 by PhD Jan af Geijerstam,
Stockholm, 26pp.

No. 93: Kurt Gladh, interview from 2007 by PhD Jan af Geijerstam,
Stockholm, 26pp.

No. 94: Gunnar Holmdahl, interview from 2008 by PhD Jan af Geijerstam,
Stockholm, 26pp.

No. 95: Hildegard Machschefes, interview from 2008 by Mats Schedin and PhD
Jan af Geijerstam, Stockholm, 27pp.

No. 96: Sten Flinke, interview from 2008 by PhD Jan af Geijerstam, Stockholm,
and Mats Schedin, Stockholm, 19pp.

No. 97: Mike Kazen, interview from 2007 by PhD Jan af Geijerstam, Stockholm,
and Kurt Gladh, Stockholm, 38pp.

No. 98: Kjell Hellberg, interview from 2008 by Gustav Sjöblom, Technology and
Society, Chalmers University, 48pp.

No. 99: Birger Kvaavik, interview from 2008 by Gustav Sjöblom, Technology and
Society, Chalmers University, 32pp.

No. 100: Gunnar Stenudd, interview from 2008 by Gustav Sjöblom, Technology
and Society, Chalmers University, 37pp.

No. 101: SM Eriksson, interview from 2008 by Gustav Sjöblom, Technology and
Society, Chalmers University, 34pp.

No. 102: Curt G Olsson, interview from 2008 by Björn Thodenius, Center for
Information Management, Stockholm School of Economics, and Anders
Rönn, 26pp.

No. 103: Jan Wallander, interview from 2008 by Rune Brandinger and Björn
Thodenius, Center for Information Management, Stockholm School of
Economics, 20pp.

No. 104: Rolf Nilsson and Bo Loftrup, interview from 2008 by Martin Emanuel,
Div. of History of Science and Technology, KTH, Stockholm, 30pp.

No. 105: Kerstin Gunnarsson, interview from 2008 by Sofia Lindgren,
Stockholm, 18pp.

No. 106: Ingvar Sundgren, interview from 2008 by Sofia Lindgren, Stockholm, 18pp.

No. 107: Gunnel Atterfelt, interview from 2008 by Sofia Lindgren, Stockholm, 27pp.

No. 108: Bengt Axelsson, interview from 2008 by Sofia Lindgren, Stockholm, 17pp.

No. 109: Tom Engström, interview from 2008 by Sofia Lindgren, Stockholm, 26pp.

No. 110: Jan Aschan, interview from 2008 by Sofia Lindgren, Stockholm, 15pp.

No. 111: Göran Rosman, interview from 2008 by Sofia Lindgren, Stockholm, 19pp.

No. 112: Gunilla Carlén, interview from 2008 by Sofia Lindgren, Stockholm, 22pp.

No. 113: Stig Medin, interview from 2007 by Björn Thodenius, Center for
Information Management, Stockholm School of Economics, and Bengt-
Åke Eriksson, 36pp.

No. 114: Per Lindberg, interview from 2008 by Sofia Lindgren, Stockholm, 20pp.

No. 115: Thord Nilsson, interview from 2008 by Sofia Lindgren, Stockholm, 19pp.

No. 116: Bengt Marnfeldt, interview from 2008 by Sofia Lindgren, Stockholm, 21pp.

No. 117:   *Per Olofsson, interview from 2007 by Sture Hallström and Björn
Thodenius, Center for Information Management, Stockholm School of
Economics, 36pp.*

No. 118:   *Rolf Holmberg, interview from 2008 by Gustav Sjöblom, Technology and
Society, Chalmers University, 43pp.*

No. 119:   *Sören Arlbring, interview from 2008 by Gustav Sjöblom, Technology and
Society, Chalmers University, 31pp.*

No. 120:   *Rune Brandinger, interview from 2008 by Björn Thodenius, Center for
Information Management, Stockholm School of Economics, 19pp.*

No. 121:   *SPP/AMF, group interview with Perolof Axelson, Jan-Erik Erenius, Birger
Fernström and Göran Krantz from 2008 by Björn Thodenius, Center for
Information Management, Stockholm School of Economics, 38pp.*

No. 122:   *Trygg Hansa, group interview with Olli Aronsson, Kjell Gunnarson and
Lars Ågren from 2008 by Björn Thodenius, Center for Information
Management, Stockholm School of Economics, 37pp.*

No. 123:   *Länsförsäkringar, group interview with Per Lind, Jan-Gunnar Persson,
Göran Öfverström and Johnny Östberg from 2008 by Björn Thodenius,
Center for Information Management, Stockholm School of Economics,
52pp.*

No. 124:   *Lennart Bernhed, interview from 2008 by Gustav Sjöblom, Technology
and Society, Chalmers University, 45pp.*

No. 125:   Christer Jacobsson, interview from 2008 by Gustav Sjöblom, Technology
and Society, Chalmers University, 32pp.

No. 126:   *Per-Olov Lindblom and Stefan Melander, interview from 2008 by Gustav
Sjöblom, Technology and Society, Chalmers University, 38pp.*

No. 127:   *Ingvar Anderberg, interview from 2007 by Björn Thodenius, Center for
Information Management, Stockholm School of Economics, and Anders
Rönn, 24pp.*

No. 128:   *Sune Vallgren, interview from 2008 by Gustav Sjöblom, Technology and
Society, Chalmers University, 30pp.*

No. 129:   *Göran Nydahl, interview from 2008 by Martin Emanuel, Div. of History
of Science and Technology, KTH, Stockholm, 27pp.*

No. 130:   *Örjan Broman and Mats Bäck, interview from 2008 by Martin Emanuel,
Div. of History of Science and Technology, KTH, Stockholm, 29pp.*

No. 131:   *K-G Ahlström, interview from 2008 by Martin Emanuel, Div. of History of
Science and Technology, KTH, Stockholm, 25pp.*

No. 132:   *Göran Kjellberg, interview from 2008 by Gustav Sjöblom, Technology
and Society, Chalmers University, 27pp.*

No. 133:   *Anita Kollerbaur, interview from 2008 by Martin Emanuel, Div. of
History of Science and Technology, KTH, Stockholm, 34pp.*

No. 134:   *Jan Boström, interview from 2008 by Martin Emanuel, Div. of History of
Science and Technology, KTH, Stockholm, 30pp.*

No. 135:   *Bengt Nilsson, interview from 2008 by Martin Emanuel, Div. of History of
Science and Technology, KTH, Stockholm, 33pp.*

No. 136: *Ulla Riis, interview from 2008 by Martin Emanuel, Div. of History of*
             Science and Technology, KTH, Stockholm, 38pp.
No. 137: *Bo Holmqvist and Fred Norling, interview from 2008 by Gustav Sjöblom,*
             Technology and Society, Chalmers University, 43pp.
No. 138: *Bernhard Gustafsson, interview from 2008 by Gustav Sjöblom,*
             Technology and Society, Chalmers University, 29pp.
No. 139: *Sture Hallström, interview from 2008 by Björn Thodenius, Center for*
             Information Management, Stockholm School of Economics, 29pp.
No. 140:   Bengt-Åke Eriksson, interview from 2008 by Björn Thodenius,
             Center for Information Management, Stockholm School of Economics,
             15pp.
No. 141: *Erik Altenstedt, interview from 1998 by Kurt Fredriksson, 9pp.*
No. 142: *Jonny Andersson, interview from 1998 by Kurt Fredriksson, 4pp.*
No. 143: *Sven Brunnander, interview from 1998 by Kurt Fredriksson, 10pp.*
No. 144: *Bengt Ek, interview from 1999 by Kurt Fredriksson 5pp.*
No. 145: *Sven Eklöf, interview from 1998 by Kurt Fredriksson 4pp.*
No. 146: *Lars-Olof Granat (formerly Karlsson), interview from 1998 by Kurt*
             Fredriksson, 14pp.
No. 147: *Stig Karlsson, interview from 1998 by Kurt Fredriksson, 18pp.*
No. 148: *Stig Larsson, interview from 1996 by Kurt Fredriksson, 6pp.*
No. 149: *Jörgen Nilsson, interview from 1999 by Kurt Fredriksson, 3pp.*
No. 150: *Lennart Palm, interview from 1998 by Kurt Fredriksson, 11pp.*
No. 151: *Nils Råberg, interview from 1998 by Kurt Fredriksson, 9pp.*
No. 152:   Birger Skog, interview from 2007 by Björn Thodenius, Center for
             Information Management, Stockholm School of Economics, and Sture
             Hallström, 32pp.
No. 153:   Thomas Glück, interview from 2007 by Björn Thodenius, Center for
             Information Management, Stockholm School of Economics, and Per Olof
             Persson, 19pp.

Oral History Interviews (Recorded, Not Edited)

Seven of the interviews conducted in the project were not edited. This was due to
one or more of the following three reasons: the content of the interview was not
considered valuable, the poor quality of the audio files, and the interviewee did
explicitly not permit the recordings or transcripts to be edited or used. The recordings and transcripts of the interviews, which are listed below, are, however, deposited in the National Museum of Science and Technology's archival collections.

Dines Bjørner, interview from 2007 by Per Lundin, Div. of History of Science and
    Technology, KTH, Stockholm.
Inger Marklund, interview from 2008 by Martin Emanuel, Div. of History of Science
    and Technology, KTH, Stockholm.

Albert Öjermark, interview from 2007 by Rune Brandinger and Björn Thodenius, Center for Information Management, Stockholm School of Economics.

Åke Sandberg, part I, interview from 2008 by Per Lundin, Div. of History of Science and Technology, KTH, Stockholm.

Åke Sandberg, part II, interview from 2008 by Per Lundin, Div. of History of Science and Technology, KTH, Stockholm.

Werner Schneider, interview from 2005 by Hans Peterson and Urban Rosenqvist.

Sven Stegfors, interview from 2008 by Sofia Lindgren, Stockholm.

Oral History Interviews (Not Recorded, Edited)

Six of the interviews conducted in the project were not recorded but edited based on notes made by the interviewer during the interview session. These six interviews, which should not be seen as edited transcripts, were used as sources for the chapter "Användarna kommer till tals" by Mats Utbult in the published report *Användarna och datorerna: En historik 1960–1985*, Vinnova Rapport VR 2009:2 (Stockholm, 2009). The interviews are listed below, but it should be noted that they are *not* deposited in the National Museum of Science and Technology's archival collections.

Martti Hakkala, interview from 2008 by Mats Utbult, Stockholm.

Christian Hörup, interview from 2008 by Mats Utbult, Stockholm.

Peter Kjellqvist, interview from 2008 by Mats Utbult, Stockholm.

Claes Leo Lindwall, interview from 2008 by Mats Utbult, Stockholm.

Sture Ring, interview from 2008 by Mats Utbult, Stockholm.

Mats Schultze, interview from 2008 by Mats Utbult, Stockholm.

Witness Seminars (Edited, Published)

In the project, 47 witness seminars were held. The resulting recordings and transcripts are all deposited in the National Museum of Science and Technology's archival collections. The edited transcripts consist of 2,417 pages of text in total. All the transcripts were edited, and 44 of them published both in print and electronic versions (2,271 pages of text). These are listed below. The electronic versions are available in KTH's working paper series TRITA-HST at the Academic Archive On-line (DiVA), http://www.diva-portal.org, or at the National Museum of Science and Technology's Web page http://www.tekniskamuseet.se.

Dávila, Milena, ed., Datorisering av medicinsk laboratorieverksamhet 1: En översikt: Transkript av ett vittnesseminarium vid Svenska Läkaresällskapet i Stockholm den 17 februari 2006, TRITA-HST 2008/5 (Stockholm, 2008), 41pp.

Dávila, Milena, ed., Datorisering av medicinsk laboratorieverksamhet 2: Massanalyser och hälsokontroller: Transkript av ett vittnesseminarium vid

Tekniska museet i Stockholm den 20 september 2006, TRITA-HST 2008/6 (Stockholm, 2008), 40pp.

Emanuel, Martin, ed., ABC 80 i pedagogikens tjänst: Exempel på tidig användning av mikrodatorer i den svenska skolan: Transkript av ett vittnesseminarium vid Cloetta Center i Linköping den 23 september 2008, TRITA-HST 2008/32 (Stockholm, 2009), 56pp.

Emanuel, Martin, ed., Folkbildning kring datorn 1978–85: Transkript av ett vittnesseminarium vid Tekniska museet i Stockholm den 9 oktober 2008, TRITA-HST 2008/36 (Stockholm, 2009), 52pp.

Emanuel, Martin, ed., Datorn i skolan: Skolöverstyrelsens och andra aktörers insatser, 1970- och 80-tal: Transkript av ett vittnesseminarium vid Tekniska museet i Stockholm den 30 oktober 2008, TRITA-HST 2008/40 (Stockholm, 2009), 62pp.

Ernkvist, Mirko, ed., Svensk dataspelsutveckling, 1960–1995: Transkript av ett vittnesseminarium vid Tekniska museet i Stockholm den 12 december 2007, TRITA-HST 2008/28 (Stockholm, 2008), 54pp.

Gribbe, Johan, ed., Att modellera slagfältet: Tidig databehandling vid FOA, 1954–66: Transkript av ett vittnesseminarium vid Tekniska museet i Stockholm den 15 oktober 2007, TRITA-HST 2007/7 (Stockholm, 2007), 39pp.

Gribbe, Johan, ed., JA 37: Pilot och system: Transkript av ett vittnesseminarium vid Tekniska museet i Stockholm den 11 december 2007, TRITA-HST 2008/1 (Stockholm, 2008), 51pp.

Gribbe, Johan, ed., NIBS: Utvecklingen av Näckens informationsbehandlingssystem, 1966–82: Transkript av ett vittnesseminarium vid Tekniska museet i Stockholm den 14 januari 2008, TRITA-HST 2008/3 (Stockholm, 2008), 46pp.

Gribbe, Johan, ed., LEO: Databehandling och operativ ledning inom försvaret, 1972–89: Transkript av ett vittnesseminarium vid Högkvarteret i Stockholm den 15 januari 2008, TRITA-HST 2008/4 (Stockholm, 2008), 59pp.

Gribbe, Johan, ed., Tidig flygradar: Transkript av ett vittnesseminarium vid Tekniska museet i Stockholm den 15 april 2008, TRITA-HST 2008/13 (Stockholm, 2008), 55pp.

Klein, Kajsa, ed., Integritetsdebatten åren kring 1984: Transkript av ett vittnesseminarium vid Tekniska museet i Stockholm den 30 november 2007, TRITA-HST 2008/9 (Stockholm, 2007), 46pp.

Larsson, Ebba, ed., Fastighetsdatasystemet: Transkript av ett vittnesseminarium vid Tekniska museet i Stockholm den 30 september 2008, TRITA-HST 2008/35 (Stockholm, 2008), 59pp.

Lindgren, Sofia, ed., Dataföreningar i Sverige: 1949–1990: Framväxt och förändbringsmönster: Transkript av ett vittnesseminarium vid Tekniska museet i Stockholm den 26 september 2008, TRITA-HST 2008/33 (Stockholm, 2008), 53pp.

Lindgren, Sofia, ed., Fackpress på dataområdet: Exempel från 1960- och 1970-talet: Transkript av ett vittnesseminarium vid Tekniska museet i Stockholm den 14 oktober 2008, TRITA-HST 2008/37 (Stockholm, 2008), 48pp.

Lindgren, Sofia and Julia Peralta, eds., Lysator: Transkript av ett vittnesseminarium vid Linköpings universitet den 21 februari 2008, TRITA-HST 2008/8 (Stockholm, 2008), 69pp.

Lindgren, Sofia and Julia Peralta, eds., Datacentralerna för högre utbildning och forskning: Transkript av ett vittnesseminarium vid Tekniska museet i Stockholm den 27 mars 2008, TRITA-HST 2008/17 (Stockholm, 2008), 55pp.

Lindgren, Sofia and Julia Peralta, eds., Högre datautbildningar i Sverige i ett historiskt perspektiv: Transkript av ett vittnesseminarium vid Tekniska museet i Stockholm den 24 januari 2008, TRITA-HST 2008/18 (Stockholm, 2008), 53pp.

Lundin, Per, ed., Att arbeta med 1950-talets matematikmaskiner: Transkript av ett vittnesseminarium vid Tekniska museet i Stockholm den 12 september 2005, TRITA-HST 2006/1 (Stockholm, 2006), 43pp.

Lundin, Per, ed., Tidig programmering: Transkript av ett vittnesseminarium vid Tekniska museet i Stockholm den 16 mars 2006, TRITA-HST 2007/1 (Stockholm, 2007), 43pp.

Lundin, Per, ed., Databehandling vid Väg- och vattenbyggnadsstyrelsen/Vägverket 1957–1980: Transkript av ett vittnesseminarium vid Tekniska museet i Stockholm den 22 maj 2006, TRITA-HST 2007/2 (Stockholm, 2007), 42pp.

Lundin, Per, ed., Administrativ systemutveckling i teori och praktik: Transkript av ett vittnesseminarium vid Tekniska museet i Stockholm den 26 november 2007, TRITA-HST 2008/19 (Stockholm, 2008), 52pp.

Lundin, Per, ed., Tidiga e-postsystem: Transkript av ett vittnesseminarium vid Tekniska museet i Stockholm den 14 februari 2008, TRITA-HST 2008/20 (Stockholm, 2008), 54pp.

Lundin, Per, ed., Den skandinaviska skolan i systemutveckling under 1970- och 1980-talen: Exemplen DEMOS och UTOPIA: Transkript av ett vittnesseminarium vid Tekniska museet i Stockholm den 31 mars 2008, TRITA-HST 2008/21 (Stockholm, 2008), 54pp.

Lundin, Per, ed., Styrbjörn: Utvecklingen och användningen av ett konstruktions- och produktionssystem för skeppsbyggnad vid Kockums under 1960- och 1970-talen: Transkript av ett vittnesseminarium vid AVEVA AB i Malmö den 2 oktober 2007, TRITA-HST 2008/30 (Stockholm, 2008), 53pp.

Nilsson, Mikael, ed., Staten och kapitalet: Betydelsen av det dynamiska samspelet mellan offentligt och privat för det svenska telekomundret: Transkript av ett vittnesseminarium vid Tekniska museet i Stockholm den 18 mars 2008, TRITA-HST 2008/10 (Stockholm, 2008), 46pp.

Nilsson, Mikael, ed., Sambandssystem 9000 ur ett användarperspektiv: Transkript av ett vittnesseminarium vid Tekniska museet i Stockholm den 13 mars 2008, TRITA-HST 2008/11 (Stockholm, 2008), 51pp.

Nilsson, Mikael, ed., Radiokommunikationsutvecklingens betydelse för mobilteleindustrin: Transkript av ett vittnesseminarium vid Tekniska museet i Stockholm den 12 mars 2008, TRITA-HST 2008/12 (Stockholm, 2008), 36pp.

Orrghen, Anna, ed., Tidiga söksystem: Transkript av ett vittnesseminarium vid Tekniska museet i Stockholm den 21 januari 2008, TRITA-HST 2008/7 (Stockholm, 2008), 62pp.

Peralta, Julia, ed., ADB i folkbokföring och beskattning: Transkript av ett vittnesseminarium vid Tekniska museet i Stockholm den 17 januari 2008, TRITA-HST 2008/14 (Stockholm, 2008), 53pp.

Peralta, Julia ed., Statskontoret: Transkript av ett vittnesseminarium vid Tekniska museet i Stockholm den 5 februari 2008, TRITA-HST 2008/15 (Stockholm, 2008), 45pp.

Peralta, Julia ed., ADB och den Allmänna försäkringen: Transkript av ett vittnesseminarium vid Tekniska museet i Stockholm den 12 februari 2008, TRITA-HST 2008/16 (Stockholm, 2008), 56pp.

Sjöblom, Gustav, ed., Systemutveckling och långtidsplanering vid SAS Data i Stockholm, 1964–1982: Transkript av ett vittnesseminarium vid Tekniska museet i Stockholm den 5 december 2007, TRITA-HST 2008/22 (Stockholm, 2008), 49pp.

Sjöblom, Gustav, ed., Standardekonomisystem för stordatorer: EPOK, EPOS & FACTS, 1969–1986: Transkript av ett vittnesseminarium vid Tekniska museet i Stockholm den 29 januari 2008, TRITA-HST 2008/23 (Stockholm, 2008), 62pp.

Sjöblom, Gustav, ed., Standardisering och integration av datasystem inom godstransportbranschen, 1970–1985: Transkript av ett vittnesseminarium vid Flygfältsbyrån i Göteborg den 11 mars 2008, TRITA-HST 2008/24 (Stockholm, 2008), 53pp.

Sjöblom, Gustav, ed., IT-konsultbranschens uppkomst och tillväxt, 1964–1985: Transkript av ett vittnesseminarium vid Tekniska museet i Stockholm den 1 april 2008, TRITA-HST 2008/25 (Stockholm, 2008), 69pp.

Sjöblom, Gustav, ed., Varuhushandelns datorisering före 1980: Transkript av ett vittnesseminarium vid Tekniska museet i Stockholm den 29 september 2008, TRITA-HST 2008/34 (Stockholm, 2009), 51pp.

Sjöblom, Gustav, ed., Dagligvaruhandelns datorisering före 1985: Transkript av ett vittnesseminarium vid Tekniska museet i Stockholm den 20 oktober 2008, TRITA-HST 2008/38 (Stockholm, 2009), 47pp.

Sjöblom, Gustav, ed., Införandet av streckkoder i Sverige: Transkript av ett vittnesseminarium vid Tekniska museet i Stockholm den 22 oktober 2008, TRITA-HST 2008/39 (Stockholm, 2009), 48pp.

Skoglund, Crister, ed., Föreställningar om informationssamhället under 1980-talets första hälft: Transkript av ett vittnesseminarium vid Tekniska museet i Stockholm den 27 maj 2008, TRITA-HST 2008/41 (Stockholm, 2008), 46pp.

Thodenius, Björn, ed., IT i bank- och finanssektorn 1960–1985: Transkript av ett vittnesseminarium vid Tekniska museet i Stockholm den 13 mars 2006, TRITA-HST 2008/2 (Stockholm, 2008), 53pp.

Thodenius, Björn, ed., Teknisk utveckling i bankerna fram till 1985: Transkript av ett vittnesseminarium vid Tekniska museet i Stockholm den 12 november 2007, TRITA-HST 2008/26 (Stockholm, 2008), 55pp.

Thodenius, Björn, ed., De viktigaste drivkrafterna för att utnyttja IT inom försäkringsbranschen mellan 1960–1985: Transkript av ett vittnesseminarium vid Tekniska museet i Stockholm den 28 november 2007, TRITA-HST 2008/27 (Stockholm, 2008), 56pp.

Thodenius, Björn, ed., Uttagsautomater: Transkript av ett vittnesseminarium vid Tekniska museet i Stockholm den 16 januari 2007, TRITA-HST 2008/31 (Stockholm, 2008), 53pp.

Witness Seminars (Edited, Not Published)

Three of the edited witness seminar transcripts are not published in print or electronically, but are available electronically at the National Museum of Science and Technology's Web page: http://www.tekniskamuseet.se.

Ernkvist, Mirko, ed., "Införandet av EDB som stöd för logistikprocessen inom Volvo 1958–1973, skildrad utifrån användarnas perspektiv: Rapport bearbetad utifrån ett vittnesseminarium på Volvo IT den 29 maj 2006" (unpublished report, 2007), 49pp.

Geijerstam, Jan af, ed., "Sandvikens Jernverks AB och IT: Transkript av ett vittnesseminarium vid Sandvik AB i Sandviken den 30 oktober 2007" (unpublished report, 2008), 49pp.

Geijerstam, Jan af, ed., "VIS/MIS – visionen om den kompletta informationen: Transkript av ett vittnesseminarium vid Chalmers tekniska högskola i Göteborg den 8 maj 2008" (unpublished report, 2008), 48pp.

Autobiographies (General Call)

As mentioned in Chap. 2 of this book, two types of calls for autobiographies were made (a general call and a number of focused calls). The general call for autobiographies, which was carried out by the research group in collaboration with the National Museum of Science and Technology and Nordiska museet, resulted in 249 replies consisting of 1,461 pages of text in total. Of the replies, 190 were considered autobiographies. The remaining replies lacked autobiographical qualities (simple inquires and the like). The 190 autobiographical entries are listed below according to the following format: [entry number], [name of autobiographer], [possible title], [number of pages]. One hundred and twenty-nine of the autobiographies are available electronically at the National Museum of Science and Technology's Web page http://www.tekniskamuseet.se/it-minnen and they are italicized in the list below. The remaining autobiographies are deposited in the museum's archival collections.

No. 1:   *Ragnar Svensson, "Mitt livs historia fram till juli 2007," 3pp.*
No. 2:   *Bo Nyqvist, "Ett yrkesliv från 1952 till 2004 med och utan IT," 3pp.*
No. 4:   *Roy Johansson, "IT-vittnen," 3pp.*
No. 7:   Bertil Ahlberg, 2pp.
No. 8:   *Göran Dahlström, 9pp.*
No. 9:   Inga-Britt Svärd, "Teknikens barfotabarn: Min livshistoria utan och med datorer," 27pp.
No. 11:   *Lennart Lövegard, "Bidrag till Datahistorik," 2pp.*
No. 12:   Thomas Ljungdell, 2pp.
No. 13:   *Yngve Larsson, "Den första användningen av datorer inom Sydkraft (EON Sverige)," 3pp.*
No. 14:   *Yngve Lossing, 5pp.*

No. 15:   Gunnel Berglund, *"Från matematikmaskin till IT,"* 2pp.
No. 16:   Jan Dahlberg, *"Produktionsplanering av Spraytorn – mitt bästa totalm-isslyckande,"* 2pp.
No. 18:   *Ulla Lord, 1pp.*
No. 19:   Åke Gustavson, "IT-minnen," 2pp.
No. 20:   Bengt Kynning, *"Upprop om IT-historia,"* 4pp.
No. 21:   Pia Gawell, 1pp.
No. 24:   Erik Elvers, 1pp.
No. 25:   Ib Lenneke, 1pp.
No. 27:   Ann Christine Lundh, 1pp.
No. 30:   *Åke Rehnberg, 3pp.*
No. 34:   Anders Lindgren, 1pp.
No. 36:   Lars B Hedberg, *"Självbiografiskt upprop om IT-historia 1958–2007,"* 34pp.
No. 38:   *Gillis Een, 13pp.*
No. 40:   Per Mikael Sternberg, 1pp.
No. 41:   *Arne Franklin, 1pp.*
No. 49:   Alexander Roussos, "Mitt liv som IT-gubbe," 6pp.
No. 51:   Torbjörn Alm, "Vad jag upplevt under mer än 50 år av datautveckling," 6pp.
No. 53:   Torgny Sundin, 1pp.
No. 54:   Erik Sandström, *"En resa i TIDas,"* 6pp.
No. 57:   *Ingvar Holmberg, 6pp.*
No. 58:   Björn Elmblad, 1pp.
No. 59:   Maria Kallin, 1pp.
No. 64:   Conny Norman, 1pp.
No. 65:   Sten Zeilon, 1pp.
No. 66:   *Kaj Vareman, 3pp.*
No. 67:   Kurt Malm, *"Minnen från en svunnen tid – ett inlägg i den svenska IT-historien,"* 2pp.
No. 68:   Janis Platbardis, 1pp.
No. 70:   Bengt-Olov Ljung, 2pp.
No. 71:   Uno Ahlström, 5pp.
No. 72:   Magnus Mogensen, *"Några anspråkslösa rader om mina datorminnen,"* 2pp.
No. 74:   Per-Åke Jansson, *"Mina IT-erfarenheter,"* 3pp.
No. 75:   *Bo Andersson, 5pp.*
No. 76:   Anita Nordstedt-Sparrvik, 1pp.
No. 77:   Jacob Palme, *"Datorer på 60-talet och 70-talet. Några svenska datormin-nen,"* 9pp.
No. 79:   Mats-Åke Hugoson, "Svenska IT-historien," 1pp.
No. 80:   Bertil Lindberg, *"Mitt liv med informationstekniken,"* 2pp.
No. 81:   Nils Erik Thorell, *"Mina tidiga erfarenheter av datorer,"* 2pp.
No. 82:   Evald Holmén, *"Erfarenheter av matematikmaskiner och datorer,"* 6pp.
No. 83:   Stig L Olsson, *"Min självbiografiska historia,"* 11pp.
No. 85:   *Ulf Jansson, 3pp.*
No. 88:   Runar Lundman, *"IT-historia,"* 18pp.
No. 91:   Ulla Toby Holm, 1pp.

No. 92:   Lars Rydberg, 2pp.
No. 93:   Anders Olsson, "Från matematikmaskin till IT," 4pp.
No. 94:   Claes Garelius, "Mina år fram till idag samt viktiga händelser," 3pp.
No. 95:   Lars Persson, "Mina dataminnen," 9pp.
No. 98:   Stig Holmberg, "Från matematikmaskin till IT," 3pp.
No. 99:   Rolf Hansson, 3pp.
No. 100:   Ulf Melin, 2pp.
No. 103:   Kim Stronkler, pseudonym, "Om fysisk närvaro," 7pp.
No. 106:   Björn Omér, "Från IT-service på 70-talet till IT-dokumentation på 00-talet," 3pp.
No. 107:   Roland Johansson, 2pp.
No. 108:   Åke Rullgård, 9pp.
No. 109:   Per-Åke Helander, 2pp.
No. 111:   Ingrid Nilsson, "Min del av den svenska IT-historien," 1pp.
No. 112:   Lars A Wern, 2pp.
No. 113:   Edvard Pröckl, 1pp.
No. 115:   Lars Kihlborg, 4pp.
No. 116:   Ulla Gustavsson, "Mina relationer till IT," 2pp.
No. 117:   Tommy Bergfors, "Mitt dataliv," 3pp.
No. 118:   Torsten Bergner, "Info om IT-utvecklingen i Sverige," 14pp.
No. 119:   Stefan Fosseus, 4pp.
No. 122:   Monica Backlund, 1pp.
No. 124:   Thomas Gustafsson, "Datoriseringen inom vården," 9pp.
No. 125:   Valborg Werneborg, 1pp.
No. 127:   Lars Asplund, "Mitt liv som programmerare," 25pp.
No. 128:   Nils-Ivar Lindström, 1pp.
No. 129:   Ove Tedenstig, "The True Story of 'Stored Force,'" 6pp.
No. 131:   Irene Husberg, 3pp.
No. 133:   Gunnar Ringmarck, 9pp.
No. 135:   Arvid Harmsen, 1pp.
No. 137:   Karl Jonsson, 3pp.
No. 138:   Per Ola Eriksson, "Min IT-historia," 15pp.
No. 139:   Bengt Moberg, 2pp.
No. 140:   Torsten Nilsson, "IT-historia Pressbyrån," 2pp.
No. 141:   Lennart Gunnarsson, "Bidrag till den svenska IT-historien," 5pp.
No. 142:   Bengt Glantzberg, 2pp.
No. 143:   Sture Linn, "Självbiografi," 2pp.
No. 144:   Gunnar Markesjö, "Självbiografi av Gunnar Markesjö skriven för Tekniska museet," 24pp.
No. 145.1:   Bertil Forss, 9pp.
No. 145.2:   Siv-Britt Widmark, 2pp.
No. 146:   Solveig Sköllermark, 1pp.
No. 147:   Bertil Norstedt, 7pp.
No. 148:   Lars Davidsson, "34 år med datorer," 1pp.
No. 149:   Gunnar Eriksson, "IT-historia," 16pp.
No. 150:   Valter Sundkvist, "Självbiografisk beskrivning av egna datorminnen," 4pp.

No. 151:   Nils-Erik Sahlström, "Den svenska IT-historien 1950–1980," 8pp.
No. 152:   Dag Swenson, "En enkel beskrivning av mina tidiga kontakter med datorer," 3pp.
No. 153:   Göran Carlsson, "Minnesanteckningar av DFS-medlem 1824," 3pp.
No. 154:   Jan Samuelsson, "Min IT-historia," 6pp.
No. 156:   Anders Thurin, 2pp.
No. 157:   Örjan Widmark, 3pp.
No. 158:   Erik Sundström, "Mina tidiga kontakter med datorer," 2pp.
No. 159:   Staffan Ersborg, "I utkanten av IT," 2pp.
No. 160:   Per Olov Olsson, 2pp.
No. 161:   Hans-Åke Ramdén, "Min IT-historia från 1963 och framåt," 15pp.
No. 162:   Henric Nordlander, "Minnen från Kreditbanken," 5pp.
No. 163:   Klas-Anders Öhlin, "Min ADB-historia," 8pp.
No. 164:   Axel Carlander, 7pp.
No. 165:   Kai Thurfors, "Bidrag till IT-historia 1950–80," 5pp.
No. 166:   Torkel Danielsson, "Min IT-historia som jag upplevt den," 9pp.
No. 167:   Åke Rinneby, "Från BESK till cd-baserad interaktiv multimedia för utbildning," 3pp.
No. 168:   Thomas Osvald, 30pp.
No. 169:   Wilford Lindgren, 2pp.
No. 170:   Jan Eklund, "Egna erfarenheter av tidig IT-verksamhet inom vården," 2pp.
No. 171:   Arne Larsson, "IT-historia," 10pp.
No. 172:   Dag Moberg, "IT-historia," 3pp.
No. 173:   Gunnar Rosengren, "Min ADB-IT-historia," 4pp.
No. 174:   Claes Thorén, 6pp.
No. 175:   Björn Grindegård, 3pp.
No. 176:   Tommy Granholm, "Om tillvaron i datorernas värld 1959–1980," 7pp.
No. 177:   Ingemar Forsgren, 4pp.
No. 178:   Börje Lemark, "Min IT-historia," 56pp.
No. 179:   Anne Cronström, 4pp.
No. 180:   Bo Foss, IT-historia, 2pp.
No. 181:   Jörgen Lindelöf, 5pp.
No. 182:   Sten Ahlberg, "Vittnen från datorernas barndom," 3pp.
No. 183:   Lars Torgny Wahlström, "IT-historia, självbiografi," 2pp.
No. 184:   Hans Laestadius, "Mina IT-minnen 1965–1980," 5pp.
No. 185:   Tommy Lundell, "Svenska IT-historien från min horisont," 4pp.
No. 186:   Ulf Bjälkefors, "Min IT-verksamhet åren 1960–1980," 12pp.
No. 188:   Anders Hagland, 4pp.
No. 189:   Paula Wallster, 2pp.
No. 190:   Ann-Sophie Qvarnström, "Datordomptörens återkomst," 2pp.
No. 192:   Gunnar Johansson, "IT-historia," 28pp.
No. 193:   Christer Nicklasson, "Min självbiografiska IT-historia," 4pp.
No. 194:   Birgitta Lagerlöf, "Minnesberättelse," 5pp.
No. 195:   Peter Olofsson, "Min datorhistoria," 12pp.
No. 196:   Leif Anders Björklund, 4pp.
No. 197:   Veine Berndtson, "Från hålkortsnisse till PC-freak," 18pp.

No. 198:   Ingeli Åkerberg, "IT-boomen blev en klassresa för mig," 4pp.
No. 199:   Bengt Kjellström, 5pp.
No. 200:   Torsten Gustafsson, 3pp.
No. 201:   Bengt Marcusson, 2pp.
No. 202:   Carl-Uno Manros, "Min IT-historia," 25pp.
No. 203:   Sam Haglund, 19pp.
No. 204:   Per-Göran Svensson, "IT-historia-självbiografi," 8pp.
No. 205:   Roger Hansson, "Min IT-historia fram till 1980," 28pp.
No. 206:   Yngve Linnér, 4pp.
No. 207:   Kerstin Öhrnell, 3pp.
No. 208:   Siwert Forslund, "IT-minnen 1958–1980," 21pp.
No. 209:   Peter Juselius, 6pp.
No. 210:   Kurt Svensson, 16pp.
No. 211:   Bo Sandén, "Lärdomar och äventyr i IT-branschen," 15pp.
No. 212:   Tom Wallin, "Självbiografiskt upprop om IT-historia," 8pp.
No. 213:   Katarina Löfstrand, 3pp.
No. 214:   Margareta Håkansson, "VIVE-STANS AB," 2pp.
No. 215:   Margit Ekman, 3pp.
No. 216:   Kjell Karlsson, 6pp.
No. 217:   Lilian Ryd, "1970-tals-IT på en nyhets-redaktion," 14pp.
No. 218:   Anders Öberg, "IT-vittnet Anders Öbergs historia," 7pp.
No. 219:   Ing-Marie Berggren-Pihlström, "En liten del av datahistorien," 15pp.
No. 221:   Ninna Widstrand, "Min IT-historia fr.o.m. 1967," 1pp.
No. 222:   Lennart Larsson, "Data i mitt liv," 140pp.
No. 223:   Lars Högberg, "Minnen av tidiga IT-system för litteratur-bevakning
              och informations-utbyte i forskningsmiljö," 8pp.
No. 224:   Bo-Gunnar Reit, 10pp.
No. 225:   Lars Bertil Owe, "Lars Bertil Owe berättar några minnen från tidiga
              datorer i Sverige," 5pp.
No. 226:   Gunvor Svartz-Malmberg, "Att söka vetenskaplig litteratur via dator," 2pp.
No. 227:   Stig Algotsson, "Mina första 10 år med datorer 1973–1983," 38pp.
No. 228:   Sten-Sture Tersmeden, "Självbiografiskt upprop om IT-historia," 32pp.
No. 229:   Birgitta Mellgren and Ingela Jernberg, 2pp.
No. 230:   Annika Rullgård, 10pp.
No. 231:   Ylva C Båve, 1pp.
No. 232:   Sven I Hansson, "Mitt liv som IT-man," 5pp.
No. 233:   Arne Hamfelt, "IT-vård 50–70-tal," 19pp.
No. 234:   Erik Stålberg, "Historisk sammanställning av IT, särskilt telemedicin vid
              Avd. för klinisk neurofysiologi, Akademiska sjukhuset, Uppsala," 5pp.
No. 235:   Lennart Edvardsson, 13pp.
No. 236:   Ove Iko, 8pp.
No. 237:   Christer Götling, "Min IT-historia," 21pp.
No. 238:   Kent Berg, "Datorminnen," 4pp.
No. 240:   Britt-Gerd Malmberg, 3pp.
No. 241:   Bertil Jacobson, "Tillkomsten av medicinsk teknik i Sverige – En högst
              personlig berättelse," 9pp.

No. 242:   *Kalle Sandqvist, "Min IT-historia," 3pp.*
No. 243:   *Anders Englund and Göran Engholm, "Ett IT-baserat journalsystem för en landstäckande företagshälsovård-användningens förändring över åren," 3pp.*
No. 244:   *Ragnar Weinz, "Några minnen av arbete med datamaskiner och datorer," 7pp.*
No. 245:   Lisbet Niklason, "Programmering inom klinisk fysiologi i Lund på 1970-talet," 6pp.
No. 246:   *Hartmut Blau, 4pp.*
No. 247:   *Lennart Hammar, "PRISMA – Ett projekt i svensk laboratorie-automation," 25pp.*
No. 248:   *Gunnar Nordström, "Mitt Liv med Datorer, 'Skillnaden mellan Gud och en dator: Gud ser i nåd till Människan,'" 56pp.*
No. 249:   Arne Larsson, "MIN IT-historia," 3pp.

Autobiographies (Focused Calls)

In addition to the project's general call for autobiographies, there were a number of calls carried out by the focus groups. These were aimed at the senior practitioners in each focus group and people in their networks. The resulting 24 autobiographies consist of 534 pages of text in total, and they are listed below. Six of the autobiographies are available electronically at the National Museum of Science and Technology's Web page http://www.tekniskamuseet.se/it-minnen, and they are italicized in the list below. The remaining autobiographies are deposited in the museum's archival collections.

Early Computers

Lars Arosenius, "Människor i datavärlden – några personliga minnen," 6pp.
Elsa-Karin Boestad-Nilsson, "Besk från FOAs horisont," 3pp.
Ingemar Dahlstrand, "To Sort Things Out," 195pp.
Gert Persson, "'Computers and Computing' i Skandinavien: Tillbakablick över de första 15 åren i ett svenskt perspektiv," 10pp.
Gunnar Stenudd, "BESK – bygge, byggare och användare," 4pp.
Gunnar Stenudd, "Forskning och utveckling efter BESK-tiden," 14pp.
Gunnar Wedell, "Dataminnen," 5pp.

Healthcare

Bengt Dahlin, "Historien om en datorjournal," 21pp.
Ingmar Jungner, "Berättelsen om AutoChemist," 77pp.
Åke Holmgård, "Hudiksvall," 4pp.

Leif Ohlsén, "Datasystem AutoChemist (ACH) och ACH-Prisma 1964–86: En historisk tillbakablick," 18pp.
Leif Ohlsén, "Datasystem Autochemist (ACH)," stencil, 20pp.
Torsten Seeman, "Datautvecklingen inom Göteborgs sjukvård 1972–1997," 14pp.

Higher Education

Bengt Olsen, "Svensk superdatorhistoria – några minnesbilder," 6pp.

Information Technology Industries

Kurt Fredriksson, "Kurt Fredrikssons tillbakablick," 14pp.

Schools

K-G Ahlström, 1pp.
Göran Axelsson, 1pp.
Robert Ekinge, 3pp.
Bengt Bruno Lönnqvist, 5pp.
Gunnar Markesjö, 2pp.
Bertil Petersson, 5pp.

Transportation Industries

Kjell Byström, "I huvet på en gammal IT-gubbe," 5pp.
Jan U Storm, "Hej Bröder i Vägsektorns historia," 2pp.

User Organizations and User Participation

Lennart Lennerlöf, "Mitt Arbetsliv: En rekonstruerad forskningshistoria," 99pp.

Writers' Web Entries

In addition to the call for autobiographies, the project developed a virtual platform, the Writers' Web, with the URL http://ithistoria.se/. Between May 2007 and February 2009, 35 autobiographies and 19 comments on these were posted on the Writers' Web site. The autobiographies and comments are listed below according to the following format: [name of autobiographer], [title], [day of the week], [date and time] by [user identity]. All entries are available at http://ithistoria.se/.

Paul Hall, "Vi datoriserade patientinformation av Paul Hall," mån, 2007-05-28 10:06 av Isabelle Dussauge.
    Comment: "'Cigarrlådan' Paul nämner," fre, 2007-10-19 08:04 av todan.

116

Appendices

Comment: "Vi på Spårvägen hade två," fre, 2007-10-26 20:28 av Lars.

Lars-Erik Lundberg, "Service av datorer och digital utrustning," tors, 2007-08-30 09:16, av Labiata.

Malcolm Thomason, "IT erfarenheter från 70 talet – minnen," ons, 2007-09-19 09:19, av Malcolm Thomason.

Comment: "Hej Malcolm! Du skriver," tors, 2007-09-20 20:06 av Lars.

Comment: "Hej Lars, Jag har kollat och," fre, 2007-09-21 06:45 av Malcolm Thomason.

Henric Nordlander, "Bidrag till IT-historia - Minnen från Kreditbanken," mån, 2007-10-01 10:57 av henricn.

"Monte Carlo funkade inte...," ons, 2007-10-10 19:48 av lmesbob.

"AKORD, Automatisk KOnstruktion och ReläsatsDokumentation," tis, 2007-10-23 20:28 av Neve.

Björn Sölving, "År 2000 hade jag jobbat 40 år med datorer," lör, 2007-10-27 11:19 av BjörnSölving.

Ingvar Holmberg, "Från OC71 till Internet," ons, 2007-11-07 19:47 av Ingvar_ Holmberg.

Thom Jaxhagen, "Från glödtråd till chips," tors, 2007-11-08 12:04 av Tjax.

B. Svante Eriksson, "Hur Sunet skapades," sön, 2007-11-18 13:00 av B.Svante.

Lars Fors, "Min IT-historia," mån, 2007-11-26 14:31 av LarsF.

Sam-Olof Sandström, Generationsbyten, ons, 2007-11-28 17:33 av Sam-Olof.

Christian Ekvall, "Självbiografi av Christian Ekvall," tors, 2007-11-29 14:54 av Anne Marcusson.

Kurt Svensson, "Från mekanik till elektronik," fre, 2007-11-30 10:38 av Kurt. Svensson.

Teddy L. Rosenthal, "IT-hågkomster med spretiga minnesbilder," fre, 2007-11-30 13:03 av TeddyLennart.

Bengt Dahlin, "Historien om en datorjournal," fre, 2007-11-30 13:17 av bengtdahlin.
Comment: mån, 2009-10-19 17:05 av PO Persson
Comment: tis, 2009-10-27 09:44 av bengtdahlin

Bertil Palmgren, "Mina 40 års verksamhet i Svensk Dator Tillverkning," lör, 2007-12-01 19:25 av Z-man.

Gunvor Svartz-Malmberg, "Att söka vetenskaplig litteratur via dator av Gunvor Svartz-Malmberg," mån, 2007-12-03 12:13 av Anne Marcusson.

Tom Wallin, "Bibliografisk IT-historia från datoranvändare på KTH-institution Tom Wallin, född 1933," tis, 2007-12-04 12:56 av Anne Marcusson.

Sven Westman, "Mössen invaderar BESK!," tors, 2007-12-06 12:18 av sgiw.

Owe Svensson, "Den första medicintekniska datorn i Lund," tors, 2007-12-13 22:03 av Owe.

Helge Eriksson, "Kommunal entré i datavärlden," fre, 2007-12-28 18:18 av helge.e.
Comment: "Gunnar Eriksson Roland," fre, 2008-11-21 19:59 av Gunnar.

"När minnesdumpar inte räckte...," ons, 2007-10-10 20:49 av lmesbob.
Comment: "Säkerhetsnivån vid," lör, 2007-11-03 13:47 av Bernte.
Comment: "OK, Bernte! Men jag minns," ons, 2007-11-07 14:19 av Lars.
Comment: "Ett av de smartare sätten," ons, 2008-01-09 15:25 av Bernte.

Comment: "Ang. Stockholms Spårvägar," tis, 2008-01-01 16:30 av helge.e.

Comment: "Jo, sådant var vanligt på," ons, 2008-01-16 22:03 av Lars.

Comment: "Jag tror han var," tors, 2008-01-17 12:31 av Lars.

Comment: "Underliga äro elektronernas," sön, 2008-01-20 18:46 av ollee.

Comment: "Jomenvisst! Vissa system," tis, 2008-01-22 19:10 av Lars.

Comment: "Jodå Olle – och du var en," tors, 2009-01-29 20:26 av Bernte.

Lars Asplund, "Som programmerare 1966-1982," mån, 2007-09-03 20:57 av Lars.

Comment: "Resten av mitt liv med," ons, 2008-01-30 21:09 av Lars.

Carl-Uno Manros, "Min IT-historia 1964 till 2001," tis, 2007-10-23 18:40 av Manros.

Comment: "Jag tycker att det är en," sön, 2007-11-18 17:44 av Lars.

Comment: "Kul och intressant historia," tors, 2008-02-07 17:12 av Niklas.

Patrik Strömberg, "Från Abc 80 till Compiz och senare Atari och Mac," mån, 2008-06-16 17:17 av Patrik_Strömberg.

"Hur hamnade jag inom IT?," lör, 2009-02-21 14:53 av Grosen.

"Min Data-historik, 43 år tillbaks," tors, 2009-07-30 16:49 av Bapsen.

"Min första kontakt med datorer var 1970," tors, 2009-10-15 10:10 av bic.

"Första generationens systemerare och datakonsult," ons, 2009-10-21 12:01, av Erik Andersson.

"Göteborg anslöt det första svenska nätet till Internet 1984," lör, 2009-11-07 16:38 av Bilting.

"Virusjakt i Luleå 1988," mån, 2009-11-23 23:38, av joheben.

"Svensk Programvaruutveckling," tors, 2010-02-11 11:05 av LeifJonas.

"Mitt liv som systemutvecklare inom Volvo. (På Volvo-Data, Volvo Reservdelar, Parts, Truck Parts och VCC Aftersales)," tis, 2010-11-09 18:27 av Piraten.

"Klok användning av datorer," sön, 2010-11-14 17:51 av LarsG.

Appendix II: List of Meta-documentation

This appendix lists documents (knowledge outlines, final reports, and publications) that primarily serve to contextualize the created and collected sources.

Knowledge Outlines

The 18 knowledge outlines completed in the project have the character of research notes, and we have, therefore, decided not to make them available online. Instead, they are deposited in the National Museum of Science and Technology's archival collections.

Carlsson, Ingemar, et al., "Inventeringsgruppen för IT i Försvaret: Inventering av IT-objekt 1945–80" (unpublished document, 2007).

Dussauge, Isabelle, "Datorer och hälsokontroller (1960- och 1970-tal)" (unpublished document, 2008), 19pp.

Dussauge, Isabelle, "Kunskapsöversikt: IT och patientjournal" (unpublished document, 2008), 25pp.

Emanuel, Martin, "Kunskapsöversikt: Datorn i skolan" (unpublished document, 2009), 22pp.

Geijerstam, Jan af, and Anne Marcusson, "Notiser ur datoriseringens historia vid Sandvikens Jernverks AB/Sandvik AB" (unpublished document, 2007), 19pp.

Klein, Kajsa, "Kunskapsöversikt: Integritetsdebatten 1966–1986" (unpublished document, 2007), 55pp.

Lindgren, Sofia, and Julia Peralta, "Introduktion till kunskapsöversikt gällande fokusområdet universitet och högskola" (unpublished document, 2008), 31pp.

Lundin, Per, "Kunskapsöversikt: IBM Nordiska Laboratorier" (unpublished document, 2007), 17pp.

Nilsson, Mikael, "Forskningsöversikt, området mobil telekom" (unpublished document, 2008), 8pp.

Orrghen, Anna, "Kunskapsöversikt: ABM: Datoranvändning för litteraturhantering" (unpublished document, 2008), 13pp.

Orrghen, Anna, "Kunskapsöversikt: Datorer och konst" (unpublished document, 2008), 26pp.

Peralta, Julia, "Offentlig förvaltning, rationaliseringsarbete och den nya ADB-tekniken" (unpublished document, 2008), 51pp.

Schedin, Mats, "IT-historia (Industrigruppen): Affärer och IT samverkade" (unpublished document, 2008), 7pp.

Sjöblom, Gustav, "Datoranvändning inom transportområdet i Sverige fram till ca 1980: Kunskapsöversikt för området *Transporter* inom projektet 'Från matematikmaskin till IT'" (unpublished document, 2008), 78pp.

Sjöblom, Gustav, "Data- och datatjänstebranschen i Sverige före ca 1980: Kunskapsöversikt för området *IT-industri* inom projektet 'Från matematikmaskin till IT'" (unpublished document, 2008), 78pp.

Sjöblom, Gustav, "Datoranvändning i handeln i Sverige fram till ca 1985: Kunskapsöversikt för området *Handel* inom projektet 'Från matematikmaskin till IT'" (unpublished document, 2009), 20pp.

Thodenius, Björn, "Bankernas IT-historia: En översiktlig karta över utvecklingen från 60-talet till 90-talet" (unpublished document, 2008), 17pp.

Thodenius, Björn, "Försäkringsbolagens IT-historia: En översiktlig karta över utvecklingen från 50-talet till 90-talet" (unpublished document, 2008), 13pp.

Final Reports

The 21 final reports on the work carried out by the 16 focus groups are available electronically at the National Museum of Science and Technology's Web page: http://www.tekniskamuseet.se.

Dussauge, Isabelle, "Slutrapport: IT inom vården" (unpublished report, 2008), 10pp.

Emanuel, Martin, "Slutrapport: Datorn i grundskolan, gymnasieskolan och i folkbildningen" (unpublished report, 2009), 11pp.

Ernkvist, Mirko, "Slutrapport: Svensk dataspelsutveckling, 1960–1995" (unpublished report, 2008), 6pp.

Geijerstam, Jan af, "Slutrapport: Industri" (unpublished report, 2008), 13pp.

Gribbe, Johan, "Slutrapport: IT i försvaret" (unpublished report, 2008), 9pp.

Klein, Kajsa, "Slutrapport: Integritetsdebatten" (unpublished report, 2008), 9pp.

Lindgren, Sofia, "Slutrapport: ABM" (unpublished report, 2009), 8pp.

Lindgren, Sofia, "Slutrapport: Media" (unpublished report, 2009), 8pp.

Lindgren, Sofia, and Julia Peralta, "Slutrapport: IT i universitet och högskolor" (unpublished report, 2008), 11pp.

Lundin, Per, "Slutrapport: Användarinflytande och användardeltagande vid utveckling av datateknik och datasystem" (unpublished report, 2008), 5pp.

Lundin, Per, "Slutrapport: Systemutveckling" (unpublished report, 2008), 8pp.

Nilsson, Mikael, "Slutrapport: Telekom" (unpublished report, 2008), 7pp.

Orrghen, Anna, "Slutrapport: ABM (arkiv, bibliotek, museer)" (unpublished report, 2008), 16pp.

Orrghen, Anna, "Slutrapport: Media" (unpublished report, 2008), 12pp.

Peralta, Julia, "Slutrapport: Offentlig förvaltning, rationaliseringsarbete och den nya ADB-tekniken" (unpublished report, 2008), 14pp.

Sjöblom, Gustav, "Slutrapport: IT-industrin" (unpublished report, 2008), 8pp.

Sjöblom, Gustav, "Slutrapport: IT i transportbranschen" (unpublished report, 2008), 8pp.

Sjöblom, Gustav, "Slutrapport: Handel" (unpublished report, 2009), 6pp.

Thodenius, Björn, "Slutrapport: Finans/Bank" (unpublished report, 2008), 19pp.

Thodenius, Björn, "Slutrapport: Finans/Bank" (unpublished report, 2009), 5pp.

Utbult, Mats, "Slutrapport: Användarreaktioner på en metallindustri, ett kommunalt energiverk, ett tidningsföretag och ett pappersmassabruk, speglade genom arbetslivsintervjuer; användarreaktioner inom kontorsarbete i statens tjänst, speglad genom en studie av fackförbundspress" (unpublished report, 2008), 6pp.

Publications on the Project

Emanuel, Martin, "Från matematikmaskin till IT," Datorn i Utbildningen 2008:6, 34.

Frejhagen, Birgitta, ed., Användarna och datorerna: En historik 1960–1985, Vinnova Rapport VR 2009:2 (Stockholm, 2009), 156pp.

Ilshammar, Lars and Kajsa Klein, "Tillbaka till framtiden: 1984 revisited," in Användarna och datorerna: En historik 1960–1985, Vinnova Rapport VR 2009:2, ed. Birgitta Frejhagen (Stockholm, 2009), 31–60.

Lundin, Per, "From Computing Machines to IT: Collecting, Documenting, and Preserving Source Material on Swedish IT-History," in History of Nordic Computing 2: Second IFIP WG9.7 Conference, HiNC2, Turku, Finland, August

21–23, 2007: Revised Selected Papers, ed. John Impagliazzo, Timo Järvi & Petri Paju (Berlin, Heidelberg & New York, 2009), 65–73.

Lundin, Per, "Inledning: Projektet och fokusgruppen," in Användarna och datorerna: En historik 1960–1985, Vinnova Rapport VR 2009:2, ed. Birgitta Frejhagen (Stockholm, 2009), 13–20.

Lundin, Per, "Metoder för att dokumentera historia," in Användarna och datorerna: En historik 1960–1985, Vinnova Rapport VR 2009:2, ed. Birgitta Frejhagen (Stockholm, 2009), 21–30.

Lundin, Per, Documenting the Use of Computers in Swedish Society between 1950 and 1980: Final Report on the Project "From Computing Machines to IT", TRITA/HST 2009/1 (Stockholm, 2009), 86pp.

Peterson, Hans and Per Lundin, "Documenting the Use of Computers in Swedish Health Care up to 1980," IMIA Yearbook of Medical Informatics (2011), 169–74.

Skoglund, Crister and Bernt Skovdahl, "Entusiasm och skepsis: Några linjer i debatten om informationssamhället åren runt 1980," in Användarna och datorerna: En historik 1960–1985, Vinnova Rapport VR 2009:2, ed. Birgitta Frejhagen (Stockholm, 2009), 88–111.

Sundblad, Yngve and Per Lundin, "Användarmedverkan i IT-utveckling: Skandinaviska skolan," in Användarna och datorerna: En historik 1960–1985, Vinnova Rapport VR 2009:2, ed. Birgitta Frejhagen (Stockholm, 2009), 61–87.

Utbult, Mats, "Användarna kommer till tals," in Användarna och datorerna: En historik 1960–1985, Vinnova Rapport VR 2009:2, ed. Birgitta Frejhagen (Stockholm, 2009), 112–38.

Appendix III: Formal Description of Organization and Work Process

Organization and Responsibilities

The project is led by *the project leader* Rolf Berndtson, chairman of the Swedish Computer Society. The project leader delegates the responsibility for collecting, creating, and editing sources to *the research group*, which is based at the Division of History of Science and Technology at KTH and is led by *the research project leader* Per Lundin. Furthermore, the project leader delegates the responsibility for administration, preservation, and dissemination of the produced sources to *the group for the management of material*, which is based at the National Museum of Science and Technology and is led by the *project leader for the management of material* Peter Du Rietz.

A *steering group* advises the project leader in his work. A *project coach* assists and advises the project leader, the research group, and the group for the management of material in their work. Per Olof Persson, Athena Konsult AB, is the project coach.

A *managerial group* consisting of the project leader, the research project leader, the project leader for the management of material, and the project coach has the operative responsibility.

The research group has two tasks. Firstly, to coordinate, develop, and evaluate the methods used, to keep the project updated on the state of the research in computing history and oral history, and to establish and maintain contacts with national and international research environments. The research group participates in ongoing discussions on methods for contemporary history and presents the project's results at national and international conferences. Secondly, to identify, collect, and create sources as well as produce edited sources. The research project leader is responsible for delegating the second task to *the research secretaries*.

The research secretaries are part of the research group. Each of the research secretaries is, in turn, responsible for a *focus group*. The focus group is related to a *focus area*. The project has identified 16 focus areas. These are early computers; healthcare; financial industries; manufacturing industries; information technology industries; systems development, user organizations, and user participation; transportation industries; defense; public administration, telecommunications industries; higher education, archives, libraries, and museums; media; schools; and retail and wholesale industries. The focus group consists of a *research secretary* and a number of practitioners with experience from the area in question. The practitioners should be representative of the focus area. The role of the practitioners is to assist and advise the research secretary in his or her work. Together, they identify important historical events and processes as well as relevant and representative witnesses of these. Furthermore, they arrange witness seminars, conduct interviews, and invite people to write autobiographies. It is the responsibility of the research secretary to devise knowledge outlines, to decide—in consultation with the practitioners—which topics should be covered, which type of collection should be carried out, and to what extent. The research secretary is also responsible for the process of collecting, creating, and editing sources, as well as publishing it when appropriate. He or she is, furthermore, responsible for presenting a final report on the work completed by the focus group.

A *scientific council* advises the research group in its methodological work. The scientific council is led by Arne Kaijser.

The research project leader and the research secretaries are assisted by a *project secretary*, who is part of the research group. The project secretary functions, foremost, as the link between the research secretaries and the group for the management of material and is responsible for delivering the collected and created sources to the group for the management of material. The project secretary also assists the managerial group.

The group for the management of material is responsible for registering and preserving the sources, which the focus groups have collected and created, in the National Museum of Science and Technology. It also has the responsibility to oversee that documentation efforts are performed along the lines that a long-term preservation practice requires. An archivist, a curator, a librarian, and a photographer are part of the group.

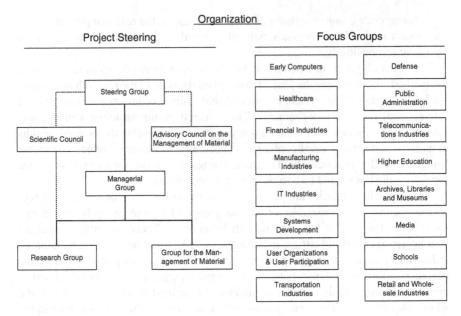

Fig. A.1 An overview of the project organization

An *advisory council on the management of material* advises the group for the management of material on its work. It is led by Anne Louise Kemdal (later replaced by Helene Sjunnesson) (Fig. A.1).

The participants in the organizational bodies described above are listed in Appendix IV: Participants in the Project.

Deliverables and Debriefing

As mentioned, each research secretary is responsible for realizing the documentation in each focus area. For *each focus area*, the project has agreed with the financiers to deliver:

- One knowledge outline
- Three witness seminars
- Ten interviews
- One final report

It should be emphasized that this composition of deliverables may vary from focus area to focus area. In some cases, it may be more relevant with more interviews and fewer witness seminars. In other cases, the reverse may be true. The composition of deliverables for each focus area is specified by the research secretary and the focus group.

Each research secretary has 25 paid weeks at his or her disposal. These are suggested to be distributed approximately as follows:

- One knowledge outline, 3 weeks
- Three witness seminars, 13 weeks (5 + 4 + 4)
- Ten interviews, 6 weeks (3 days for each interview)
- One final report, 1 week
- Research group/focus group activities, 2 weeks

The project has, besides these deliverables, agreed to deliver about 200 autobiographies. These are collected and created by the research group with the help of questionnaires according to the methodology developed by Nordiska museet as well as the specially designed Writers' Web.

Debriefing

Research secretaries and the project secretary debrief the research project leader in the form of a monthly status report, while the research project leader, the project leader for the management of material, and the project coach, in turn, debrief the project leader in the form of a monthly status report.

Work Process for a Focus Area

The work within a focus area is divided into three phases: *initiation*, *realization*, and *finalization*. The initiation phase is estimated to take 3 months, the realization phase 12, and the finalization phase 2.

Initiation

The work within a focus area begins with producing a *project plan*. The project plan includes a preliminary study of the focus area in question. It also contains a budget, deliverables, and a time schedule. The project plan is prepared by the managerial group. The plan is approved by the project leader.

A research secretary is employed after the project plan has been prepared and approved. The managerial group handles this task. The project leader decides who to employ. A focus group is assembled after the project plan has been prepared and approved and a research secretary has been employed. The research secretary and the project coach together carry out this task.

The initiation phase is completed when a project plan has been approved, a research secretary employed, and a focus group assembled.

Realization

The focus group devises a detailed *plan of action* for the realization of the work according to the overarching guidelines laid down in the project plan. The plan of action specifies the number of deliverables. The research secretary is responsible for the preparation of the plan of action, which, in turn, is approved by the research project leader. The process of creating and collecting sources according to the criteria and methods established by the project can then start.

The realization phase is completed when the deliverables (including a final report) have been produced. The research secretary's involvement comes to an end with the completion of the realization phase.

Finalization

The focus group's involvement on a nonprofit basis may continue for a while after the research secretary's involvement has come to an end. That the group's continued involvement is limited to only 2 months is due to the National Museum of Science and Technology's limited capacity to manage sources over and above the group for the management of material's tasks.

Management of Created and Collected Sources

The group for the management of material at the National Museum of Science and Technology is responsible for the management of the created and collected sources. It receives these from the focus groups, and weeds out low-quality sources and possible duplicates in dialogue with the research secretaries. It makes sure that the sources are consistent with the Personal Data Act (*personuppgiftslagen, PUL*), and in consultation with the donor, its project leader clarifies the copyrights for sources that may be copyright protected. The group also classifies the sources, provides them with metadata, and stores them digitally.

Sources that cannot be incorporated in the National Museum of Science and Technology's collections should either be returned to the donor or be forwarded to another interested party. It is the responsibility of the project leader for the management of material to make these decisions in consultation with the donor.

The group for the management of material registers the received sources in the National Museum of Science and Technology's collections databases (the picture and artifact database, the archives database, and the library catalogue).

Information Management

The project uses Projektplatsen at http://www.projektplatsen.se as a tool for managing internal information. We have designed Projektplatsen so that it contains different sections for shared information, for the research group and for each and every one of the focus groups. The Web site also contains a general description of the project, its current status and news. The section for shared information contains the project manual, protocols from the steering group's meetings, and funding information. The section for the research group contains information on methodology, reference literature, and protocols from the research group's meetings. The sections for the different focus groups contain information on the activities of each group.

Each research secretary is responsible for documenting the meetings in his or her focus group and uploading the protocols onto Projektplatsen. The project secretary is the Web site administrator.

External information on the project is found on the Web portal http://ithistoria.se, which links to the Web pages of the Swedish Computer Society (http://www.dfs.se), the Division of History of Science and Technology at KTH (http://www.teknikhistoria.se), and the National Museum of Science and Technology (http://www.tekniskamuseet.se). The project leader is responsible for updating the information on the Web portal and the project secretary for administering it.

Appendix IV: Participants in the Project

Steering Group

Rolf Berndtson (chairman)	The Swedish Computer Society
Per Olof Persson (secretary)	Athena Konsult P O Persson AB
Peter Du Rietz	The National Museum of Science and Technology
Anne-Marie Fransson[a]	IT & Telekomföretagen
Inger Gran	The Swedish Computer Society
Gunnar L. Johansson	former President AB Volvo, former chairman of the Federation of Swedish Industries
Arne Kaijser	Div. of History of Science and Technology, KTH
Per Lundin	Div. of History of Science and Technology, KTH
Per Olofsson	formerly CEO IBM Sweden
Helene Sjunnesson[b]	The National Museum of Science and Technology

[a]Fransson replaced Ylva Hambraeus-Björling, IT & Telekomföretagen, in 2007
[b]Sjunnesson replaced Anne Louise Kemdal, the National Museum of Science and Technology, in 2008

Managerial Group

Rolf Berndtson (chairman)	The Swedish Computer Society
Sofia Lindgren[a] (secretary)	The Swedish Computer Society
Peter Du Rietz	The National Museum of Science and Technology

(continued)

(continued)

Per Lundin	Div. of History of Science and Technology, KTH
Per Olof Persson	Athena Konsult P O Persson AB

[a]Lindgren replaced Cecilia Calmfors in 2007. Calmfors had earlier replaced Åsa Hiort af Ornäs

Scientific Council

Arne Kaijser (chairman)	Div. of History of Science and Technology, KTH
Per Lundin (secretary)	Div. of History of Science and Technology, KTH
Boel Berner	Dept. of Technology and Social Change, Linköping University
Isabelle Dussauge	Div. of History of Science and Technology, KTH
Jan Garnert	The National Museum of Science and Technology
Lars Ilshammar	Labour Movement Archives and Library
Jenny Sundén	Media Technology and Graphic Arts, KTH

Advisory Council on the Management of Material

Helene Sjunnesson[a] (chairman)	The National Museum of Science and Technology
Peter Du Rietz (secretary)	The National Museum of Science and Technology
Torbjörn Hörnfeldt	The National Archives
Per Olof Persson	Athena Konsult P O Persson AB

[a]Sjunnesson replaced Anne Louise Kemdal, the National Museum of Science and Technology, in 2008

Research Group

Per Lundin (chairman)	Div. of History of Science and Technology, KTH
Milena Dávila	Div. of History of Science and Technology, KTH
Isabelle Dussauge	Div. of History of Science and Technology, KTH
Martin Emanuel	Div. of History of Science and Technology, KTH
Mirko Ernkvist	Dept. of Economic History, University of Gothenburg
Jan af Geijerstam	Div. of History of Science and Technology, KTH
Johan Gribbe	Div. of History of Science and Technology, KTH
Kajsa Klein	Dept. of Journalism, Media and Communication, Stockholm University
Ebba Larsson	The Swedish Computer Society

(continued)

(continued)

Sofia Lindgren	The Swedish Computer Society
Mikael Nilsson	Div. of History of Science and Technology, KTH
Anna Orrghen	School of Culture and Communication, Södertörn University
Julia Peralta	Dept. of Economic History, Uppsala University
Gustav Sjöblom	Technology and Society, Chalmers University
Crister Skoglund	School of Culture and Communication, Södertörn University
Björn Thodenius	Center for Information Management, Stockholm School of Economics
Mats Utbult	Arbetslivsjournalisterna

Group for the Management of Material

Peter Du Rietz (chairman)	The National Museum of Science and Technology
Ellinor Algin	The National Museum of Science and Technology
Martin Lindberg	The National Museum of Science and Technology
Anne Marcusson	The National Museum of Science and Technology
Peter Westerberg	The National Museum of Science and Technology

Project Secretary

Sofia Lindgren[a]   The Swedish Computer Society

[a]Lindgren replaced Cecilia Calmfors in 2007. Calmfors had earlier replaced Åsa Hiort af Ornäs

Focus Groups

Early Computers

Lars Arosenius, Bo Lindestam, Tord Jöran Hallberg, Gunnar Holmdahl, Stig Holmberg, Thomas Höglund, Kurt Katzeff, Per Lundin, Gert Persson, Per Olof Persson, Pär Rittsel, Gunnar Stenudd, Gunnar Wedell

Healthcare

Isabelle Dussauge, Bengt Olsen, Hans Peterson, Urban Rosenqvist

Financial Industries

Banking Industries Group: Rune Brandinger, Bengt-Åke Eriksson, Sture Hallström, Per Olof Persson, Fredrik Runnquist, Anders Rönn, Björn Thodenius
   Insurance Industries Group: Olli Aronsson, Perolof Axelson, Göran Carlsson, Anders Kleverman, Per Lind, Göran Lindberg, Per Olof Persson, Björn Thodenius

Manufacturing Industries

Jan af Geijerstam, Kurt Gladh, Peter Lundh, Bernt Malmkvist, Per Olof Persson, Mats Schedin, Anders Svedberg, Ingvar Söderlund

Information Technology Industries

Lars Arosenius, Gunnar Hesse, Per Olof Persson, Gustav Sjöblom, Anders Skarin, Thord Wilkne, Gunnar Wedell, Viggo Wentzel

Systems Development

Janis Bubenko, Harold "Bud" Lawson, Per Lundin, Tomas Ohlin, Lars Wiktorin, Ulf Åsén

User Organizations and User Participation

Klas Barklöf, Peter Docherty, Birgitta Frejhagen, Lars Ilshammar, Ove Ivarsen, Cecilia Katzeff, Kajsa Klein, Lennart Lennerlöf, Per Lundin, Jenny Maniette, Christer Marking, Bengt Sandblad, Cecilia Sjöberg, Crister Skoglund, Yngve Sundblad, Per Tengblad, Peter Ullmark, Mats Utbult, Åke Walldius, Gunnela Westlander, Anders Wiberg

Transportation Industries

Roger Bydler, Dag Ericson, Esbjörn Hillberg, Bo Midander, Anders Rydberg, Per Olof Persson, Gustav Sjöblom, Rune Svensson, Ingvar Söderlund, Bengt Wennerberg

Defense

Jonas Agerberg, Tomas Ahlberg, Ingemar Carlsson, Helge Gard, Johan Gribbe, Sigurd Håkanson, Malte Jönson, Gunnar Lindqvist, Sven Olof Olson, Gert Persson, Gert Scyborger, Carl-Olof Ternryd, Bertil Wennerholm, Christina Winblad

Public Administration

Olli Aronsson, Göran Ernmark, Dag Osterman, Julia Peralta, Gert Persson, Per Olof Persson, Nils Qwerin

Telecommunications Industries

Göran Kihlström, Per Lundgren, Mikael Nilsson

Higher Education

Ingemar Dahlstrand, Sofia Lindgren, Julia Peralta

Archives, Libraries, and Museums

Sofia Lindgren, Anna Orrghen

Media

Peter Blom, Mirko Ernkvist, Lars Kjelldahl, Sofia Lindgren, Anna Orrghen, Pär Rittsel

Schools

Martin Emanuel, Ulla Riis

Retail and Wholesale Industries

Rolf Holmberg, Per Olof Persson, Gustav Sjöblom

References

Aaltonen, S.: Tunteita, tulkintoja ja tietotekniikkaa: 'Milloin kuulit ensimmäistä kertaa tietokoneista?' -kyselyn tuloksia (Emotions, Interpretations, and Information Technology: Results from a Survey: "When Did You First Hear about Computers?"). Turku (2004)

Ågren, M.: Synlighet, vikt, trovärdighet – och självkritik: Några synpunkter på källkritikens roll i dagens historieforskning. Historisk tidskrift **125**(2), 249–262 (2005)

Åkerman, S.: Mjukdata. In: Qviller, B., Wahlin, B. (eds.) Usynlig historie: Foredrag fra den 17. Nordiske fagkonferensen for historisk metodelære i Tranum Klit 19.–23. mai 1981, pp. 47–59. Universitetsforlaget, Oslo (1983)

Albert, G.: Appropriating America: Americanization in the history of European computing. IEEE Ann. Hist. Comput. **32**(2), 4–7 (2010)

Andersson-Skog, L.: Från normalspår till bredband: Svensk kommunikationspolitik i framtidens tjänst 1850–2000. In: Andersson-Skog, L., Krantz, O. (eds.) Omvandlingens sekel: Perspektiv på ekonomi och samhälle i 1900-talets Sverige, pp. 117–143. Studentlitteratur, Lund (2002)

Annerstedt, J.: Staten och datorerna: En studie av den officiella datorutvecklings- och datorforskningspolitiken. Kommittén för forskningsorganisation och forskningsekonomi, Stockholm (1969)

Annerstedt, J., Forssberg, L., Henriksson, S., Nilsson, K.: Datorer och politik: Studier i en ny tekniks politiska effekter på det svenska samhället. Zenith & Bo Cavefors, Lund (1970)

Appelquist, J.: Informationsteknik och organisatorisk förändring: Teknik, organisation och produktivitet inom svensk banksektor 1975–2003. Almqvist & Wiksell International, Lund (2005)

Asker, B.: ALGOL-GENIUS: An early success for high-level languages. In: Bubenko, J. Jr., Impagliazzo, J., Sølvberg, A. (eds.) History of Nordic Computing: IFIP WG9.7 First Working Conference on the History of Nordic Computing (HiNC1), 16–18 June 2003, Trondheim, Norway, pp. 251–260. New York (2005)

Aspray, W., Ceruzzi, P.E. (eds.): The Internet and American Business. MIT Press, Cambridge, MA (2008)

Åström, K.J.: Early control development in Sweden. Eur. J. Control. **13**, 1–24 (2007)

Atlestam, B.: Datornät. In: Atlestam, B. (ed.) Infrastruktur för informationssamhället: Teknik och politik, pp. 113–127. NUTEK, Stockholm (1995)

Avelin, L.: Oral history and E-research: Collecting memories of the 1960s and 1970s youth culture. In: Kurkowska-Budzan, M., Zamorski, K. (eds.) Oral History: The Challenges of Dialogue, pp. 35–46. John Benjamins, Amsterdam (2009)

Bansler, J.: Systemutveckling: Teori och historia i skandinaviskt perspektiv, trans. Johansson, G. Studentlitteratur, Lund (1990)

Brändström, A., Åkerman, S. (eds.): Icke skriftliga källor: Huvudtema I. Historiska institutionen, Umeå universitet, Umeå (1991)

Broman, P.O.: Kort historik över framtidens musik: Elektronmusiken och framtidstanken i svenskt 1950- och 60-tal. Gidlunds förlag, Stockholm (2007)

131

Bubenko, J. Jr., Impagliazzo, J., Sølvberg, A. (eds.): History of Nordic Computing: IFIP WG9.7 First Working Conference on the History of Nordic Computing (HiNC1), 16–18 June 2003, Trondheim, Norway. New York (2005)

Burström, M.: Samtidsarkeologi: Introduktion till ett forskningsfält. Studentlitteratur, Lund (2007)

Caminer, D. (ed.): User-Driven Innovation: The World's First Business Computer. McGraw Hill, London (1996)

Carlsson, A.: Tekniken – politikens frälsare?: Om matematikmaskiner, automation och ingenjörer vid mitten av 50-talet. Arbetarhistoria 23, 23–30 (1999)

Carlsson, A.: Elektroniska hjärnor: Debatten om datorer, automation och ingenjörer 1955–58. In: Widmalm, S. (ed.) Artefakter: Industrin, vetenskapen och de tekniska nätverken, pp. 245–285. Gidlunds förlag, Hedemora/Möklinta (2004)

Center for History and New Media, http://chnm.gmu.edu/. Accessed 10 June 2009

Center for History of Physics, http://www.aip.org/history/. Accessed 10 June 2009

Ceruzzi, P.E.: A History of Modern Computing, 2nd edn. MIT Press, Cambridge, MA (2003)

Ceruzzi, P.E.: Internet Alley: High Technology in Tysons Corner, 1945–2005. MIT Press, Cambridge, MA (2008)

Cohen, D.J., Rosenzweig, R.: Digital History: A Guide to Gathering, Preserving, and Presenting the Past on the Web. University of Pennsylvania Press, Philadelphia (2006)

Computer History Collection, http://americanhistory.si.edu/collections/comphist/. Accessed 10 June 2009

Cortada, J.W.: The Digital Hand: How Computers Changed the Work of American Manufacturing, Transportation, and Retail Industries. Oxford University Press, Oxford (2004)

Cortada, J.W.: The Digital Hand: Volume 2, How Computers Changed the Work of American Financial, Telecommunications, Media, and Entertainment Industries. Oxford University Press, Oxford (2006a)

Cortada, J.W.: The digital hand: How information technology changes the way industries worked in the United States. Bus. Hist. Rev. 80(4), 755–766 (2006b)

Cortada, J.W.: Studying the role of IT in the evolution of American business practices: A way forward. IEEE Ann. Hist. Comput. 29(4), 28–39 (2007)

Cortada, J.W.: The Digital Hand: Volume 3, How Computers Changed the Work of American Public Sector Industries. Oxford University Press, Oxford (2008)

Cowan, R.S.: The consumption junction: A proposal for research strategies in the sociology of technology. In: Bijker, W.E., Hughes, T.P., Pinch, T. (eds.) The Social Construction of Technological Systems: New Directions in the Sociology and History of Technology, pp. 261–280. MIT Press, Cambridge, MA (1989)

Cubitt, G.: History and Memory. Manchester University Press, Manchester (2007)

Dædalus 1978/79: Tekniska museets årsbok. Stockholm (1978–79)

de Chadarevian, S.: Using interviews to write the history of science. In: Söderqvist, T. (ed.) The Historiography of Contemporary Science and Technology, pp. 51–70. Harwood Academic, Amsterdam (1997)

De Geer, H.: På väg till datasamhället: Datatekniken i politiken 1946–1963. Kungl. Tekniska högskolan, Stockholm (1992)

Dexter, L.A. (ed.): Elite and Specialized Interviewing. Northwestern University Press, Evanston (1970)

Doel, R.E., Söderqvist, T. (eds.): The Historiography of Contemporary Science, Technology, and Medicine: Writing Recent Science. Routledge, New York (2006)

Dong, H., Clarkson, J.P., Cassim, J., Keates, S.: Critical user forums: An effective user research method for inclusive design. Des. J. 8(2), 49–59 (2005)

Dussauge, I., Gribbe, J., Kaijser, A., Lundin, P., Peralta, J., Sjöblom, G., Thodenius, B.: Precursors of the IT nation: Computer use and control in Swedish society, 1955–1985. In: Impagliazzo, J., Lundin, P., Wangler, B. (eds.) History of Nordic Computing 3: Third IFIP WG9.7 Conference, HiNC 3, Stockholm, Sweden, 18–20 Oct 2010: Revised Selected Papers, pp. 425–432. Heidelberg (2011)

Edgerton, D.: From innovation to use: Ten eclectic theses on the historiography of technology. Hist. Technol. **16**, 111–136 (1999)

Edgerton, D.: The Shock of the Old: Technology and Global History Since 1900. Oxford University Press, Oxford (2007)

Edwards, P.N.: A Vast Machine: Computer Models, Climate Data, and the Politics of Global Warming. MIT Press, Cambridge, MA (2010)

Evans, R.: In Defence of History, new edn. Granta, London (2000)

Focus group, http://en.wikipedia.org/wiki/Focus_group. Accessed 3 Nov 2011

Fogelberg, H.: Research on IT Use and Users in Sweden, with Particular Focus on 1990–2010. KTH, Stockholm (2011)

Fogerty, J.E.: Oral history and archives: Documenting context. In: Charlton, T.L., Myers, L.E., Sharpless, R. (eds.) History of Oral History: Foundations and Methodology, pp. 197–226. Rowman & Littlefield, Lanham (2007)

Gaunt, D.: Oral history och levnadsöden. In: Brändström, A., Åkerman, S. (eds.) Icke skriftliga källor: Huvudtema I, pp. 63–72. Historiska institutionen, Umeå universitet, Umeå (1991)

Ginzburg, C.: Clues, Myths and the Historical Method, English trans. John and Anne Tedeschi, pp. 96–125. Johns Hopkins University Press, Baltimore (1989)

Glimell, H.: Återerövra datapolitiken! En rapport om staten och informationsteknologin under fyra decennier. Universitetet i Linköping, Linköping (1989)

Green, A.: Individual remembering and 'collective memory': Theoretical presuppositions and contemporary debates. J. Oral Hist. Soc. **32**(2), 35–44 (2004)

Grele, R.J.: Oral history as evidence. In: Charlton, T.L., Myers, L.E., Sharpless, R. (eds.) History of Oral History: Foundations and Methodology. Rowman & Littlefield, Lanham (2007)

Gribbe, J.: Controlling the battlefield: Computing and operational command in the Swedish armed forces, 1966–1989. In: Impagliazzo, J., Lundin, P., Wangler, B. (eds.) History of Nordic Computing 3: Third IFIP WG9.7 Conference, HiNC 3, Stockholm, Sweden, 18–20 Oct 2010: Revised Selected Papers, pp. 22–27. Heidelberg (2011a)

Gribbe, J.: Stril 60: Teknik, vetenskap och svensk säkerhetspolitik under det kalla kriget. Gidlunds förlag, Hedemora (2011b)

Hagström, C., Marander-Eklund, L.: Att arbeta med frågelistor. In: Hagström, C., Marander-Eklund, L. (eds.) Frågelistan som källa och metod, pp. 9–29. Studentlitteratur, Lund (2005a)

Hagström, C., Marander-Eklund, L. (eds.): Frågelistan som källa och metod. Studentlitteratur, Lund (2005b)

Haigh, T.: Inventing information systems: The systems men and the computers, 1950–1968. Bus. Hist. Rev. **75**(1), 15–61 (2001a)

Haigh, T.: The chromium-plated tabulator: Institutionalizing an electronic revolution. IEEE Ann. Hist. Comput. **23**(4), 75–104 (2001b)

Haigh, T.: The historian for hire: Conducting a career oral history series in a technical area. Lecture at the summer school oral history and technological memory: Challenges in studying European pasts, Turku, Finland, 10–15 Aug 2009

Hallberg, T.J.: IT-gryning: Svensk datahistoria från 1840- till 1960-talet. Studentlitteratur, Lund (2007)

Hammarlund-Larsson, C.: Samlingarna och samlandet. In: Medelius, H., Nyström, B., Stavenow-Hidemark, E. (eds.) Nordiska museet under 125 år, pp. 180–239. Nordiska museets förlag, Stockholm (1998)

Hamngren, I., Odhnoff, J., Wolfers, J.: De byggde Internet i Sverige, 2nd edn. ISOC-SE, Stockholm (2009)

Hasselberg, Y., Müller, L., Stenlås, N.: History from a Network Perspective: Three Examples from Early Modern and Modern History c. 1700–1950. Centrum för transport- och samhällsforskning, Borlänge (1997)

Henriksson, S.: Datapolitikens död och återkomst. In: Atlestam, B. (ed.) Infrastruktur för informationssamhället: Teknik och politik. NUTEK, Stockholm (1995)

Henriksson, S.: De galna åren – en efterskrift. In: Atlestam, B. (ed.) Informationssamhället – åter till framtiden. Vinnova, Stockholm (2004)

Hessenbruch, A.: The trials and promise of a web-history of materials research. In: Grandin, K., Wormbs, N., Widmalm, S. (eds.) The Science–Industry Nexus: History, Policy, Implications, pp. 397–413. Science History Publications, Sagamore Beach (2004)

Hessenbruch, A.: The Mutt Historian': The perils and opportunities of doing history of science on-line. In: Doel, R.E., Söderqvist, T. (eds.) The Historiography of Contemporary Science, Technology, and Medicine: Writing Recent Science, pp. 279–298. Routledge, New York (2006)

Hoddeson, L.: The conflict of memories and documents: Dilemmas and pragmat-ics of oral history. In: Doel, R.E., Söderqvist, T. (eds.) The Historiography of Contemporary Science, Technology, and Medicine: Writing Recent Science, pp. 187–200. Routledge, New York (2006)

Höjeberg, M. (ed.): Dædalus 2002: Tekniska museets årsbok: Dator till vardags. Stockholm (2001)

Holmgren, K.: Datorverksamheten vid Kockums under efterkrigstiden. In: Vårt Kockums, pp. 279–310. Varvshistoriska föreningen i Malmö, Malmö (2010)

Hounshell, D.: The medium is the message, or how context matters: The RAND corporation builds an economics of innovation, 1946–62. In: Hughes, T.P., Hughes, A.C. (eds.) Systems, Experts and Computers: The Systems Approach in Management and Engineering, World War II and After. MIT Press, Cambridge, MA (2000)

Howell, M., Prevenier, W.: From Reliable Sources: An Introduction to Historical Methods. Cornell University Press, Ithaca (2001)

Iggers, G.G.: Historiography in the Twentieth Century: From Scientific Objectivity to the Postmodern Challenge, with a new epilogue by the author. Wesleyan University Press, Middletown (2005)

Ilshammar, L.: Från supervapen till supermarket: Utvecklingen av Internet 1957–1997. In: Blomkvist, P., Kaijser, A. (eds.) Den konstruerade världen: Tekniska system i historiskt perspektiv, pp. 323–343. Brutus Östlings bokförlag Symposion, Stockholm/Stehag (1998)

Ilshammar, L.: Offentlighetens nya rum: Teknik och politik i Sverige 1969–1999. Örebro universitet, Örebro (2002)

Impagliazzo, J., Lundin, P., Wangler, B. (eds.): History of Nordic Computing 3: Third IFIP WG9.7 Conference, HiNC 3, Stockholm, Sweden, 18–20 October 2010: Revised Selected Papers. Springer, Heidelberg (2011)

IT-ceum: Det svenska datamuseet, http://www.itceum.se/. Accessed 15 June 2009

Ivanov, K.: Systemutveckling och ADB-ämnets utveckling. Linköping (1984)

Johansson, M.: Early analog computers in Sweden—with examples from Chalmers University of technology and the Swedish aerospace industry. IEEE Ann. Hist. Comput. 18(4), 27–33 (1996)

Johansson, M.: Smart, Fast and Beautiful: On Rhetoric of Technology and Computing Discourse in Sweden 1955–1995. Linköping University, Linköping (1997)

Johansson, M.: Big blue gets beaten: The technological and political controversy of the first large Swedish computerization project in a rhetoric of technology perspective. IEEE Ann. Hist. Comput. 21(2), 14–30 (1999)

Johansson, C. (ed.): Tema gudar. Datasaabs vänner, Linköping (2002)

Johansson, J.: Du sköna nya tid?: Debatten om informationssamhället i riksdag och storting under 1990-talet. Linköpings universitet, Institutionen för Tema, Linköping (2006)

Johansson, C., Nissen, J.: Människa, informationsteknik, samhälle: MITS – en forskargrupp. Linköpings universitet, Linköping (1996)

Jordanova, L.: History in Practice, 2nd edn. Hodder Arnold, London (2006)

Kaiserfeld, T.: Computerizing the Swedish welfare state: The middle way of technological success and failure. Technol. Cult. 37, 249–279 (1996)

Karlsson, M.: The Liberalisation of Telecommunications in Sweden: Technology and Regime Change from the 1960s to 1993. Linköping University, Linköping (1998)

Karlsson, S.: Nödvändighetens väg: Världsbildande gränsarbete i skildringar av informationssamhället. Karlstad University Press, Karlstad (2005)

Karlsson, M., Sturesson, L. (eds.): The World's Largest Machine: Global Telecommunications and Human Condition. Linköpings universitet, Linköping (1995)

Kingery, D.W.: Learning from Things: Method and Theory of Material Culture Studies. Smithsonian Institution Press, Washington, DC (1996)

Kjeldstadli, K.: Det förflutna är inte vad det en gång var, trans. Sven-Erik, T. Studentlitteratur, Lund (1998)

Kline, R., Pinch, T.: Users as agents of technological change: The social construction of the automobile in the rural United States. Technol. Cult. 37(4), 763–795 (1996)

Knutsson, B. (ed.): Tema bank: Datasaab och bankerna. Datasaabs vänner, Linköping (1996)

Kopytoff, I.: The cultural biography of things: Commoditization as process. In: Appadurai, A. (ed.) The Social Life of Things: Commodities in a Cultural Perspective, pp. 64–91. Cambridge University Press, Cambridge (1986)

Krige, J.: Review: How users matter: The co-construction of users and technology by Nelly Oudshoorn & Trevor Pinch. Contemp. Sociol. 35(1), 31–32 (2006)

Lamb, R., Kling, R.: Reconceptualizing users as social actors in information systems research. MIS Q. 27(2), 197–236 (2003)

Lehtisalo, K.: The History of NORDUnet: Twenty-Five Years of Networking Cooperation in the Nordic Countries. NORDUnet, Hørsholm (2005)

Lennersand, M.: Historikern som arkivarie. Arkiv, samhälle och forskning 2, 62–66 (2008)

Lindgren, M.: Glory and Failure: The Difference Engines of Johann Müller, Charles Babbage and Georg and Edvard Scheutz, trans. McKay, C. G., 2nd edn. MIT Press, Cambridge, MA Cambridge (1990)

Lindkvist, K.: Datateknik och politik: Datapolitiken i Sverige 1945–1982. Forskningspolitiska institutet, Lund (1984)

Lindqvist, S.: A cost-benefit analysis of science: The dilemma of engineering schools in the twentieth century. In: Grenthe, I., et al. (eds.) Science, Technology and Society: University Leadership Today and for the Twenty-First Century, pp. 105–116. Tekniska högskolan i Stockholm, Stockholm (1998)

Lindström, K.: 50 gram fattas mig i Berlin, http://computersweden.idg.se/2.2683/1.414848/50-gram-fattas-mig-i-berlin. Accessed 20 Nov 2011

Lubar, S., Kingery, D.W. (eds.): History from Things: Essays on Material Culture. Smithsonian Institution Press, Washington, DC (1993)

Lummis, T.: Structure and validity in oral evidence. In: Perks, R., Thomson, A. (eds.) The Oral History Reader, 2nd edn, pp. 255–260. Routledge, New York (2006)

Lund, J.: Från kula till data. Gidlunds förlag, Stockholm (1989)

Lundin, P.: Bilsamhället: Ideologi, expertis och regelskapande i efterkrigstidens Sverige. Stockholmia, Stockholm (2008)

Lundin, P.: Documenting the use of computers in Swedish society between 1950 and 1980: Final report on the project "From Computing Machines to IT". KTH, Stockholm (2009a)

Lundin, P.: From computing machines to IT: Collecting, documenting, and preserving source material on Swedish IT-History. In: Impagliazzo, J., Järvi, T., Paju, P. (eds.) History of Nordic Computing 2: Second IFIP WG9.7 Conference, HiNC2, Turku, Finland, August 21–23, 2007: Revised Selected Papers, pp. 65–73, Berlin/Heidelberg/New York (2009b)

Lundin, P.: Inledning: Projektet och fokusgruppen. In: Frejhagen, B. (ed.) Användarna och datorerna: En historik 1960–1985, pp. 13–20. Vinnova, Stockholm (2009c)

Lundin, P.: Metoder för att dokumentera historia. In: Frejhagen, B. (ed.) Användarna och datorerna: En historik 1960–1985, pp. 21–30. Vinnova, Stockholm (2009d)

Lundin, P.: Designing democracy: The UTOPIA-Project and the role of labor movement in technological change during the 1970s and the 1980s. In: Impagliazzo, J., Lundin. P., Wangler, B. (eds.) History of Nordic Computing 3: Third IFIP WG9.7 Conference, HiNC 3, Stockholm, Sweden, 18–20 Oct 2010: Revised Selected Papers, pp. 187–195. Heidelberg (2011)

Lundin, P., Stenlås, N.: Technology, state initiative and national myths in cold war Sweden: An introduction. In: Lundin, P., Stenlås, N., Gribbe, J. (eds.) Science for Welfare and Warfare: Technology and State Initiative in Cold War Sweden, pp. 1–34. Science History Publications, Sagamore Beach (2010)

Lundin, P., Stenlås, N., Gribbe, J. (eds.): Science for Welfare and Warfare: Technology and State Initiative in Cold War Sweden. Science History Publications, Sagamore Beach (2010)

Marcus, G.E.: Elite as a concept, theory, and tradition. In: Marcus, G.E. (ed.) Elites: Ethnographic Issues, pp. 7–13. University of New Mexico Press, Albuquerque (1983)

McMahan, E.: Elite Oral History Discourse: A Study of Cooperation and Coherence. University of Alabama Press, Tuscaloosa (1989)

Mellberg, K., Wedell, G., Lindestam, B.: Fyrtio år av den svenska datahistorien: Från Standard radiofabrik till …? Veteranklubben Alfa, Stockholm (1997)

Miliband, R.: The State in Capitalist Society. Basic Books, London (1969)

Misa, T.J.: Understanding 'how computing changed the world'. IEEE Ann. Hist. Comput. 29(4), 52–63 (2007)

Misa, T.J.: Organizing the history of computing: 'Lessons Learned' at the Charles Babbage Institute. In: Impagliazzo, J., Järvi, T., Paju, P. (eds.) History of Nordic Computing 2: Second IFIP WG9.7 Conference, HiNC2, Turku, Finland, 21–23 Aug 2007: Revised Selected Papers, pp. 1–12. Berlin/Heidelberg/New York (2009)

Misa, T.J., Zepcevski, J.: Realizing user-centered computer history: Designing and using NSF's FastLane (1990–Present). Paper presented at the SHOT meeting, 12–14 Oct 2008, Lisbon, Portugal

Molin, K.: Den moderne patriarken: Om arbetsledarna och samhällsomvandlingen 1905–1935. Almqvist & Wiksell International, Stockholm (1998)

Morrissey, C.: The two-sentence format as an interviewing technique in oral history field work. Oral Hist. Rev. 15, 43–54 (1987)

Myrdal, J.: Source pluralism as a method of historical research. In: Fellman, S., Rahikainen, M. (eds.) Historical Knowledge: In Quest of Theory, Method and Evidence. Cambridge Scholars, Publishing Cambridge (2012)

Naur, P.: Datamaskinerna och samhället, med ett tillägg om svenska förhållanden av Sten Henriksson, trans. Henriksson, S. Studentlitteratur, Lund (1969)

Nilsson, M.: Tools of Hegemony: Military Technology and Swedish-American Security Relations 1945–1962. Santérus Academic Press, Stockholm (2007)

Nilsson, B.G., Waldetoft, D., Westergren, C. (eds.): Frågelist och berättarglädje: Om frågelistor som forskningsmetod och folklig genre. Nordiska museets förlag, Stockholm (2003)

Nissen, J.: Pojkarna vid datorn: Unga entusiaster i datateknikens värld. Symposion graduale, Stockholm (1993)

Norberg, A.L.: A perspective on the history of the Charles Babbage Institute and the Charles Babbage Foundation. IEEE Ann. Hist. Comput. 23(4), 12–23 (2001)

Norberg, A.L.: Computers and Commerce: A Study of Technology and Management at Eckert-Mauchly Computer Company, Engineering Research Associates, and Remington Rand, 1946–1957. MIT Press, Cambridge, MA (2005)

Norberg, A.: How to conduct and preserve oral history, http://www.ithistory.org/resources/norberg-article.pdf. Accessed 15 Aug 2009

Nurminen, M.I.: People or Computers: Three Ways of Looking at Information Systems (1986), trans. Käpylä, P., Valle, E. Studentlitteratur, Lund (1988)

Nybom, T.: Det nya statskontorets framväxt 1960–1965. In: Granholm, A., Rydén, M. (eds.) Statskontoret 1680-1980: En jubileums- och årsskrift, pp. 133–179. Statskontoret, Stockholm (1980)

Odén, B.: Den 'osynliga' historien. In: Qviller, B., Wåhlin, B. (eds.) Usynlig historie: Foredrag fra den 17. Nordiske fagkonferensen for historisk metodelære i Tranum Klit 19.–23. mai 1981, pp. 9–24. Universitetsforlaget, Oslo (1983)

Olsson, L.: Det datoriserade biblioteket: Maskindrömmar på 70-talet. Tema, Linköpings universitet, Linköping (1995)

Oral Histories Collection, http://www.computerhistory.org/collections/oralhistories/. Accessed 4 Nov 2011

Oral History Collection, http://www.chemheritage.org/exhibits/ex-nav2.html. Accessed 4 Nov 2011

Oral History Database, http://www.cbi.umn.edu/oh/index.phtml. Accessed 15 June 2009

Oral-History: IEEE Oral History Collection, http://www.ieeeghn.org/wiki/index.php/Oral-History:IEEE_Oral_History_Collection. Accessed 4 Nov 2011

Oral History@MIT, http://libraries.mit.edu/archives/oral-history/index.html. Accessed 17 Oct 2007

Oral History on Space, Science, and Technology, http://www.nasm.si.edu/research/dsh/oralhis-tory.cfm. Accessed 10 June 2009

Oral History Skeleton Question List, http://www.aip.org/history/oral_history/questions.html. Accessed 20 July 2009

Orrghen, A.: Collaborations between engineers and artists in the making of computer art in Sweden, 1967–1986. In: Impagliazzo, J., Lundin, P., Wangler, B. (eds.) History of Nordic Computing 3: Third IFIP WG9.7 Conference, HiNC 3, Stockholm, Sweden, 18–20 Oct 2010: Revised Selected Papers, pp. 127–136. Heidelberg (2011)

Oudshoorn, N., Pinch, T.: Introduction: How users and non-users matter. In: Oudshoorn, N., Pinch, T. (eds.) How Users Matter: The Co-Construction of Users and Technologies, pp. 1–25. MIT Press, Cambridge, MA (2003)

Oudshoorn, N., Pinch, T.: User-technology relationships: Some recent developments. In: Hackett, E.J., Amsterdamska, O., Lynch, M., Wajcman, J. (eds.) The Handbook of Science and Technology Studies, 3rd edn, pp. 541–565. MIT Press, Cambridge, MA (2008)

Paju, P.: National projects and international users: Finland and early European computerization. IEEE Ann. Hist. Comput. 30(4), 77–91 (2008)

Paju, P., Malmi, E., Honkela, T.: Text mining and qualitative analysis of an IT history interview collection. In: Impagliazzo, J., Lundin, P., Wangler, B. (eds.) History of Nordic Computing 3: Third IFIP WG 9.7 Conference, HiNC 3, Stockholm, Sweden, 18–20 Oct 2010: Revised Selected Papers, pp. 433–443. Heidelberg (2011)

Perks, R., Thomson, A. (eds.): The Oral History Reader, 2nd edn. Routledge, New York (2006)

Persson, G.: Från Svenska Dataföreningen till Dataföreningen Sverige. In: Bruhn, E. (ed.) EDB historik: I nordisk perspektiv. DATAaktieselskabet, København (1988)

Persson, P.A.: Transformation of the analog: The case of the Saab BT 33 artillery fire control simu-lator and the introduction of the digital computer as control technology. IEEE Ann. Hist. Comput. 21(2), 52–64 (1999)

Pettersson, O.: Byråkratisering eller avbyråkratisering: Administrativ och samhällsorganisatorisk strukturomvandling inom svenskt vägväsende 1885–1985. Uppsala universitet, Uppsala (1988)

Petersson, T.: I teknikrevolutionens centrum: Företagsledning och utveckling i Facit, 1957–1972. Ekonomisk-historiska institutionen, Uppsala universitet, Uppsala (2003)

Petersson, T.: Facit and the BESK boys: Sweden's computer industry (1956–1962). IEEE Ann. Hist. Comput. 27(4), 23–30 (2005)

Petersson, T.: Private and public interests in the development of the early Swedish computer industry: Facit, saab and the struggle for national dominance. In: Lundin, P., Stenlås, N., Gribbe, J. (eds.) Science for Welfare and Warfare: Technology and State Initiative in Cold War Sweden, pp. 109–129. Science History Publication, Sagamore Beach (2010)

Pickstone, J., Bowker, G.: The Manchester heritage. IEEE Ann. Hist. Comput. 15(3), 7–8 (1993)

Portelli, A.: The death of Luigi Trastulli: Memory and the event. In: The Death of Luigi Trastulli and Other Stories, pp. 1–26. State University of New York Press, Albany (1991)

Ritchie, D.A.: Doing Oral History: A Practical Guide, 2nd edn. Oxford University Press, Oxford (2003)

Ritchie, D.A. (ed.): The Oxford Handbook of Oral History. Oxford University Press, New York (2011)

Rolandsson, B.: Facket, informationsteknologin och politiken: Strategier och perspektiv inom LO 1976–1996. Department of Sociology, Göteborg University, Göteborg (2003)

Rosenzweig, R.: Scarcity or abundance? Preserving the past in a digital era. Am. Hist. Rev. 108, 735–762 (2003)

Sandqvist, U.: Digitala drömmar: En studie av svenska dator- och tv-spelsbranschen 1980–2005, Occasional papers in economic history 12, Ekonomisk-historiska institutionen, Umeå univer-sitet, Umeå (2007)

Schama, S.: Landscape and Memory. A.A. Knopf, London (1996)

Schrum, K., Brennan, S., Halabuk, J., Leon, S.M., Scheinfeldt, T.: Oral history in the digital age. In: Ritchie, D.A. (ed.) The Oxford Handbook of Oral History, pp. 499–515. Oxford University Press, New York (2011)

Seldon, A., Pappworth, J.: By Word of Mouth: 'Élite' Oral History. Methuen, London (1983)
Sheridan, D.: Ordinary lives and extraordinary writers: The British mass-observation project. In: Nilsson, B.G., Waldetoft, D., Westergren, C. (eds.) Frågelist och berättarglädje: Om frågelistor som forskningsmetod och folklig genre, pp. 45–55. Nordiska museets förlag, Stockholm (2003)
Shopes, L.: Making sense of oral history. History Matters: The U.S. Survey Course on the Web, http://historymatters.gmu.edu/mse/oral/, February 2002. Accessed 9 Mar 2009
Shopes, L.: Oral history and the study of communities: Problems, paradoxes, and possibilities. In: Perks, R., Thomson, A. (eds.) The Oral History Reader, 2nd edn. pp. 261–270. Routledge, New York (2006)
Silicon Genesis: An Oral History of Semiconductor Technology. http://silicongenesis.stanford.edu/index.html. Accessed 4 Nov 2011
Sjöblom, G.: The programming priesthood comes to Sweden: Computer training in the 1950s. Unpublished manuscript, presented at the Division of History of Science and Technology, KTH, 2 Nov 2009
Sjöblom, G.: The totally integrated management information system in 1960s Sweden. In: Impagliazzo, J., Lundin, P., Wangler, B. (eds.) History of Nordic Computing 3: Third IFIP WG9.7 Conference, HiNC 3, Stockholm, Sweden, 18–20 Oct 2010: Revised Selected Papers, pp. 83–91. Heidelberg (2011)
Sjöblom, G.: Informationsteknikens materialitet, http://gustavsjoblom.blogspot.com/2011/11/informationsteknikens-materialitet.html. Accessed 20 Nov 2011
Skovdahl, B.:, Den digitala framtiden: Om förutsagda informationssamhällen och framväxande IT-realiteter. Institutet för framtidsstudier, Stockholm (2009)
Slim, H., Thompson, P., Bennett, O., Cross, N.: Ways of listening. In: Perks, R., Thomson, A. (eds.) The Oral History Reader, 2nd edn, pp. 143–154. Routledge, New York (2006)
Söderlind, Å.: Personlig integritet som informationspolitik: Debatt och diskussion i samband med tillkomsten av Datalag (1973:289). Valfrid, Borås (2009)
Söderqvist, T.: Preface. In: Söderqvist, T. (ed.) The Historiography of Contemporary Science and Technology. Harwood Academic, Amsterdam (1997)
Soojung-Kim Pang, A.: Oral history and the history of science: A review essay with speculations. Int. J. Oral Hist. 10(3), 270–285 (1989)
Sources for History of Quantum Physics, http://www.amphilsoc.org/library/guides/ahqp/. Accessed 10 June 2009
Stone, L.: Prosopography. Daedalus 100(1 Winter), 46–79 (1971)
Sundin, B., Sörlin, S.: Landskapets värden: Kring miljö- och kulturmiljövård som historiskt problemfält. In: Pettersson, R., Sörlin, S. (eds.) Miljön och det förflutna: Landskap, minnen, värden, pp. 3–19. Institutionen för idéhistoria, Umeå universitet, Umeå (1998)
Svensson, G.: Digitala pionjärer: Datorkonstens introduktion i Sverige. Carlsson, Stockholm (2000)
Szabó, M.: Fältarbeten och forskning. In: Medelius, H., Nyström, B., Stavenow-Hidemark, E. (eds.) Nordiska museet under 125 år, pp. 240–271. Nordiska museets förlag, Stockholm (1998)
Tansey, E.M.: Witnessing the witnesses: Potentials and pitfalls of the witness seminar in the history of twentieth-century medicine. In: Doel, R.E., Söderqvist, T. (eds.) The Historiography of Contemporary Science, Technology, and Medicine: Writing Recent Science, pp. 260–278. Routledge, New York (2006)
Tansey, T.: Telling like it was, New Scientist, 16 Dec 1995, 49
Ternryd, C-O, Hallmén, B., Waernér, G.: Fotogrammetri och datamaskiner i vägplaneringen i USA och Kanada: Erfarenheter från studieresa 3.8.–5.10. 1958. Stockholm (1958)
Thompson, P.: The Voice of the Past: Oral History. Oxford University Press, Oxford (1978)
Thomson, A.: Four paradigm transformations in oral history. Oral Hist. Rev. 34(1), 49–70 (2006)
Tosh, J.: The Pursuit of History: Aims, Methods and New Directions in the Study of Modern History, 4th edn. with Seàn Lang. Pearson Education, Harlow (2006)
Tweedale, G.: The national archive for the history of computing. J. Soc. Arch. 10(1), 1–8 (1989)
UK National Archive for the History of Computing, http://www.chstm.manchester.ac.uk/research/nahc/. Accessed 10 June 2009

Veà, A.: Internet History and Internet Research Methods: Engineering the Worldwide WiWiW Project. Paper prepared for the SHOT meeting, 12–14 Oct 2008, Lisbon, Portugal

Vittnesseminarier: Samtidshistoriska institutet. Unpublished document

von Hippel, E.: Democratizing Innovation. MIT Press, Cambridge, MA (2005)

Waldemarsson, Y.: Politiska makthavare som historisk källa. Arkiv, samhälle och forskning 2, 6–23 (2007)

Waldemarsson, Y.: Den redigerade källan. Arbetarhistoria 1, 32–35 (2008)

Waldetoft, D. (ed.): Framtiden var vår: Civilingenjörer skriver om sitt liv och arbete. Nordiska museet i samarbete med Sveriges civilingenjörsförb, Stockholm (1993)

Wellcome Witnesses to Twentieth Century Medicine, http://www.ucl.ac.uk/histmed/publications/wellcome_witnesses_c20th_med. Accessed 10 June 2009

Wentzel, V. (ed.): Tema D21. Datasaabs vänner, Linköping (1994)

Wentzel, V. (ed.): Tema flyg: Flygets datorpionjärer. Datasaabs vänner, Linköping (1995)

What Is a Witness Seminar? http://www.ccbh.ac.uk/witnessseminars.php. Accessed 15 June 2009

WiWiW project, wiwiw.org/. Accessed 4 Nov 2011

Yates, J.: Structuring the Information Age: Life Insurance and Technology in the Twentieth Century. Johns Hopkins University Press, Baltimore (2005)

Yates, J.: How business enterprises use technology: Extending the demand side turn. Enterp. Soc. 7(3), 422–455 (2006)

Yngvell, S. (ed.): Tema D22–D23: Tunga linjens uppgång och fall. Datasaabs vänner, Linköping (1997)

Young, R.S.: Oral history at CHF. Chem. Herit. 23(2), 34–35 (2005)

Interviews and Correspondence

Allison, D.K.: E-mail, 23 Oct 2007.

Douglas, D.: Personal communication, 25 Oct 2007.

Kaijser, L.: E-mail, 2 Nov 2009.

Misa, T.J.: Personal communication, 25 May 2007

Nebeker, F.: Personal communication, 22 May 2007

Nilsson, T.: Personal communication, 24 Aug 2007

Paju, P.: E-mail, 22 June 2009

Sumner, J.: E-mail, 19 June 2009

Tashev, K.,Spicer, D.: Personal communication with Peter Du Rietz and Per Olof Persson, 25 May 2007

Index

P. Lundin, *Computers in Swedish Society: Documenting Early Use and Trends*,   141
History of Computing, DOI 10.1007/978-1-4471-2933-2, © Springer-Verlag London 2012